Accessible Technology
in Today's Business
CASE STUDIES FOR SUCCESS

Gary Moulton
LaDeana Huyler
Janice Hertz
Mark Levenson

Contributing Authors
Jane Glasser and
Thea Rhiannon

PUBLISHED BY
Microsoft Press
A Division of Microsoft Corporation
One Microsoft Way
Redmond, Washington 98052-6399

Library of Congress Cataloging-in-Publication Data
Accessible Technology in Today's Business : Case Studies for Success / Gary Moulton ... [et al].
     p. cm.
   Includes index.
   ISBN 0-7356-1501-2
   1. Computers and people with disabilities.   2. Computerized self-help devices for people with disabilities. I. Moulton, Gary, 1949–.

HV1569.5 .A23   2002
658.3'8--dc21   2002019718

Printed and bound in the United States of America.

1 2 3 4 5 6 7 8 9   QWE   7 6 5 4 3 2

Distributed in Canada by Penguin Books Canada Limited.

A CIP catalogue record for this book is available from the British Library.

Microsoft Press books are available through booksellers and distributors worldwide. For further information about international editions, contact your local Microsoft Corporation office or contact Microsoft Press International directly at fax (425) 936-7329. Visit our Web site at www.microsoft.com/mspress. Send comments to mspinput@microsoft.com.

Cover images: Corbis® and Digital Imagery© copyright 2002 PhotoDisc®, Inc. Encarta, FrontPage, Microsoft, Microsoft Press, NetMeeting, Outlook, and Windows are either registered trademarks or trademarks of Microsoft Corporation in the United States and/or other countries. Other product and company names mentioned herein may be the trademarks of their respective owners.

The inclusion in this book of a profile of the Department of Defense does not imply the Department of Defense's endorsement of Microsoft Corporation or of *Accessible Technology in Today's Business.*

The example companies, organizations, products, domain names, e-mail addresses, logos, people, places, and events depicted herein are fictitious. No association with any real company, organization, product, domain name, e-mail address, logo, person, place, or event is intended or should be inferred.

Acquisitions Editor: Alex Blanton
Project Editor: Jenny Moss Benson

Body Part No. X08-68166

Contents

Foreword

As a critical thinker and decision maker in your organization, you're always looking for ways to maximize the effectiveness of your business. Right? I know I am. That's why I'm so excited about this book. We all know that our employees are our most important asset and are central to a company's ability to succeed and grow. If you're like me, you want to be able to tap into the largest possible pool of hiring candidates with the greatest minds and talents. You also want to retain the great people you already have.

So what does this have to do with accessibility and technology? I believe this book offers a very compelling answer. Today, technology is making it possible for people of all physical capabilities and ages to be productive in every field imaginable.

Microsoft has always had the goal of making software easier for people to use. As a leader in the technology industry, we have long recognized that we have a responsibility to develop products and information technologies that are accessible to and usable by all people, including those with disabilities. Indeed, for more than a decade, Microsoft has been making accessibility a consideration at every phase of the software development process. Especially in the last few years, we've seen huge advances in accessibility features and assistive technologies that allow people with disabilities to enjoy many of the benefits of technology.

In the long run, designing accessible products yields better products overall. For example, high-contrast color schemes were designed for people with visual impairments, but they can also be useful to anyone with tired eyes at the end of a long day. Providing keyboard access is essential for people with disabilities but also provides a productivity boost for power users. As technology advances and the capabilities and scope of assistive technology advance as well, the possibilities are virtually limitless.

Think about it: do your employees regularly communicate with each other using e-mail or instant messaging? If so, is there a noticeable difference if one of them is blind, deaf, or mobility impaired? There isn't if they can use the e-mail and messaging software like their colleagues. With forthcoming advances in speech recognition software and products, for example, a deaf or hard-of-hearing employee can attend meetings with a laptop instead of a sign language interpreter, and an employee with a spinal cord injury will be able to come back to work and continue to use his or her computer as productively as before the accident.

We believe that within the next 10 to 15 years, technology will virtually eliminate barriers due to disability or limitations brought on by accidents or as a natural part of the aging process. This is a good thing because, as the baby boomer generation advances in age, so does your workforce. Your 40- to 50-year-old employees are already facing increased visual limitations, perhaps some dexterity loss, and even the beginnings of hearing loss. Yet, as more and more people live and work longer due to healthcare advances and evolving societal norms, your employees will be working to an older age. At the same time, due to changing demographic trends, there will be fewer young candidates in the pipeline. Fortunately, advances in accessible technology will coincide with these demographic changes on the horizon.

At Microsoft, we strive to hire and retain the best and the brightest people in their fields. Naturally, an increasing number of our best employees also happen to be blind, visually impaired, deaf, hard-of-hearing, or mobility impaired. We hope this book will help you determine how you can also tap talented new resources among people with disabilities and at the same time retain your most important employees as they grow older. Accessibility, like technology, is all about removing barriers and providing the benefits of technology for everyone.

Steven A. Ballmer
Chief Executive Officer, Microsoft Corporation

Preface

At a disability conference late last year, Microsoft representatives met with an assistive technology manufacturer. The manufacturer had just published a new catalog of its products. The company had hundreds of copies to hand out at the event. It was the perfect place for such a distribution. Gathered in one place was a virtual assistive technology "choir" that included teachers, parents, clinicians, individuals with disabilities, disability advocates, and representatives of disability-specific organizations. Collectively they represented the "computer science," if you will, of being more independent at home, at work, at school, and at play.

The assistive technology catalog was beautiful. It contained pictures showing individuals with disabilities using PC technology in offices, classrooms, and at home. The product descriptions revealed remarkable things that could be done with a computer. Anyone looking through the catalog could think "Individuals with disabilities are truly extraordinary—they can even use a computer." However, anyone looking through the catalog and thinking that way would be wrong.

Yes, the catalog contained extraordinary products that made the computer accessible to individuals with disabilities. But the catalog contained only products that allowed individuals with disabilities to do what anyone else might want to, or indeed was already doing, with a computer. Why should that be so remarkable? After all, isn't the personal computer more than 25 years old? What could be so significant about products that allow individuals with disabilities to do anything they want to on a computer? Truth be told, nothing.

Point of fact, no matter what an individual's disability, no matter how severe or rare, there is an assistive technology product that will allow that individual to use a computer to learn, to work, to think, and to play—today, right this very moment, in every classroom, living room, and office around the world. As a result of the work of a group of assistive technology heroes, this book could be written, and it was indeed the time to write it. Many of these heroes we have had the pleasure of knowing, knowing of, or working with over the years.

Trust us—the assistive technology "hero" list is a long one. We'll confine ourselves to the heroes we consulted with regularly during the writing of this book. They include Madelyn Bryant McIntire, Rob Sinclair, Bonnie Kearney,

Laura Ruby, Heather Swayne, and the rest of Microsoft's very talented Accessible Technology Group, Alan Brightman, Jane Lee, Pam Patton, Peter Green, Robin Coles of Apple's old Disability Solutions Group, and Steve Jacobs of NCR who first chronicled the "bet-you-didn't-know-who-is-a-PC-success-story-who-also-happens-to-have-a-disability" list.

Assistive technology does have a fantastic history, and if its history is ever written, it will contain the story of an engineer and his college roommate. Two years after graduation this particular engineer's roommate was severely injured in a diving accident. The engineer recalled from an anatomy class taken during his junior year that the part of the body we as humans have the most fine-motor control over, after our fingers, is our tongue. So, he figured if his former roommate could no longer type with his fingers, why couldn't he type with his tongue? With the help of a dentist who was a family friend, the engineer designed, prototyped, and built an intra-oral device that could be used to type on a computer and control a power wheelchair, bed, television, and all the other appliances in the house. In fact, this device could also control the doors and the thermostat.

This is just one example; there are uncountable others. We've attempted to bring these real stories to life in a way that not only makes sense for the audience, but also engages the reader in such a way that it motivates him or her to change the way business is done. We hope to compel business leaders to think, perhaps for the first time, about the positive impacts of recruiting, hiring, and accommodating individuals with disabilities for their business.

As authors of this book, we have had no small amount of help in sharing the stories of the organizations included in this book. Special thanks to those who helped on this book project: Alex Blanton, Jenny Moss Benson, Tess McMillan, and Patricia Bradbury at Microsoft Press, as well as Dean Katz, Ellen Meyer, Karl Bridge, Peggy O'Farrell, Cheryl Wells, and Anita Williams at Microsoft Corporation.

We'd like to especially acknowledge those at the organizations featured in the case studies: Skip Simonds at UnumProvident; Diana Burke and Dorothy Rekman at RBC Financial Group; Compaq's Michael Takemura; Gloria Johnson and Susan Palmer at Cingular Wireless; Elizabeth Grotz and Willie Jones of General Motors; Janice Drummond and Judy Antonicic at Sears; Hunter Ramseur at the Georgia Center for Assistive Technology and Environmental Access; Layne Thorne at Home Depot; Dinah Cohen of CAP at the U.S. Department of Defense; and Jeff Berry at iCan.

Most individuals would believe that if someone can't see a computer monitor, hear its speakers, or use its keyboard and mouse, he or she simply can't use a computer. The fact of the matter is that it is no small technical challenge, for example, to make the computer's graphical user interface accessible for individuals who are blind, but it's been done. The ability to make point, click, and drag options usable by someone who can't use his or her arms and hands was a daunting technical challenge, but it was accomplished. Because the typical assumption is that technology can't be used by individuals with disabilities, it wasn't always easy for the accessible technology pioneers. For individuals and organizations who have persevered in riding the roller coaster that is technology evolution, they have had to lay their own parallel track of assistive technology for individuals with disabilities to make certain that no one was left behind. These pioneers have often had to balance the fact that individuals with disabilities can use computer technology, but not with all products or at least not the latest versions until the assistive technology catches up. But this landscape is changing, as you'll see in this book.

A number of groups are dedicated to helping individuals with disabilities find employment and accessible technology that meet their needs. We would like to recognize those who helped us with this project: the Alliance for Technology Access, the Assistive Technology Industry Association, and the Sierra Group, Inc. We would like to also recognize the hundreds of assistive technology manufacturers and thousands of individuals with disabilities who were never afraid to install a beta in spite of the sometimes dire consequences. While we can't mention them all, many are mentioned in the chapters that follow.

Anyone who has been involved in a book project knows the time such an effort takes. But how many individuals are that fortunate to have had the experience? Counting us, there are four more. We are each grateful to have had the experience and would like to personally thank those who have lived with us during this project.

Personal thanks from Gary Moulton: Although Joanne bought me my first computer, she had no idea it would become a full-time job. Neither did she know that it would ultimately send our oldest, Dennis, on an entrepreneurial path in the same vicinity as his father. Nor did she realize that our youngest son, Robert, would want to parlay his time on a PC-based flight simulator into a commercial pilot career, or that we would eventually learn so much about instant messaging from our daughter, Breanne. With this book, you all pretty much know all that I know.

Personal thanks from LaDeana Huyler: This project was every bit as challenging as I expected, but even more rewarding than I imagined. I'd like to thank each of you on the book team—the synergy between us was instrumental in bringing this book to life and made this project even more rewarding for me. And, special thanks goes to my husband, Mark, who brightens the colors of all my endeavors with his support, and always knows just how to inspire and respond. Here's to the new journeys ahead we will embark on together.

Personal thanks from Janice Hertz: This has been a great team to work with, and I have to say that "you guys are the best!" We've all collaborated so well on this book that it has become bigger than any one of us foresaw when we started this endeavor. It's been fantastic being a part of something like this. To our colleagues in the Accessible Technology Group at Microsoft: I hope this book helps validate the great work you keep doing—you guys rock. To my husband, Brian Trede: thanks for always being there and not getting fed up with hearing me gush about how much fun this book has been and how it's going to be so wonderful when it's done! After the completion of this book, I am retiring from my technology career to enter the next phase of my life. The last six plus years at Microsoft have been the perfect culmination for a 27-year career in technology, and this book has been a great "last project."

Personal thanks from Mark Levenson: I extend thanks to LaDeana Huyler and Gary Moulton of Microsoft who brought me onto the team for this project, to Alex Blanton of Microsoft Press who made that "draft pick" official, to Jane Glasser and Thea Rhiannon who pitched in when the work was long and the time was short, and to all the people at Compaq Computer, Cingular Wireless, General Motors, and UnumProvident who shared their stories with me and facilitated my work. Thanks as well to my wife, AnneBeth, for everything.

Gary Moulton

LaDeana Huyler

Janice Hertz

Mark Levenson

Redmond, Washington

February 2002

Introduction

Many books are available today that address how to provide physical accessibility accommodations for people with disabilities. Other books describe computer accessibility and explain how to assess the needs of individuals with disabilities and provide accommodation with accessible technology. Few, if any, books show the business value of integrating accessible technology across organizations or explain how to accomplish this mission.

Microsoft Press, in conjunction with Microsoft's Accessible Technology Group, published this book for one primary reason. That reason is to demonstrate to organizations that not only are accessible solutions available *today* that provide people with disabilities the essential tools they need to work, but also that it makes good business sense to do so.

About This Book

Many people are still unaware of products that provide access to computers for individuals with disabilities. Consider the employee who is blind and uses a computer through the use of assistive technology products, such as a screen reader. This employee can work at a bank and provide banking assistance to a customer over the phone as well as access the bank's computer system through the screen reader. Or consider an employee who has an impairment that prevents him from speaking. He can still communicate with his coworkers through e-mail and instant messaging. Also, consider the impact of an accessible Web site that would allow consumers who cannot drive to order products online and have them delivered to their homes. In this book, we will explore business scenarios and solutions for providing accessible technology in today's businesses.

This book provides

- A discussion of the business value of providing accessible technology in your organization. You'll learn how accessible technology can help you retain your most valued employees, recruit the most talented minds, and attract new customers.

- An overview of what accessible technology means, including information about assistive technology products available today, and how individuals with disabilities and whole organizations can benefit from using these products.

- In-depth case studies that showcase solutions implemented in health-care, retail, manufacturing, government, and financial organizations. These case studies feature best practices and lessons learned from organizations such as Cingular Wireless, Compaq Computer Corporation, General Motors, RBC Financial Group, Sears, the State of Georgia, UnumProvident, and the U.S. Department of Defense.

- An outline of a five-step process your organization can use to develop and execute a strategic accessible technology plan as well as ideas on how to measure progress and sustain the plan over time.

- A list of important purchase considerations and tools to help you identify solutions that will work well for your organization.

- A prediction of what the future holds for accessible technology based on today's research trends.

Audience

You'll find this book compelling if you are interested in retaining your most valuable employees and continuing to increase productivity with an aging workforce. This book also explains ways accessible technology will help you grow your business and attract a new customer segment that your competition might be unaware of. And, if you want to increase your pool of talented candidates for positions, you'll find this book useful.

In general, anyone interested in providing accessible technology solutions for employees and customers with accessibility needs will find the information in this book informative, particularly

- Business managers and executives

- Government procurement officers

- Human resource managers and employees with disabilities

- Education technology coordinators, educators, trainers, and rehabilitation specialists

Case Studies and Personal Profiles

Case studies are organized by industry. Case studies from your industry will probably be of the most interest to you, but we encourage you to read others as well.

Within each case study, a number of profile stories are included that feature individuals using accessible technology. To learn about specific types of disabilities, reading case studies of other organizations might prove very helpful. To identify profile stories by type of impairment, see Table I-1.

Table I-1.   *Finding profiles within case studies by type of impairment*

Type of Impairment	Profile within case studies
Visual impairments	Chapter 3, "Accessible Technology in the Healthcare Industry" (pages 61–64) Chapter 4, "Accessible Technology in the Financial Industry" (pages 75–76, 80–81, 85–89) Chapter 6, "Accessible Technology in the Retail Industry" (pages 125–127, 136–138) Chapter 7, "Accessible Technology in the Manufacturing Industry" (pages 152–157, 162–165)
Hearing impairments	Chapter 6, "Accessible Technology in the Retail Industry" (pages 133–134) Chapter 7, "Accessible Technology in the Manufacturing Industry" (pages 143–145, 157–159)
Mobility impairments	Chapter 3, "Accessible Technology in the Healthcare Industry" (pages 55–57, 58–61, 65–68) Chapter 5, "Accessible Technology in Government" (pages 93, 107, 109–112, 114–115) Chapter 6, "Accessible Technology in the Retail Industry" (pages 119–121, 131–132)
Learning impairments	Chapter 5, "Accessible Technology in Government" (pages 105–108)
Language impairments	Chapter 5, "Accessible Technology in Government" (pages 113–114) Chapter 6, "Accessible Technology in the Retail Industry" (pages 131–132)

About the CD

The accompanying CD includes in-depth accessibility resources to support integrating accessible technology into your organization. The companion CD, located at the back of this book, contains

- An electronic version (eBook) of this book

- Appendices with sample accessibility requirements, tools to help you select the right assistive technology, and an interview with Michael Fiore of the Sierra Group

- Technology planning resources for organizations integrating accessible technology.

- Guide to features and accessibility options in Microsoft products

- Step by step tutorials for accessibility features and options in Microsoft products

- Information about assistive technology products compatible with Microsoft products

- Resource guides organized by disability type

- Articles about people with disabilities who successfully use computers

- Background information about Microsoft's role in the area of accessibility

If the CD is missing from your copy of this book or for updates, these resources are also available at *http://www.microsoft.com/enable*.

System Requirements

To view most of the content on the CD, you'll need Microsoft Internet Explorer version 2.0 or later or Netscape Navigator version 4.0 or later.

To view the appendices on the CD, you'll need Adobe Acrobat. You can download Adobe Acrobat Reader for free at *http://www.adobe.com/products/acrobat/readstep.html*.

To view the eBook, you must have Microsoft Internet Explorer 5.01 or later and the proper HTML Help components installed. If your computer does not have Internet Explorer 5.01 or later, the eBook setup wizard will offer to install Internet Explorer 5.5 for you.

If your system is running Microsoft Windows NT 4.0 or later (including Microsoft Windows 2000 and Microsoft Windows XP), you will need administrative privileges to install the eBook.

For more information about eBook installation, refer to the Readme.txt file in the \enable\eBook folder.

How to Use the CD

To view the contents of the CD on your computer, complete the following steps:

1. Insert the CD into your CD-ROM drive. A Web page to the resources on the CD will launch automatically in your browser window.
2. If the Web page doesn't automatically appear, open the file default.htm (or default-u.htm for a text-only version) in the \enable folder to launch the Web page.
3. Navigate the contents of the CD just like you would navigate a Web site.
4. To see a description of the electronic version of this book, click the link Electronic Version of This Book. Launch the eBook setup by clicking the link on the page that appears. In the File Download dialog box that appears, click Run This Program From Its Current Location or Open, depending on your version of Internet Explorer. Finally, click Setup when the eBook wizard appears, and follow the instructions that appear on your screen.

On the Web

For more information about Microsoft Press, visit our site at *http://www.microsoft.com/mspress*. You will find descriptions of our books, information about ordering, notice of special features and events, additional content for Microsoft Press books, and much more.

For updated information about Microsoft's product accessibility, visit the Microsoft Accessibility Web site at *http://www.microsoft.com/enable*.

For developers and IT professionals, information about how to create accessible technology is also available on the Microsoft Developer Network at *http://msdn.microsoft.com/at*.

Corrections and Comments

Extensive efforts were made to ensure the accuracy of this book and the contents found on the CD. Microsoft Press provides comments and corrections for its books on the Web at *http://www.microsoft.com/mspress/support/*.

If you have comments, questions, or ideas regarding this book or the CD, please send them by e-mail to *mspinput@microsoft.com* or by postal mail to

Microsoft Press
Attn: Accessible Technology in Today's Business Editor
One Microsoft Way
Redmond, WA 98052-6399

Please note that support for Microsoft products is not offered through the preceding addresses. For help with Microsoft products, contact Microsoft Support Online at *http://support.microsoft.com*.

The Value of Accessible Technology

The Business Value of Integrating Accessible Technology into Your Organization

If you want to be a business leader and want access to top talent and enhanced market opportunity, you should absolutely promote accessibility.

*—John Cleghorn, former Chairman and CEO,
RBC Financial Group*

More than 500 million people in the world have a permanent disability or impairment—so sooner or later, it's likely you'll encounter someone among your employees, suppliers, customers, family, and friends for whom **accessible technology** is beneficial. Add to that number the people who experience temporary impairments caused by illness or accident and people affected by aging, and it is clear that most organizations will have employees and customers with disabilities.

This chapter outlines how accessible technology enhances your organization's ability to

- **Retain the Most Valued Employees.** Accessible technology increases an individual's productivity, enhances collaboration and communication among all employees—including those with disabilities—and helps you retain your most talented employees.

- **Recruit the Most Talented Minds.** Increase your potential pool of candidates by enhancing your organization's ability to hire the best minds for the job and to diversify your workforce.

- **Attract New Customers.** A diverse workforce helps you meet the needs of a wider customer base.

- **Understand Regulations That Promote Accessibility.** Even if you aren't convinced that accessible technology is important to your business, there are regulations that you'll need to pay attention to regardless. You'll learn what role technology plays in your accommodation strategy and appreciate that it's not just ramps and physical access that are required.

Retain Your Most Valued Employees

By providing accessible technology, you facilitate collaboration and communication among all members of your organization—whether they have disabilities or not. This results in greater overall organizational productivity. In addition, accessible technology helps you retain your most talented employees when employees become temporarily disabled or as they develop impairments due to the natural aging process. Retaining employees helps eliminate the high cost of hiring and training replacements, and it improves employee morale. In this section, you'll see how the workforce is changing and how accessible technology can make your organization more effective and efficient.

Intel's overall workforce objective is to reinforce a concept of diversity that everyone can identify with, and create a work environment that respects and values everyone. "This type of corporate culture," Gustavo De La Torre, Diversity Director at Intel Corporation, says, "aligns well with the culture already in place at Intel, and enhances the company's ability to recruit, hire, integrate, develop, and retain employees."

How Your Workforce Is Changing

Most organizations, at one time or another, will face the need to accommodate an employee or customer with a disability. Some disabilities might not have been present when you first hired your employee or worked with your customer. Certain disabilities occur as people age or as a result of accidents.

Everyone ages and your employees are no exception. Consider those employees you have invested in for years who know your business exceptionally well and are growing older. As more of your employees move into their 40s and 50s, they begin to feel the natural limitations that come with aging: reduced visual acuity, hearing, and mobility. They likely will not self-identify as having an impairment, and they probably won't mention that they aren't as productive as they used to be. Unless they are aware of the accessible technology available to them, they will not know that there are ways to address these limitations so they can be as productive as they used to be when they were younger. Consider the temporary disabilities that occur every day: a top sales executive breaks her wrist in a skiing accident. Or, what happens when your most trusted lieutenant is in a car accident that results in a spinal cord injury? He's irreplaceable. You need to integrate accessible technology to keep your business running smoothly.

Let's look at how accessible technology can help you prepare for the aging workforce—whether disabilities are temporary or permanent—and open up your pool of qualified candidates like never before.

The Aging Workforce

The likelihood of developing a disability increases with age. In the United States, people age 45–54 have an 11.5 percent chance of developing a disability. Your chances dramatically increase after age 55. People age 55–64 have a 21.9 percent chance of developing a disability. (National Organization on Disability 2001) Consider the 76 million baby boomers born between 1946 and 1964. The first "wave" turned 55 in 2001. This population will dramatically impact the median age of your workforce. Figure 1-1 on the next page shows the increased likelihood of developing a disability as you age.

Did You Know?   In 2005, the American workforce will include 27 million people between the ages of 50 and 59, compared to 20 million in 1997. The median age of the workforce will be over 40 by 2005, compared to 34.7 in 1979. (Economist 1998)

With the onset of impairments due to aging, you can't ignore your employees' need for accessible technology. Baby boomers on your staff will require technology adjusted to meet their needs. They will expect that technology will make them more productive in the workplace. With readily available technology, you can retain your most talented and experienced employees, make them as productive as possible regardless of their age, harness their intellect, and overcome the functional limitations people acquire as they grow older.

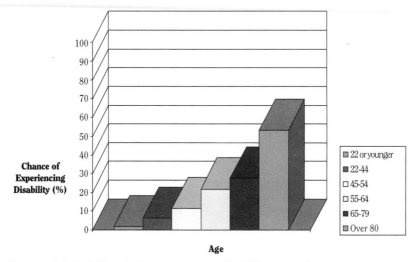

Figure 1-1. *Likelihood of experiencing a disability as age increases*

"...the boomers aren't just numerous, they're also critically important to most companies. If they leave, most of your organization's intellectual capital walks out the door."

—*Jerry McAdams, Consultant, Watson Wyatt Worldwide*

Employees Who Develop Temporary Disabilities

Having accessible technology in your organization provides you with the ability to help lower the costs of time lost and money spent when an employee develops a temporary disability. Providing accessible technology also allows an employee with a temporary disability to remain productive and up-to-date, and prevents you from having to hire a temporary replacement or letting the work pile up while the employee is recovering.

If a key employee has a serious accident and can come back to her previous position because accessible technology is provided, think of the gains associated with this situation. Her morale and that of her colleagues is improved and further evidence is given of what a great company they work for. In addition, you'll have retained the knowledge and talents of your key contributor without incurring the high cost of hiring and training a replacement.

The U.S. Department of Defense has benefited from a strong accommodation program that includes employees who develop temporary disabilities. The department "has lowered its operating costs by installing computers in the homes of temporarily disabled employees, allowing them to continue to be productive at a cost of approximately $5,000 per installation—thereby avoiding the average $28,000 per workers' compensation claim." (Gray 2000)

Enhance Productivity for All Employees

Providing employees with accessible technology that is adjustable to meet their needs increases productivity, job satisfaction, and employee morale. The range of what "accessible" is varies from person to person. When choosing technology, it is critical to consider the diverse needs and preferences of all your employees, not just "special cases" flagged by the human resources department. For some, accessible technology might simply mean the ability to easily change font size, icon size, colors, sounds, and speed of the mouse cursor on their PC. For others, additional **assistive technology products** might be needed in order for them to access a computer.

Myth vs. Fact

Myth: Employees with disabilities are less reliable and dependable.

Fact: The U.S. President's Committee on Employment of People with Disabilities reports that "employees with disabilities in the workplace are safer, more reliable, more dependable, more punctual, and more loyal employees than their nondisabled counterparts." (Gray 2000)

Accessible technology encompasses three elements:

- **Accessibility features.** An operating system and software that includes accessibility features, which allow you to adjust and customize to your own accessibility needs.

- **Assistive technology products.** Compatible assistive technology product(s) chosen specifically to accommodate an individual's disability or multiple disabilities.

- **Compatibility.** An operating system and software that are compatible with a specific type of assistive technology products.

An accessibility feature is an option within a product that allows you to adjust the product settings to your personal accessibility needs—for example, vision, hearing, mobility, language, and learning needs.

Assistive technology products (also known as "accessibility aids") refer to particular products developed to work with a computer's operating system to accommodate specific impairments. Assistive technology products are chosen specifically to accommodate the disability, or multiple disabilities, so that an individual can effectively access a computer. It is critical that the assistive technology be compatible with the operating system and other software. Assistive technology can include products such as a different type of pointing device to use instead of a mouse, or a system equipped with a Braille display and screen reader. Not all users with accessibility needs require assistive technology products.

More Info   In Chapter 2, "Understanding Accessible Technology and Disabilities," we define the various types of assistive technology that are available for specific types of disabilities.

Because assistive technology cannot be added to just any computer—it must be compatible with the computer's operating system and additional software products—it is important that your organization select software that is accessible. If your organization is running systems incompatible with assistive technology, it can be very difficult, and costly, to add assistive technology through reverse engineering. With up-front planning and implementation, you will be able to provide accessible technology to your entire workforce based on your organization's standard.

"Assistive technology, and information technology in general, is removing a major barrier to having managers recruit, hire and retain individuals with disabilities."

—Ophelia Falls, Director of the U.S. Department of Agriculture's Accessible Technology Program

When choosing technology for your organization, select an operating system and software that meet the range of accessibility needs of your workforce.

The following examples describe four individuals with various accessibility needs typical in an organization today:

- **Nancy**, who began wearing glasses last year when she turned 47, changed the font settings on her laptop so that she could more easily read words on her monitor. She now finds that she feels better at the end of the day because she's no longer straining to see the smaller fonts. Prior to being able to change the font size, she was increasingly reluctant to work overtime because her eyes were so tired that she didn't feel safe driving home afterwards.

- **Max**, who is hearing impaired, could not hear the sound notification when new e-mail messages arrived. He was able to change his computer settings to receive visual notification when new e-mail arrives. Another benefit of accessible technology is that he can now capture conversations with coworkers. Although Max can read lips, he prefers to have conversations with coworkers through e-mail and instant messaging to ensure he picks up all the words and has a record of conversations for later reference.

- **Josh**, who is blind, uses a screen reader to navigate his computer and does not use a monitor at all. His screen reader translates the user interface and documents into speech. He doesn't use a mouse but rather his keyboard and keyboard shortcuts to navigate the computer. Keyboard shortcuts (also known as "shortcut keys") provide an alternative way to navigate the computer, such as selecting Alt+Tab to move between open documents and programs. Keyboard shortcuts are a requirement for people who cannot use a mouse, such as Josh, and are widely used by others who find keyboard shortcuts faster and easier than a mouse.

- **Katie**, who recently broke her wrist and is in a cast, can type only with her right hand. As an editor, she needs to continue to use her computer. Katie uses keyboard shortcuts and keyboard settings, which allow her to type with one hand. Katie uses keyboard settings such as MouseKeys, which allows her to use her numeric keypad in place of her mouse. She is pleased to be able to continue working during her recovery.

In these examples, all four employees use the same operating system and productivity software, but each adjusts his or her computer to meet unique accessibility needs. Max and Nancy were able to accommodate their needs independently because the technology was accessible. Only Josh and Katie needed to consult with an HR representative—Josh consulted with HR to select and purchase his screen reader, and Katie consulted HR about continuing to work during recovery and to learn about keyboard shortcuts and settings.

These individuals represent just a few examples of different accessibility needs that are prevalent in most organizations today. With planning and integration, all employees can use the same accessible operating system and productivity software. For more extensive accessibility needs, assistive technology products are easily added, such as Josh's screen reader.

"Hard facts about the productivity of employees with disabilities are a chief driver of progress, and an irreversible one. The CEO of Marriott International, Inc. recently said that the 5,000 employees with disabilities who work for his company would be among the last to go if layoffs loomed. Why? Because, he said, they have proven themselves as excellent performers, more loyal and more responsive to customers.

Washington Mutual, a financial services company, documented similar facts: better retention among employees with disabilities saves the company $15,000 per new employee in training costs."

—*National Organization on Disability 2001*

Enhance Collaboration and Communication Among All Employees

Accessible technology further empowers your employees to share documents and collaborate on projects as well as to communicate among one another. When all employees have the power to customize their computers to meet their individual needs, they can more easily communicate with coworkers. For example, employees who can modify the way information is presented to them visually, aurally, and tactilely (in the case of Braille output) can more fluidly communicate with coworkers. With productivity software, it's also easier to collaborate on projects.

Take our examples of Nancy, Max, Josh, and Katie, who are able to communicate via e-mail and instant messaging. Previously, Josh and Max needed an interpreter to communicate because Max communicates with sign language and Josh is blind. Katie, who knows a little sign language, cannot sign with her arm in a cast. Katie and Max can still communicate via their computers until Katie recovers. Max and Josh can communicate directly online without an interpreter because they both feel comfortable using e-mail. For real-time discussions, they use instant messaging. In addition to easier communication with his coworkers, Josh is able to fully collaborate with the rest of his group in the writing and editing of a business plan by using his screen reader software.

Myth vs. Fact

Myth: Employees with disabilities will be absent a lot and have below-average job performance.

Fact: A Dupont study shows that 90 percent of employees with disabilities have above-average job performance. (Dupont 1996)

Another benefit of using the same operating system and productivity software throughout the company is that it is easy for employees with disabilities to use other computers within your organization. There are occasions when employees must use a computer other than their own, for example, when giving a presentation, attending a training course, or using a computer lab. Because all the computers are equipped with the same operating system and productivity software, employees with accessibility needs can use another machine within your organization, either temporarily for a training course or permanently to replace obsolete or faulty hardware. This flexibility lowers costs and increases productivity.

With an accessible operating system, employees with specific accessibility needs can save their profile settings, including their accessibility settings, so that when they log onto another machine on the network, their settings are automatically applied. Computers without built-in accessibility prevent or interrupt the activities of people who need such accommodations, resulting in lost time and money.

Recruit the Most Talented Minds

Accessible technology makes the difference between being able to use a computer or not for many people with disabilities or functional limitations. What if, for example, you find the perfect candidate by using an online search? You then discover, however, that because your organization uses inaccessible technology, the candidate cannot use your company's computer systems. And, what if you determine that hiring this candidate would make a significant difference to your bottom line for the next 5 to 10 years? Worse yet, you realize that your archenemy competitor wants to hire him too—and that company *is* standardized on accessible technology. You would have a serious business problem.

Did You Know?   A 1995 poll of 300 chief executive officers and human resource managers in Fortune 500 companies found that 73 percent of the top industries across the United States are currently hiring people with disabilities. (National Council on Disability 2001)

Providing highly effective, low-cost accessible technology allows you to hire from the largest pool of exceptional candidates possible—including people with disabilities. If you want proven problem solvers for your company's open positions, consider that people with disabilities, regardless of age, are successful in managing the obstacles brought on by their disabilities on a daily basis. So, tapping into this overlooked resource pool is a valuable option. Without accessible technology, Cambridge, England, and the rest of the world wouldn't have the brilliant insights of Steven Hawking, a leading figure in modern cosmology who has Lou Gehrig's disease. Who is the Steven Hawking in your industry?

Myth vs. Fact

Myth: People with disabilities have lower job performance ratings and lower job retention.

Fact: People with disabilities have equal, or higher, job performance ratings, higher retention rates, and lower absenteeism. (National Organization on Disability 2001)

Myth vs. Fact

Myth: Accommodating employees with disabilities is expensive.

Fact: According to the U.S. President's Committee on Employment of People with Disabilities, the majority of accommodations cost less than $500 US, and many have little or no cost at all. (Job Accommodation Network 2000) However, the average recruiting cost equals more than 13 percent of an employee's annual salary. (Employment Management Association 2000)

Attracting New Employees: The Power of a Good Public Image

Your organization's public image plays a crucial role in its ability to recruit and retain talented employees. With a strong reputation and thoughtful human resource practices, your company can draw top talent to new positions and retain your most talented employees. Job candidates naturally evaluate the entire compensation package offered including human resource programs, work/life balance, community involvement, and the diversity of your organization and how it accommodates the diverse needs and styles of its workforce.

Organizations that promote accessibility for their employees are recognized by word-of-mouth and in top publications, helping to draw candidates to their doorsteps and consumers to their storefronts.

Did You Know?
"Cause programs"—programs that address various social issues—increase sales and positively impact an organization's bottom line in the short term, and increase customer loyalty, employee pride, and brand image in the long term. (Cone/Roper Cause Related Trends Report 1999)

For minority groups, various magazines publish annual lists of the top organizations for which to work. One such publication is *Careers & the disABLED* magazine, which for 10 years has surveyed readers and published a list of the top 50 companies and 20 government agencies that are positive working environments for people with disabilities. When your organization is recognized for promoting accessibility, word gets out, and it helps your company attract future employees.

The Benefits of a Diverse Workforce and the Growing Demand for Accessible Products

Fostering a diverse workforce—which includes people with disabilities— enhances your ability to provide products and services that appeal to a broader range of customers. Having people with disabilities on staff helps your organization relate to its customers with disabilities. And your competitors probably already consider diversity an integral part of the business and a critical link to serving customers.

"Diversity is important not only because it enriches the workplace and enhances the lives of our employees, but also because it enables Microsoft to better serve the needs of customers and communities."

—*Steve Ballmer, CEO, Microsoft Corporation*

As the demand for accessible products grows, businesses that are already experienced with and attuned to the needs of customer segments with accessibility requirements are naturally in a stronger position. A diverse workforce gives you market insights you might not otherwise gain. In the end, a diverse workforce provides a competitive edge. According to the National Organization on Disability, an organization benefits from having people on its teams who understand "disability culture" when approaching American consumers with disabilities. (Gray 2000)

Attract New Customers

In 1998, *Fortune* magazine reported that the aggregate income of people with disabilities in the world would exceed $1 trillion in 2001. Although unemployment remains high for people with disabilities, their discretionary income stands at $176 billion. (Digh 1998) Those are exorbitant numbers and represent a huge opportunity. Your ability to attract new customers in part lies in the public image of your organization and how easy it is for customers to access your products and services.

Did You Know? Corporate citizenship, if strategically managed and communicated, can have a positive impact on brand awareness and consumer loyalty. Fourteen percent of the U.S. population seeks out good corporate citizens when making purchases. (Council on Foundations 1996)

Home Depot, a national home improvement retailer, found that its commitment to employing a diverse workforce directly helped its store customers: "The presence of associates with disabilities fosters strong associate morale, helps us foster good community relations, and provides our shoppers with disabilities someone who better understands their needs. It's a win-win for Home Depot," says Layne Thome, Director of Associate Services at Home Depot. Thome adds, "A war for talent is on, and by targeting recruitment programs at the disabled community, we tap into a new pool of candidates. We have found that hiring qualified individuals with disabilities offers many advantages: it increases our recruitment pool in a tight employment market; and the associates with disabilities are typically long-term associates with high commitment and good attendance records." The positive ripple effect is caused when shoppers with disabilities refer others to their Home Depot store because of outstanding customer service.

"When he travels, Urban Miyares likes to stay in Marriott Hotels, not because of their ad campaigns but 'because they hire people with disabilities,' he says. Miyares is president of the San Diego-based Disabled Businesspersons Association. The Marriott Foundation for People with Disabilities facilitates the employment of young people with disabilities."

—*Patty Digh, Fortune*

Additionally, if you are a retailer who provides an online catalog of your products, whereas a competitor does not, your "online storefront" might be the one chosen by a person with a mobility impairment or a person who is blind if your Web site is accessible. Both customers are likely to purchase most of their goods online because of the difficulty of finding transportation. There is a domino effect created when careful attention is made to the accessibility of your products and services. What's more, providing accessible Web sites for customers or employees benefits all customers and employees. Companies such as Wells Fargo have seen the positive impact. "An accessible IT [information technology] site or service is almost always easier to use by a greater majority of people," claims Neil Jacobson, a senior vice president for IT at Wells Fargo Bank in San Francisco. (Anthes 2001) People who might otherwise be intimidated by your online service are more likely to find it usable if it is also accessible.

"Companies marketing to people with disabilities can reach as many as 4 in every 10 consumers. Corporate America can't afford to ignore or stereotype this market."

—Patty Digh, Fortune

Understand Regulations That Promote Accessibility

Even if you aren't convinced that accessible technology is important to your business, there are still regulations that you'll need to pay attention to. It might surprise you that regulations concerning accessibility deal as much with access to information as they do with physical access to facilities. Recent regulations impact how organizations accommodate people with disabilities.

Did You Know?   In the United States, a company can receive tax benefits for hiring and accommodating people with disabilities. (U.S. Department of Labor 1997)

In little more than a decade, crucial new U.S. and Canadian legislation has been enacted to expand the rights and protections of people with disabilities. Other nations including Japan and the European Union are also in the process of adopting laws and regulations.

U.S. and Canadian accessibility regulations focus on employment and access to products and services of government and private organizations and increase the ability of people with disabilities to work and use technology. The following sections provide overviews of select disability access laws and regulations you should be aware of when you begin to consider your technology choices. Also included is a list of resources for more information.

The access laws and regulations in the United States include

- Americans with Disabilities Act (ADA)
- Section 508 of the Rehabilitation Act
- Section 255 of the Telecommunications Act

The access laws and regulations in Canada include

- Employment Equity Act
- Human Rights Act

Americans with Disabilities Act (ADA)

Signed into law in 1990, the ADA prohibits discrimination on the basis of disability. The Act is divided into five sections: employment, state and local government and transportation, public accommodations and services, tele-communications, and miscellaneous issues.

The employment section states that "employers shall not discriminate against people with disabilities in regards to job application procedures, hiring, advancement or discharge of employees, compensation, training and other terms and conditions of employment."

This protection against discrimination for individuals with disabilities is similar to the protection provided in other legislation on the basis of race, gender, age, nationality, and religion. The U.S. Equal Employment Opportunity Commission, Department of Justice, and Federal Communications Commission (FCC) are responsible for enforcing their respective titles of this law.

The ADA defines disability functionally as any condition that substantially limits major life activities such as seeing, hearing, walking, or working, and it covers nearly 900 specific disabilities. Among the rights and protections addressed in the ADA is the requirement that an employer with 15 or more employees provide qualified individuals with disabilities an equal opportunity to benefit from the full range of employment-related opportunities available to others. Qualified individuals with disabilities are those that meet the general requirements of the position and can perform the essential functions of the job with or without a reasonable accommodation. The ADA defines reasonable accommodation as some modification in a job's task or structure, or in the workplace environment, which enables the qualified employee with a disability to perform the essential functions of the job. The modification, which can include the use of accessible technology, must be made unless it creates an undue hardship for the employer.

Accessible technology enables your business to provide accommodations for people with disabilities as required by the ADA and can benefit everyone—not just those individuals with disabilities. As mentioned earlier in this chapter, standardizing your business on a foundation of accessible technology makes it easier to quickly meet the changing needs of your workforce. You can also add additional assistive technology products required by individuals with particular disabilities, respond to employees who develop temporary disabilities, and enhance your organization's ability to hire people with disabilities.

Section 508 of the Rehabilitation Act

Commonly referred to as Section 508, Section 508 of the Rehabilitation Act of 1973 (with additional 1998 amendments) strengthens the Rehabilitation Act by requiring the federal government to make the technology it uses accessible to persons with disabilities. The Rehabilitation Act predates the ADA, and it applies to the Executive Branch of the government including executive agencies.

Section 508 requires that federal departments or agencies develop, procure, maintain, or use electronic and information technology. These requirements ensure that the electronic and information technology allows federal employees with disabilities to have access to and use information and data that is comparable to the access to and use of information and data by federal employees who are not individuals with disabilities, unless an undue burden would be imposed on the department or agency. Section 508 also requires that "individuals with disabilities, who are members of the public seeking information or services from a federal department or agency, have access to and use of information and data that is comparable to that provided to the public who are not individuals with disabilities." The 1998 amendments to Section 508 directed the Architectural and Transportation Barriers Compliance Board (known as the Access Board) to develop and publish standards by February 7, 2000. These standards set forth a definition of electronic and information technology, and delineate the technical and functional performance criteria necessary for achieving accessibility to such technology and information by individuals with disabilities. The legislation also instructed the Access Board and the General Services Administration (GSA) to provide technical assistance to federal agencies and consumers once the standards were implemented in December 2000.

A number of states have voluntarily adopted Section 508 as a "best practice" for evaluating and procuring electronic and information technology.

Section 255 of the Telecommunications Act

In 1996, Section 255 of the Telecommunications Act was signed into law. This law requires that telecommunications equipment and customer premises equipment must be designed, developed, and fabricated to be accessible to and usable by individuals with disabilities, if readily achievable. The U.S. Government Access Board developed accessibility guidelines for Section 255 compliance for telecommunications manufacturers and service providers. The FCC then created rules to implement and enforce the Access Board guidelines. These rules went into effect January 28, 2000.

Section 255 has significantly increased the availability of accessible telecommunications products and services to people with disabilities both in the workplace and at home.

Employment Equity Act

The purpose of Canada's Employment Equity Act is to achieve equality in the workplace so that no person shall be denied employment opportunities or benefits for reasons unrelated to ability. It seeks to correct the conditions of disadvantage in employment experienced by women, aboriginal peoples, persons with disabilities, and members of visible minorities by giving effect to the principle that employment equity means more than treating persons in the same way. It also requires special measures and the accommodation of differences.

Human Rights Act

The Canadian Human Rights Act states, "[A]ll individuals should have an opportunity equal with other individuals to make for themselves the lives that they are able and wish to have and to have their needs accommodated, consistent with their duties and obligations as members of society, without being hindered in or prevented from doing so by discriminatory practices...." The Canadian Human Rights Commission administers the Canadian Human Rights Act and ensures that the principles of equal opportunity and nondiscrimination are followed in all areas of federal jurisdiction.

Under the Canadian Human Rights Act, it is against the law for any employer or provider of service that falls within federal jurisdiction to make unlawful distinctions based on the following prohibited grounds: race, national or ethnic origin, color, religion, age, sex (including pregnancy and childbirth), marital status, family status, mental or physical disability (including previous or present drug or alcohol dependence), pardoned conviction, or sexual orientation.

Everyone is protected by the Canadian Human Rights Act in dealings with the following employers and service providers: federal departments, agencies and Crown corporations, Canada Post, chartered banks, national airlines, interprovincial communications and telephone companies, interprovincial transportation companies, and other federally regulated industries, such as certain mining operations.

The most recent national initiative, the Federal Task Force on Disability Issues (also known as "the Scott Task Force") was established in June 1996 by the Ministers of Human Resources Development, Finance, Revenue, and Justice. Its mandate was to define and make recommendations on the role of the Government of Canada as it relates to persons with disabilities. The Scott Task Force organized public consultations throughout the country and commissioned research papers focused on five key issues: national civil infrastructure/citizenship, legislative review, labor market integration, income support, and the tax system. In October 1996, the Scott Task Force issued its report entitled Equal Citizenship for Canadians with Disabilities: The Will to Act.

Accessibility and Regulations in Other Countries

A number of countries, such as Australia, Portugal, and Japan, have recently adopted, or are in the process of adopting, laws and policies regarding accessible design of electronic and information technology and the Web. In fact, many countries are considering adopting the United States' Section 508 Accessibility Standards for Electronic and Information Technology as a basis for evaluating and procuring accessible technology.

In the European Union, the year 2003 is designated as the "European Year of People with Disabilities." Ninety-seven percent of Europeans surveyed said they thought more could be done to integrate people with disabilities—three out of five noted they personally knew someone with a disability. (The European Union 2001)

For More Information About Laws and Regulations

Use the following resources to find more information about accessibility laws and regulations.

United States—Americans with Disabilities Act

For more information about the Americans with Disabilities Act, see the following Web sites:

- Department of Justice ADA: *http://www.usdoj.gov/crt/ada/adahom1.htm*
- Office of Disability Employment Policy: *http://www.dol.gov/dol/odep*

United States—Section 508 of the Rehabilitation Act

For more information about Section 508 of the Rehabilitation Act, see the following Web sites:

- Section 508 Accessibility Standards: *http://www.access-board.gov/news/508-final.htm*
- Federal IT Accessibility Initiative: *http://www.section508.gov*
- Department of Justice 508: *http://www.usdoj.gov/crt/508/508home.html*
- Microsoft and Section 508: *http://www.microsoft.com/enable/microsoft/section508.htm*

United States—Section 255 of the Telecommunications Act

For more information about Section 255 of the Telecommunications Act, see the following Web sites:

- FCC Section 255 Report and Order: *http://www.fcc.gov/cib/dro/section255.html*
- Section 255 Access Board Guidelines: *http://www.access-board.gov/telecomm/html/telfinal.htm*

Canada—Human Rights Act

For more information about the Human Rights Act, see the following Web sites:

- Employment Equity Act: *http://laws.justice.gc.ca/en/E-5.401/ 43300.html#rid-43309*
- Canadian Human Rights Commission: *http://www.chrc-ccdp.ca/ publications/chra_guide_lcdp.asp*
- Policy on the Provision of Accommodation for Employees with Disabilities: *http://www.tbs-sct.gc.ca/pubs_pol/hrpubs/TB_852/ ppaed_e.html*
- Canadian Human Rights Act: *http://laws.justice.gc.ca/en/H-6/ 26172.html*

International Accessibility Laws and Regulations

For more information about international accessibility laws and regulations, see the following Web sites:

- International Center for Disability Resources on the Internet: *http:// www.icdri.org/global_legal_resources.htm*
- Disability World: *http://www.disabilityworld.org*

Summary

It is clear that organizations providing accessible technology solutions for their employees and customers reap many benefits. Successfully integrating accessible technology will help you retain your most valued employees, recruit the most talented minds, and help you attract new customers.

Accessible technology increases the productivity of your employees and enhances collaboration and communication among all employees. It allows you to retain your most talented employees and increase your potential pool of candidates by enhancing your organization's ability to hire the most talented minds for the job and to diversify your workforce. And, a diverse workforce that includes people with disabilities allows your organization to better serve the needs of your customers with accessibility needs.

Now that you understand the business value of integrating accessible technology, you need to create a vision and plan to help your organization integrate accessible technology. The main purpose of this book is to provide you with the information needed to do just that.

Understanding Accessible Technology and Disabilities

To be accessible, technology must be flexible enough to meet the individual needs and preferences of a diverse set of people with many different types of abilities. When selecting technology for your organization, it is important to consider **accessibility features** and **assistive technology products** that will be helpful to individuals with specific disabilities. It is also important to plan for the onset of age-related impairments and temporary disabilities that will inevitably occur.

In this chapter, we discuss what **"accessibility"** and **"disability"** mean. We also describe various **impairments** and the specific accessibility features of mainstream computer products and assistive technology products available to help make computing possible and accessible for everyone.

What Is Accessibility?

Simply put, accessibility means providing access—making products and services available to, and usable by, everyone. Accessibility is about removing barriers. A more accessible environment benefits everyone—including people with disabilities and those without. All people benefit from an environment in which it is easier and safer to move and function. Ensuring accessibility is another way of accepting and encouraging diversity in our society.

Alan Kay, the Xerox researcher who invented **SmallTalk** (a groundbreaking object-oriented programming language) and who went on to work for companies such as Apple Corporation and Disney, stated, "A new point of view is worth 80 IQ points." If you think through a product design from different points of view, you will be able to design a better product. Accessibility is all about point of view.

When a product or service is not accessible to or usable by all people, you could argue that it is that product or service that is flawed—not the person trying to use it. It might very well be poor design rather than mere physical and mental limitations of people that creates a "disability." Through creativity and ingenuity, it is the responsibility of the people who design products, services, and facilities to make an individual's disability irrelevant.

Consider an ordinary book. The National Federation of the Blind, which is based in Baltimore, Maryland, maintains the premier Braille book library. Looking at the abundance of books, you might think it contained thousands of titles. Similar to a typical library with shelves of books from floor to ceiling, there is not an inch of wall space that is not covered by books. However, because one printed page is the equivalent of four Braille embossed pages, literally one half of one wall contains a *single* encyclopedia. As a result, you can't help thinking about all the books that aren't there. The veritable wealth of reading material assembled by humanity has been, for all intents and purposes, essentially unavailable to individuals who are blind.

Now consider the new **electronic book technology**, which is as fundamental to individuals who have visual impairments as Gutenberg's creation of the first printing press to people who are sighted. Through the use of a liquid plasma screen with the capability of 1200 dots per inch (dpi) that supports an amazing viewing angle of 160 degrees, this technology enables a device the size of an ordinary book to be read in the bright sunlight of the beach or in the darkness of a bedroom. This valuable device allows people who have extreme difficultly seeing text on a regular book page to read without strain or discomfort. The high resolution and design allows them to adjust the text to their needs. Eventually, this same technology will make a variety of books, including recently published titles, accessible to individuals who are blind by using text-to-speech technology to read the book aloud. This is an example of point of view: thanks to accessible design, the "disability" of the individual becomes irrelevant. The design of the product merely addresses the needs of all users.

What Is Accessible Technology?

As discussed in Chapter 1, "The Business Value of Integrating Accessible Technology into Your Organization," accessible technology encompasses three elements: accessibility features, assistive technology products, and compatibility between the operating system, software, and assistive technology products.

Accessibility features are options within a product that allow you to adjust the product settings to your own individual accessibility needs. These needs might include vision, hearing, mobility, language, and learning needs. Examples of accessibility features include the ability to increase font size, change font settings, and choose different colors for your computer screen. Another example is the option to receive announcements from your computer through sound notifications (a "ding" when new e-mail messages arrive), visual notifications (a dialog box that appears, notifying you of new e-mail messages), or both. These features are included in commonly used technology, but they might not be obvious to you unless you have a need for them. Microsoft products, such as Microsoft Windows XP, Microsoft Office XP, and Microsoft Internet Explorer 6, include such accessibility features and are compatible with a wide range of assistive technology products.

Assistive technology products are specially designed products chosen specifically to accommodate an individual's disability or multiple disabilities. Assistive technology products (also known as "accessibility aids") are developed to work with a computer's operating system and software. Assistive technology can be anything from using a different type of pointing device instead of a mouse, to a system equipped with a Braille display and screen reader. Not all users with accessibility needs require assistive technology products.

Compatibility between the operating system, software, and assistive technology products is a critical component of accessible technology.

Accessibility Is Good Usability

There is a fine line between **usability** (the measure of a product's convenience and ease of use) and accessibility. The two concepts often overlap. What might be a usability function for one user might be an accessibility requirement for another. Most accessibility features benefit all users by providing increased usability.

A common example is curb cuts in sidewalks. Curb cuts are an accessibility requirement for people in wheelchairs. They also greatly improve the usability and accessibility of city streets for people pushing baby strollers, shopping carts, and luggage, and even people on in-line skates.

(continued)

Accessibility Is Good Usability   *(continued)*

Let's take a software example. Allowing for the adjustment of font size or color schemes might be a convenience that improves usability for most users, but this feature makes the difference in whether or not content can be seen for users with visual impairments. Likewise, keyboard shortcuts are a productivity improvement for power users but a requirement for many users with disabilities.

Features that are initially designed to enhance accessibility usually result in improved usability and performance for all users.

Defining "Disability"

A quick Internet search on the question "What is the definition of disability?" is likely to net thousands of matches. From the U.S. federal government to individual plaintiff's attorneys and from educators to advocates of people with disabilities, the interpretations and variations of the word "disability" are seemingly endless and dependent on context. Each person who tackles the question does so from a particular perspective and bias. In fact, most of us already have formed our own definition of what disability means to us based on our own frame of reference. In many cases, the definition is all about legal contracts and insurance benefits.

One Definition of Disability

"A disability is a condition caused by an accident, trauma, genetics or disease, which can affect or limit a person's ability. A disability can affect or limit a person's mobility, hearing, breathing, vision, speech or mental function. A disability can be visible, such as a spinal cord injury necessitating wheelchair use, or invisible, such as diabetes, epilepsy, hearing loss, mental retardation or a learning disability." (Kailes 1993)

The Definition of Disability Is Personal

The definition of disability is really a personal one for individuals and how they think of themselves. Some people may or may not consider themselves "disabled" if they have everything they need to be completely independent at work, at school, and at home. In fact, many people who might by some legal, or common, definition be considered disabled do not "self-identify" or even consider themselves so.

For example, consider an employee in her 50s who experiences hearing loss, visual impairment, and mobility limitations as a result of the natural aging process. Because she does not have any problems performing her work, she does not recognize that these age-related conditions are anything but a natural part of the aging process and a part of who she is. Because her impairments are relatively minor and do not require much accommodation, she simply turns up the volume of the speakers on her computer, increases the size of the font, changes the contrast on her monitor, and uses a nonstandard keyboard.

Another example might be a person who has a learning impairment such as dyslexia. Because his employer's standard word processing software includes automatic spelling and grammar checking capabilities, his dyslexia does not impact his productivity. He doesn't think of himself as "disabled," even though a legal definition might suggest otherwise.

Many deaf people also do not identify themselves as "disabled." Many of those who are deaf consider themselves a part of a unique and important society or culture, and, in fact, would not choose to join the hearing world if given the chance.

Of those who do not self-identify as disabled and are employed, many do not seek any accommodations from their employers. As mentioned, many do not see themselves needing accommodations beyond what should easily be within their own power to change in their workplace. In other cases, they make their own accommodations to avoid drawing attention to themselves or to their impairment.

Prevalence of People with Disabilities

The definition of disability is not consistent throughout the world, nor are the statistics surrounding it. This is true because statistics are collected for different purposes by various organizations with different capabilities and resources. For example, the World Health Organization collects worldwide statistics, the U.S.

government collects statistics on a wide range of subjects, and various special interest groups collect information with the purpose of advancing their own causes. Consequently, study sizes, sampling techniques, and reliability of the data also vary widely. In addition, collecting data on people with disabilities has often been neglected. Even cultural attitudes toward what constitutes a disability make consistent statistics difficult to come by. Still, organizations such as the U.S. Census Bureau and the World Health Organization are making significant gains in gathering useful statistics that help us to frame our discussion. Consider that

- In the United States, nearly one in five Americans has some level of disability
- In Canada, it is one in six

Attitude Impacts Employment Rates

Often, the most daunting challenge that people with disabilities face is the attitudes and assumptions others maintain about their capabilities. This attitude impacts employment rates of people with disabilities. Although many people with disabilities can perform the functions of their chosen career with little or no accommodation, employment rates remain low, largely because of conjectures people form about the abilities of people with impairments. In the United States, one recent U.S. Census Bureau study showed that in the prime employable years, ages 21–64,

- 82 percent of people *without a disability* had a job or business
- 77 percent of people *with a nonsevere disability* had a job or business

    But, only 26 percent of people *with a severe disability* had a job.

    Contrary to what these figures indicate, some organizations, as you'll read about in this book, and the U.S. federal government in particular, have left no stone unturned in recruiting the best employees possible—including those with disabilities.

Did You Know?   According to the U.S. President's Committee on Employment of People with Disabilities, the majority of accommodations cost less than $500 US, and many have little or no cost at all. (Job Accommodation Network 1998)

The U.S. federal government is the largest employer of individuals with disabilities in the world. Hundreds of employees with disabilities work in federal government offices in Washington, D.C., and internationally. It must be emphasized that these employees were not hired *because* they have a disability. As a matter of fact, these employees might have acquired a disability while employed and were able to continue their careers. They were hired because some recruiter or hiring manager found them to be the best persons for a particular job. Subsequently, it proved beneficial to the organization to invest the time and energy in locating the resources that were necessary to accommodate these employees to continue to do their jobs successfully. Indeed, a small group of recruiters and other human resource professionals in companies all around the world are experts in recruiting, hiring, and accommodating individuals with disabilities. The information and experience they have acquired is highly valuable in maintaining the best possible workforce for their individual organizations.

Understanding Impairment Types

The definition of a disability, however it is defined, is relevant in this discussion only because we are addressing how accessible technology can help break down barriers. Before determining how your organization can integrate accessible technology, it is beneficial to understand the types of physical and mental impairments that impact how people access and use computers.

In this section, we outline the different types of impairments including visual, mobility, hearing, language, learning, and age-related impairments. We provide specific examples of accessibility features and assistive technology products that are useful to people with each type of impairment. We also provide definitions of the assistive technology products.

See Also   To learn more about choosing assistive technology, see Chapter 8, "Developing an Accessible Technology Plan."

Visual Impairments

Visual impairments include low vision, color blindness, and blindness. People who are blind cannot use a computer monitor and must receive information from their computers via another sense—hearing or touch. People with low vision can also receive information through sound or touch, or they can modify their computer displays so the screen is more legible.

Low Vision

A person is said to have low vision if ordinary eyeglasses, contact lenses, or intraocular lens implants are unable to provide the person with clear vision. People with low vision still have useful vision that can often be improved with software or hardware. For example, if you have low vision, you might use a utility that increases the font size and other objects on your computer screen. Microsoft Windows XP, for example, includes a basic screen magnifying utility called Microsoft Magnifier. Figure 2-1 shows Microsoft Magnifier in Windows XP with a magnification level of 2 and inverted colors selected. Although not designed, or appropriate, to use in place of full-featured **screen enlargers** (defined in the "Blindness" section later in the chapter), such built-in utilities enable individuals with visual impairments to easily use a colleague's computer or share computers in an office. In addition, these utilities provide the means for these individuals to use computers at public and school libraries as well as computers at any other location where computers are maintained for general use.

More Info   Windows XP comes with built-in accessibility utilities including Magnifier, Narrator, On-Screen Keyboard, and Utility Manager. These utilities provide accessibility support to individuals who temporarily need to use a machine other than their own or to log on and set up their machine for the first time. They are not intended as replacements for full-featured assistive technology products. To find these utilities in Windows XP, click Start, point to Programs, point to Accessories, point to Accessibility, and then select one of the utilities from the menu.

For additional information about how to use these utilities and other accessibility features in Windows XP and other Microsoft products, see the Step by Step Tutorials for Windows XP on this book's companion CD-ROM.

Figure 2-1. *Microsoft Magnifier in Windows XP*

Color Blindness

People who are color-blind often have difficulty seeing particular colors or distinguishing between certain color combinations. Computer programs that allow users to choose the display's color combinations that work best for them and to adjust screen contrast to their individual needs, help color-blind users work with their computers more comfortably and effectively. Individuals with visual impairments frequently find it easier to read white text on a black background instead of black on white. In Windows XP, users can use the Invert Colors and High Contrast color scheme options to improve legibility to meet their personal needs.

Blindness

Blindness occurs in a variety of degrees, and many people who are considered blind do have some measure of sight. For example, a person whose level of sight is equal to or less than 20/200—even with corrective glasses or lenses—is considered "legally blind" in the United States. A person who is completely sightless is considered "blind."

Did You Know?   Visual acuity is expressed as a fraction. The top number refers to the distance you stand from the vision chart, which is usually 20 feet. So, 20/200 vision indicates that the line you correctly read at 20 feet could be read by a person with normal vision at 200 feet.

Many diseases and conditions contribute to, or cause, blindness, including cataracts, cerebral palsy, diabetes, glaucoma, and multiple sclerosis. Accidents, diabetes, and macular degeneration account for most blindness in the United States. Worldwide, vitamin A deficiency is the leading cause of blindness, mental retardation, and other diseases. (USFDA 2000)

For people who are blind, the ability to interact with their computers through keyboards or voice rather than by using a mouse and visual display, as well as the use of assistive technologies for both input and output, is very important.

Accessibility features built into the Windows XP operating system, which include keyboard shortcuts, text-to-speech capabilities, and sound notification, along with additional assistive technology products can enable blind users to fully utilize computer technology. Even though earlier versions of Windows also included accessibility features, Windows XP offers the widest range. For the operating system or an application to be accessible to someone who is blind, it needs to provide information about its interactions with the user in a manner that assistive technology can then present in an alternative format. For example, if a sighted user sees a list box containing several selections to choose from, the assistive technology needs the necessary information so it can inform the blind user that he or she needs to choose from a list of selections. The list of selections might be spoken or presented in a tactile fashion with a Braille display.

A number of assistive technology products with different capabilities are available to help people with visual impairments. Some assistive technology products provide a combination of capabilities that help specific individuals. Assistive technology products that are helpful to people with visual impairments are described in the following list.

- **Screen enlargers** (or screen magnifiers) work like a magnifying glass. They enlarge a portion of the screen, increasing the legibility for some users. Some screen enlargers allow a person to zoom in and out on a particular area of the screen.

- **Screen readers** are software programs that present graphics and text as speech. Because a monitor is irrelevant to a computer user who is blind, a screen reader is used to verbalize, or "speak," everything on the screen including names and descriptions of control buttons, menus, text, and punctuation. As the user moves the cursor from point to point by pressing the Tab key, for example, each new command button is described. The text is read aloud, for example, "OK" or "Enter." In essence, a screen reader transforms a **graphic user interface (GUI)** into an **audio interface**.

- **Speech recognition systems**, also called voice recognition programs, allow people to give commands and enter data using their voices rather than a mouse or keyboard. Voice recognition systems use a microphone attached to the computer, which can be used to create text documents such as letters or e-mail messages, browse the Internet, and navigate among applications and menus by voice. Historically the stuff of science fiction, speech recognition technology is evolving to the point that all individuals will be able to eliminate their keyboards in the future.

- **Speech synthesizers** receive information going to the screen in the form of letters, numbers, and punctuation marks, and then "speak" it out loud. Often referred to as text-to-speech (TTS), the voice of the computer is synthesized speech—a distinctive, sometimes monotone voice that is the joining together of preprogrammed letters and words. Using speech synthesizers allows blind users to review their input as they type.

- **Refreshable Braille displays**, as shown in Figure 2-2 on the next page, provide tactile output of information represented on the computer screen. A Braille "cell" is composed of a series of dots. The pattern of the dots and the various combinations of the cells are used in place of letters. Unlike conventional Braille, which is permanently embossed onto paper, refreshable Braille displays mechanically lift small, rounded plastic or metal pins as needed to form Braille characters. The user reads the Braille letters with his or her fingers, and then, after a line is read, can refresh the display to read the next line.

- **Braille embossers** transfer computer generated text into embossed Braille output. Braille translation programs convert text scanned in or generated via standard word processing programs into Braille, which can be printed on the embosser. Because of the size of the "cells" that are used in place of letters and the formatting of documents to be read by individuals who are blind, the amount of text normally contained on one 8.5-by-11-inch sheet of paper results in multiple pages when printed in Braille.

- **Talking and large-print word processors** are software programs that use speech synthesizers to provide auditory feedback of what is typed. Large-print word processors allow the user to view everything in large text without added screen enlargement. Individuals with learning disabilities often use these special featured word processors to assist them with their spelling and grammar and/or to provide the auditory feedback they require to be able to write.

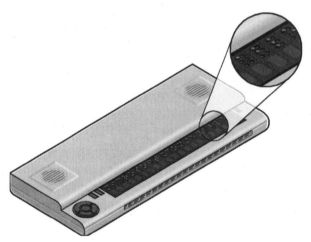

Figure 2-2.   *Refreshable Braille display*

Profile

Doris is a human resources manager at a large forest products company in British Columbia. Doris has been visually impaired since age 20 as a result of glaucoma. She is able to see text and images on her computer screen when they are enlarged to about 1.5 inches in height. Doris can effectively view and interact with personnel records—an important part of her job—by using a screen enlargement program. The program is a software add-on to her personal computer, which uses the Windows XP operating system. The PC she uses is standard for her department and requires no additional hardware or software other than the enlarger for her accommodation.

Mobility Impairments

Mobility impairments can be caused by a wide range of common illnesses and accidents such as arthritis, stroke, cerebral palsy, Parkinson's disease, multiple sclerosis, loss of limbs or digits, spinal cord injuries, and repetitive stress injury, among others. As a result of these accidents or conditions, individuals might be unable to use (or be without) arms or fingers to interact with their computers using the standard keyboard or mouse. People who have some motion impairment in their hands might be unable to type key combinations that require one key to be held down while pressing another. Others might strike multiple keys or repeat keys unintentionally. Some people might have use of their hands and arms but have a limited range of motion. All of these conditions make using a standard mouse or keyboard difficult, if not impossible.

Accessibility features built into Windows XP that are useful to people with mobility impairments include **keyboard filters** that compensate somewhat for erratic motion, tremors, slow response time, and similar conditions. For example, StickyKeys allows the user to enter key combinations without having to hold one key down while a depressing a second. Other options allow users to adjust how quickly a letter appears on the screen when they hold down a key. In addition, Windows XP allows users to adjust mouse properties such as button configuration, double-click speed, pointer size, and how quickly the mouse pointer responds to movements of the mouse. These options are available in Windows XP on the Keyboard tab in the Accessibility Options dialog box, which is shown in Figure 2-3 on the next page. Users can also increase the size of screen elements to provide a larger target, which can benefit people who have disabilities related to fine motor skills.

The Origin of StickyKeys

Microsoft's first work in the area of accessibility started in 1988 with a partnership between Microsoft and the Trace Research and Development Center at the University of Wisconsin in Madison. Trace requested assistance from Microsoft in creating a product that would make the Microsoft Windows 2.0 operating system accessible for people who are deaf or hard-of-hearing, or who have limited dexterity.

(continued)

The Origin of StickyKeys   *(continued)*

Funded by the National Institute on Disability and Rehabilitation Research (NIDRR) and IBM, the "Windows 2.0 Project" was carried out with technical assistance from the Microsoft Windows management team. The result was the "Access Utility for Windows 2.0" add-on program that enhanced keyboard and mouse operations (**StickyKeys**, **FilterKeys**, and **MouseKeys**), provided visual feedback when the computer made sounds (**ShowSounds**), and allowed specialized devices to operate the computer through a serial port (**SerialKeys**). These features are now built into the most recent versions of the Windows operating system.

Figure 2-3.   *Windows XP Accessibility Options dialog box, Keyboard tab*

Assistive technology products used with computers by people with mobility impairments are described in the following list.

- **Speech recognition programs**, as mentioned earlier, allow users to write text, navigate the Web, send e-mail, and use applications by using voice commands rather than a mouse or keyboard. These programs are often very helpful to people who do not have use of their hands and therefore have difficulty using a keyboard and mouse. Some individuals with mobility impairments like carpal tunnel use speech recognition in conjunction with a keyboard and mouse, allowing them to reduce their keyboard and mouse usage.

- **On-screen keyboard programs** provide an image of a standard or modified keyboard on the computer screen. The user selects the keys with a mouse, touch screen, trackball, joystick, switch, or electronic pointing device. On-screen keyboards often have a scanning option. With the scanning capability turned on, the individual keys on the on-screen keyboard are highlighted. When a desired key is highlighted, an individual with a mobility impairment is able to select it by using a switch positioned near a body part that the individual has under his or her voluntary control.

- **Keyboard filters** include typing aids, such as word prediction utilities and add-on spelling checkers. These products can often be used to relieve the user from having to make a lot of keystrokes. As an example, imagine you have to type the letter "g." However, in order to type the letter, you first have to move your finger over the entire first row of your keyboard and halfway across the second row. Along the way, you might accidentally depress "r," "p," or "d," but you only want the letter "g." Keyboard filters enable users to quickly access the letters they need and to avoid inadvertently selecting keys they don't want.

- **Touch screens** are devices placed on the computer monitor (or built into it) that allow direct selection or activation of the computer by touching the screen. These devices can benefit some users with mobility impairments because they present a more accessible target. It is easier for some people to select an option directly rather than through a mouse movement or keyboard. Moving the mouse or using the keyboard for some might require greater fine motor skills than simply touching the screen to make a selection. Other people with mobility impairments might make their selections with assistive technology such as mouth sticks.

Alternative input devices allow individuals to control their computers through means other than a standard keyboard or pointing device. Examples are described in the list on the following page.

- **Alternative keyboards** are available in different sizes with different keypad arrangements and angles. Larger keyboards are available with enlarged keys (see the example shown in Figure 2-4), which are easier to access by people with limited motor skills. Smaller keyboards are available with smaller keys (or keys placed closer together) to allow someone with a limited range of motion the ability to reach all the keys. Many other keyboards are also available—some with keypads located at various angles and others that include split keyboards, which offer the keypad split into different sections.

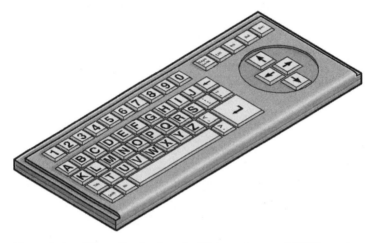

Figure 2-4.   *Alternative keyboard with large keys and ABC layout*

- **Electronic pointing devices** allow the user to control the cursor on the screen using ultrasound, an infrared beam, eye movements, nerve signals, or brain waves. When used with an on-screen keyboard, electronic pointing devices also allow the user to enter text or data.

- **Sip-and-puff systems**, shown in Figure 2-5, refer to just one of many different types of switch access. In typical configurations, a dental saliva extractor is attached to a switch. An individual uses his or her breath to activate the switch. For example, a puff generates the equivalent of a keystroke, the pressing of a key, a mouse click, and so on. Maintaining constant "pressure" on the switch (more like sucking than sipping) is the equivalent of holding a key down. With an on-screen keyboard, the user "puffs" out the letters. Moving the cursor over a document's title bar and "sipping" enables the user to drag items around on the screen just as you would with a mouse (often used with on-screen keyboards).

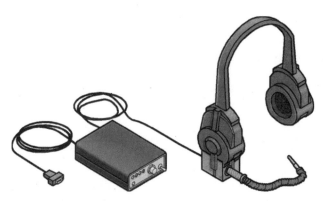

Figure 2-5.   *Sip-and-puff device*

- **Wands and sticks** are typing aids used to strike keys on the keyboard. They are most commonly worn on the head, held in the mouth, strapped to the chin, or held in the hand. They are useful for people who need to operate their computers without the use of their hands or who have difficulty generating fine movements.

- **Joysticks** can be plugged into the computer's mouse port and used to control the cursor on the screen. Joysticks benefit users who need to operate a computer with or without the use of their hands. For example, some people might operate the joystick with their feet or with the use of a cup on top of the joystick that can be manipulated with their chin.

- **Trackballs** look like an upside down mouse with a movable ball on top of a stationary base. An example of a trackball is shown in Figure 2-6. The ball can be rotated with a pointing device or a hand. People who have fine motor skills but lack gross motor skills can use these devices.

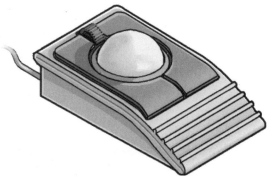

Figure 2-6.   *Trackball*

Profile

Robert is a safety manager for a southeast regional department of transportation. At 25, he lost a hand in an industrial accident. The accident prompted Robert's interest in safety, which led to his current position, but it was his mobility impairment that prompted him to learn about assistive technology. After his accident, Robert trained for and was hired for an administrative position at the department of transportation, which required him to work with a computer. Because Robert already knew how to type and had the use of one hand, he was able to accomplish his typing requirements quickly and efficiently using a low-cost assistive technology device called a Half Qwerty keyboard. The keyboard is half the size of a regular keyboard, and each key allows access to two letters. The Shift key allows switching back and forth between the two letters. Robert's typing speed is now even faster than when he had the use of both hands.

Deaf and Hard-of-Hearing

Hearing impairments encompass a range of conditions—from slight hearing loss to deafness. People who have hearing impairments might be able to hear some sound, but might not be able to distinguish words. People with this type of hearing impairment can use an amplifying device to provide functional hearing. Other people might not be able to hear sound at all.

Accessibility features in Windows XP include settings that allow the user to change sound notification to visual notification and control volume. Accessibility options include SoundSentry and ShowSounds, which allow users to choose to receive visual warnings and text captions, for example, rather than sound messages for system events. Applications such as Microsoft's Encarta encyclopedia have captions built in, and individuals with hearing impairments can use it with one or both of the previously mentioned utilities turned on. The Sound tab found in the Accessibility Options dialog box in Windows XP is shown in Figure 2-7.

There are no specific assistive technology products for people who are deaf or hard-of-hearing because generally people can interact perfectly with computers as long as they can choose to receive information visually or adjust sounds and volume to meet their hearing needs. Sound options are built into Windows, making technology accessible to people who are deaf and hard-of-hearing.

Figure 2-7.   *Windows XP Accessibility Options dialog box, Sound tab*

Assistive technology for people who are deaf and hard-of-hearing includes **captioning**, which is a standard capability of modern televisions. All televisions are equipped with a decoder. When the decoder is turned on, a captioned broadcast can be read on the screen. This same capability also allows an individual to watch television late into the night without disturbing a sleeping spouse. In a noisy environment, such as an airport where it might be impossible to turn up the volume, captioning is also beneficial.

Profile

Steve, deaf since birth, is a research assistant who works in the corporate library of a large financial corporation. His specialty is world economics, and he spends most of his day searching and reading statistical information over the Internet. Also, Steve frequently views video training programs and takes advantage of built-in video captioning, which provides textual descriptions of information otherwise communicated orally. Steve works very effectively with his computer and uses some built-in Windows XP accessibility options to meet his particular needs. Because he is deaf, he does not need any sound information from his computer, so he has completely turned off the sound.

(continued)

Profile   *(continued)*

He wants to ensure that he visually obtains information that would otherwise be conveyed by sound, so he uses SoundSentry to provide visual warnings for system sounds, ShowSounds to display captions for speech and sounds, and Notification to provide visual warnings when features are turned on or off.

Computer Use Among People Who Are Both Deaf and Blind

Although it's not well known, people who are both deaf and blind can also use computers with the aid of assistive technology. To someone who is both deaf and blind, captioning and other sound options are of no use, but Braille assistive technology products are critical. People who are both deaf and blind can use computers by using refreshable Braille displays and Braille embossers.

Myth vs. Fact

Myth: People who are both deaf and blind cannot use a computer.

Fact: People who are deaf and blind can access computers with the help of various Braille assistive technology products.

Language Impairments

Language impairments include conditions such as **aphasia** (loss or impairment of the power to use or comprehend words, often as a result of brain damage), delayed speech (a symptom of cognitive impairment), and other conditions resulting in difficulties remembering, solving problems, or perceiving sensory information. For people who have these impairments, complex or inconsistent visual displays or word choices can make using computers more difficult. For most computer users, in fact, software that is designed to minimize clutter and competing objects on the screen is easier to use, more inviting, and more useful.

Some individuals with language disabilities do not have the ability to communicate orally. These individuals can use **augmentative** and **assistive communication devices** to "speak" for them. To communicate, these individuals either type out words and phrases they wish to "say" or select from a series of images that, when arranged in a particular way, generate a phrase. For example, an individual could use the combination of a picture of an apple and a representation of McDonalds' golden arches to order a hot apple pie. Pairing the picture of the arches with a picture of a car could "say," "Let's take a ride to McDonalds." Users of augmentative and assistive communication devices can also use the SerialKeys option in the Windows XP Accessibility Options dialog box to select alternative devices to the standard keyboard and mouse.

Microsoft Windows XP has a simplified new user interface that reduces clutter on the screen. This benefits people with language and learning disabilities in particular because it reduces the interference of competing information on the screen, which can be confusing. Other options that allow for abbreviated menus and customized toolbars, for example, also help reduce the number of competing elements on the screen. Spelling and grammar checkers are also helpful for those who commonly switch the order of letters because of dyslexia and other learning impairments.

Assistive technology products used with computers by people with language impairments are described in the following list.

- **Keyboard filters**, defined earlier, which include word prediction utilities and add-on spelling checkers, can help people with language impairments.

- **Speech recognition programs**, defined earlier, allow people to use their voice to operate a computer and compose text. This technology is useful to people with a wide range of disabilities including those with visual, mobility, language, and learning impairments. Some individuals with learning impairments often find speech recognition easier to use for writing text.

- **Screen review utilities** make on-screen information available as synthesized speech and pairs the speech with a visual representation of a word, for example, highlighting a word as it is spoken. Screen review utilities convert the text that appears on screen into a computer voice. This helps some people with language impairments by giving them information visually and aurally at the same time.

- **Touch screens** are devices placed on the computer monitor (or built into it) that allow direct selection or activation of the computer by touching the screen. Earlier we discussed how touch screens benefit people with mobility impairments, but they also benefit users with language disabilities. The ability to touch the computer screen to make a selection is advantageous for people with language and learning disabilities because it is a more simple, direct, and intuitive process than making a selection using a mouse or keyboard.

- **Speech synthesizers**, defined earlier, provide the user with information through a computer voice. Also known as text-to-speech (TTS), the speech synthesizer receives information in the form of letters, numbers, and punctuation marks, and then "speaks" it out loud to the user in a monotone "computer voice."

Profile

John is a dental assistant who is recovering from a slight stroke that occurred six months ago. He has some weakness and mobility loss as a result of the stroke but is improving in strength and flexibility each day. John's employer has assisted him in his recovery process by allowing a shorter workday and rearranging the workplace for easier access and mobility. John's job requires him to work for some part of each day entering and retrieving data from his computer. As a result of the stroke, John has some difficulty processing information and finds complicated computer displays confusing. To assist their friend and coworker, John's officemates experimented with ways to modify his Windows XP-based computer to configure an easier to understand visual display. They used various Control Panel tools to make icons larger and menus shorter, and to minimize the number of toolbars that appeared on screen. They also made custom toolbars that included only the buttons John needed to do his job and turned off sound, which was also distracting to him. They reduced the number of items on his Start menu and turned off the feature that reorders frequently used items on toolbars and menus because the constant updating was confusing to John. They also turned off animations and video by selecting Internet Options from Internet Explorer's Tools menu and adjusting settings on the Advanced tab. As John recovers, he can easily reconfigure his display according to his needs and preferences.

Learning Impairments

Learning impairments can range from conditions such as dyslexia and attention deficit disorder to retardation. Processing problems are the most common and have the most impact on a person's ability to use computer applications. These conditions interfere with the learning process. Many people with these impairments are perfectly capable of learning if information is presented to them in a form and at a pace that is appropriate to them individually. Information that is presented in short, discrete units is often easier to understand. In addition, many individuals with learning disabilities learn more efficiently using their visual abilities rather than their auditory skills. Many individuals are primarily visual or auditory learners, whereas other learners are "ambidextrous." During the learning process, individuals with learning difficulties benefit from having a multisensory experience of audio speech paired with a visual representation.

Did You Know?   According to the American Council on Education, the number of college students reporting learning disabilities has risen significantly since 1988. In fall 2001, 2.4 percent of approximately 1.1 million college freshmen in the United States attending four-year schools self-reported a learning disability. That's more than double the number who self-reported learning disabilities in 1988. In that year, only 1.0 percent of the same group self-reported a learning disability. (Henderson 2001)

The simplified interface introduced in Microsoft Windows XP benefits people with learning impairments, as well as people with language impairments, because it helps reduce the number of competing elements on the screen. Complicated user interfaces can interfere with learning. User interface engineers found that an emphasis on a consistent user experience had the greatest positive impact on individuals with processing problems. Consider the individual who can't read his own handwriting but can edit for others by using a computer. Additional computer settings such as adjustable text and screen element sizes, speech capabilities, choice of visual or sound warnings for system events, and Internet display options can benefit those with learning impairments.

Assistive technology products used with computers by people with learning disabilities are described in the following list.

- **Word prediction programs** allow the user to select a desired word from an on-screen list located in the prediction window. This list, generated by the computer, predicts words from the first one or two letters typed by the user. The word can then be selected from the list and inserted into the text by typing a number, clicking the mouse, or scanning with a switch. These programs help users increase written productivity and accuracy, and increase vocabulary skills through word prompting.

- **Reading comprehension programs** focus on establishing or improving reading skills through ready-made activities, stories, exercises, or games. These programs can help users practice letter sound recognition and can increase the understanding of words by adding graphics, sound, and possibly animation.

- **Reading tools and learning disabilities programs** include software designed to make text-based materials more accessible for people who struggle with reading. Options can include scanning, reformatting, navigating, or speaking text out loud. These programs help people who have difficulty seeing or manipulating conventional print materials; people who are developing new literacy skills or who are learning English as a foreign language; and people who comprehend better when they hear and see text highlighted simultaneously.

- **Speech synthesizers**, as mentioned previously, are helpful not only for people with visual and learning impairments, but also for those with language impairments. Speech synthesizers (also known as text-to-speech) speak information aloud in a computerized voice. Individuals who have lost the ability to communicate orally can use speech synthesizers to communicate by typing information and letting the speech synthesizer speak it aloud.

- **Speech recognition programs**, as mentioned earlier, are helpful for people with a variety of impairments. Individuals can enter data, write text, and navigate applications with the use of their voice. People who have difficulty typing or reading text because of a language or learning impairment can often successfully work with computer documents using a speech recognition program along with the powerful features of modern word processing programs, such as Microsoft Word 2002.

Profile

Clair is a lead program manager at a large software company in California. Clair has a learning impairment that affects her reading and writing skills, especially her organization and reference skills. She began using a computer at age six to help her learn to read and write. The computer is now an essential tool that helps her capture her thoughts "in the moment" and organize them at a later time. Clair uses a PC equipped with Windows XP and Microsoft Office XP. Clair frequently uses the built-in spelling and grammar checkers in Microsoft Word 2002 as well as the graphical toolbars and icons in all of the Office programs. She finds icons more useful than menus. She often uses Microsoft PowerPoint to capture her thoughts and organize them. Clair also appreciates the customization options for files and folders that allow her to organize and view them in ways that better suit her particular sense of organization.

Age-Related Impairments

The likelihood of developing a disability increases with age. People age 45–54 have an 11.5 percent chance of developing a disability. Your chances dramatically increase between the ages of 55–64. (LaPlante, Carlson 1992) The incidence of physical impairments increases with age, and physical mobility begins declining during the middle age years. The incidence of conditions such as heart disease, back problems, arthritis, orthopedic impairment, and others that cause activity limitation increase with age. Functional impairments that normally do not affect job performance—such as deterioration of eyesight and mild hearing loss—also increase with age. Rates of activity limitation are incrementally lower among younger people:

- Ages 55–64   28.4 percent
- Ages 25–54   14.1 percent

Numerous accessibility features built into Windows XP can help people with mild age-related disabilities use their computers more comfortably and effectively.

These accessibility features include

- Visual options such as the choice of screen display options involving scroll bars, icons, mouse pointers, and type display

- Mobility options such as keyboard shortcuts to reduce reliance on the mouse

- Hearing options such as ShowSounds and SoundSentry to receive sound information visually

---

Profile

Julia is a claims representative in the southwest regional office of a major American insurance company. At age 55 with 30 years to her credit, she decided to take advantage of her company's early retirement option. After a few years off, Julia decided she really missed the camaraderie of the workplace and decided to return to the workforce. She accepted a position with another insurance company that was eager to hire her because of her vast experience. Her current job suits her needs for workplace camaraderie and affords her additional income to supplement her retirement benefits. Julia's job requires many hours on the telephone and at the computer. Julia is physically active and exercises regularly but has begun to develop arthritis. To lessen the need to enter data using her computer keyboard or mouse, which is sometimes painful for her, Julia uses a voice input program. By using the voice recognition software program and a microphone plugged into her computer, Julia is able to give commands and enter and edit text by voice.

Occurrence of Different Types of Impairments

Considering all sources of activity limitation that affect an individual's computer use, Table 2-1 provides the number of people with different types of impairments. (Disability Statistics Center [UCSF] 1992)

Table 2-1. *Number of People Affected by Types of Impairments*

Back problems	7.7 million
Arthritis	5.7 million
Orthopedic impairment of lower extremity	2.8 million

Table 2-1. *Number of People Affected by Types of Impairments (continued)*

Diabetes	2.6 million
Disorders of the eye (not visual impairments)	1.6 million
Learning disabilities/mental retardation	1.6 million
Visual impairments	1.3 million
Orthopedic impairments of the shoulder and upper extremity	1.2 million
Hearing impairments	1.2 million

For More Information

If you are interested in additional information about disabilities and assistive technology products, we recommend the following resources and conferences:

- **Alliance for Technology Access (ATA)**, *http://www.ataccess.org*—The ATA is a network of community-based resource centers, developers and vendors, affiliates, and associates dedicated to providing information and support services to children and adults with disabilities and increasing their use of standard, assistive, and information technologies.

- **Assistive Technology Industry Association (ATIA)**, *http://www.atia.org*— The ATIA is a not-for-profit membership organization, which consists of organizations that manufacture or sell technology-based assistive products for people with disabilities. Some organizations also provide services associated with or required by people with disabilities. Among its primary goals was the establishment and continuation of an annual assistive technology conference.

- **CSUN's Technology and Persons with Disabilities Annual Conference**, *http://www.csun.edu/cod/*—This annual conference, sponsored by the Center on Disabilities at California State University, Northridge (CSUN), is the largest technology conference for people with disabilities. It is held annually in Los Angeles, California, in the spring.

- **Closing the Gap, Annual Conference and Resource Directory**, *http:// www.closingthegap.com/*—Closing the Gap, Inc., is an organization that focuses on computer technology for people with special needs through its resource directory, Web site, and annual conference. The annual international conference, Computer Technology in Special Education and Rehabilitation, is held each fall in Minneapolis, Minnesota. It explores the many ways that technology is being used to enhance the lives of people with special needs. The Closing the Gap Resource Directory contains over 2,000 product listings. It is a guide to the selection of the latest computer related products available for children and adults with special needs.

Leading by Example

The following five chapters provide case studies of how accessible technology was integrated into organizations in the healthcare, financial, government, retail, and manufacturing industries. Organizations such as Cingular Wireless, Compaq Computer Corporation, General Motors, RBC Financial Group, Sears, State of Georgia, UnumProvident, and U.S. Department of Defense openly share the challenges, best practices, and lessons learned to help other organizations implement accessible technology solutions.

Business Case Studies

CHAPTER 3

Accessible Technology in the Healthcare Industry

A wrestling accident at the age of 17 left Glenn Higgins quadriplegic. But it didn't stop him. Thirty-six years later, Dr. Glenn Higgins is vice president and medical director for UnumProvident, the $9.4 billion provider of income protection insurance, return-to-work products and services, and **income-protection services** for employees who become injured or ill and unable to work. In a company dedicated to helping people with disabilities, he demonstrates that having a physical disability doesn't need to be an impediment to succeeding in a high-level job.

Higgins's experience has given him perspective on the evolution and status of assistive technology, and he is unwavering in his assessment.

"What I can do now with assistive technology is a thousand times beyond what was possible 20 years ago, 10 years ago," he says. "Early solutions were remarkable but incredibly slow, frustrating, and not ready for prime time. The current state of continuous-speech recognition solutions is amazing, fantastic, and something I could only hope for as recently as three or four years ago."

Indeed, when Higgins first used computers in graduate school, in the pre-PC era, assistive technology consisted pretty much of "locking keys" on a keyboard and using a mouth stick to control the Caps Lock, Shift, Alt, and Ctrl keys as well as similar functions. Even that was an advance over the first typewriter-based technology Higgins used during his initial hospitalization and rehabilitation, which required puffing Morse code into a straw to work the typewriter. Higgins tried that solution but was quickly discouraged.

Today, in contrast, Higgins is fully productive with little more than his **puff-stick** and the Dragon Naturally Speaking 4.5 speech recognition system running on Microsoft Windows 98 on his office PC. Higgins augments Dragon with a headset, a keyboard-anchored microphone, a **tele-dictation system** that allows him to dictate long memos and receive the text in e-mail, a scanner that allows him to manage visual records and forms as Microsoft PowerPoint images, and the accessibility features built into Windows including StickyKeys and keyboard shortcuts.

Together, these tools allow Higgins, who holds a Ph.D. in neuropsychology, to direct medical affairs for UnumProvident. Higgins reviews evidence on the quality of insurance claims to confirm that alleged impairments are supported by medical evidence. In addition to meeting with claims payers to discuss individual cases, the bulk of his day is spent reviewing files and writing reports—activities for which his assistive technology solution is essential.

Knowing when and how to use his assistive technology tools is one key to Higgins's success. For relatively short input—three or four paragraphs—Higgins prefers to use Dragon, speaking into a Norcomm desktop microphone, which is especially adept at filtering out extraneous noise that can impede Dragon's accuracy, that sits on top of his keyboard. Higgins finds this solution to be 90 percent accurate.

But 90 percent "still leaves room for a lot of mistakes" when working on longer documents, mistakes that usually can't be corrected by a spelling checker because they're not misspelled words, just the wrong words. Sometimes Higgins finds an unintelligible phrase in the middle of a fairly long sentence—a problem that he says could be curbed if he reviewed his work during dictation and took the time to train Dragon more thoroughly to his voice. Meanwhile, for input longer than a few paragraphs, Higgins finds it quicker to use his tele-dictation system, creating audio that is sent to a manual dictation service, which is then transcribed and returned to him in e-mail. He can then review the dictated text files and edit them using Dragon. Similarly, Higgins sometimes uses a Web-based transcription service, *http://www.idictate.com*, that automates the process of converting audio files to text.

Higgins also needs to work with great amounts of information that originate in paper form. For example, from a typical file a half-inch thick, he might need to review up to 70 pieces of paper. To make that possible, his assistant scans the required documents using a scanner. The files are then stored in PaperPort image management software from which Higgins can work with them as PaperPort images, using his mouth-stick as a navigational tool.

Despite relying on some fairly sophisticated tools, Higgins doesn't overlook basic accessibility features in Windows software, without which he says he'd be at a major loss. StickyKeys can be controlled with his mouth-stick. Keyboard shortcuts allow him to use Dragon or his mouth-stick to handle much of the navigation and management of drop-down lists, dialog boxes, buttons, and other interface elements that would otherwise require a mouse.

"For example, formatting a document in Word is something I can do with a keyboard shortcut instead of the mouse," he says. "No one shortcut is a big deal, but they do add up to make me much more productive. And they're features I don't find as much in the Apple Macintosh, where there are many things you can't do without a mouse."

Higgins also reserves praise for his employer, UnumProvident.

"They've been very good about helping me," he says. "An **occupational therapist** reviewed my workspace needs when I first joined the company. A disability manager reviewed the therapist's proposal for assistive technology and came up with the solution I use. The company set it up and hired an outside trainer to train me on Dragon. The trainer is still available to me for ongoing training if I wish. They've been extremely supportive of everything I need to do the job that they and I want me to do."

A Company Committed to People with Disabilities

UnumProvident's commitment to Glenn Higgins is hardly unique for the company. With more than a century of industry leadership, UnumProvident is the nation's number one provider of insurance products and services that help employees protect their incomes if they become injured or ill and unable to work. The company also provides extensive resources to help those employees get back to work whenever possible.

UnumProvident knows that employee disability can be a significant drain on a company's productivity. Its WorkRX Return-to-Work program is designed to find innovative ways to get employees back on the job, restoring their dignity and their company's productivity at the same time. Innovative support for employees with disabilities—including assistive technology—is high on UnumProvident's list.

The company estimates that out of a nationwide workforce of 12,000, it has about 550 employees with some level of disability. Most of these employees require only modest accommodation, such as a change in job or the addition of ergonomic support. About 10 percent of its disabled employees, approximately 50, use some form of assistive technology. Half use speech recognition technology to compensate for repetitive motion injuries, such as **carpal tunnel syndrome**. The remainder use screen magnifiers, screen readers, and other devices to compensate for visual impairment.

UnumProvident tells its customers what it knows itself: that the use of assistive technology to attract or retain qualified employees who have disabilities is more than the moral or legal thing to do—it's the sound business thing to do.

"It makes absolutely no business sense to take people with expertise and training for specific jobs and put them out on short- or long-term disability, at significant portions of their pay, when a modest investment in assistive technology could keep them on the job," says Joel Proper, disability manager for UnumProvident. "You may be talking about a person who's learned 20 custom applications and systems specific to UnumProvident. We have every reason to invest in retaining that person."

For example, the company invested $1,900 in speech recognition technology to accommodate an employee with **tendonitis**; this both gained her continued productivity and saved the $31,000 per year it would have cost to put her on long-term disability. In other cases, assistive technology makes the difference between an employee's ability to work part time or full time. In all, UnumProvident estimates that its approximate $50,000 annual investment in assistive technology hardware and software returns hundreds of thousands of dollars in productivity and savings.

In other cases, such as that of vice president and medical director Glenn Higgins, assistive technology isn't a way to keep a good employee on the job, it's a way to attract and hire the best qualified candidate in the first place.

"Dr. Higgins is a highly trained and skilled neuropsychologist with extensive background in private practice and hospital work," points out Proper. "Assistive technology enables us to give him the tools he needs to be a tremendous asset to the company. It's a win-win for him and for UnumProvident."

Deborah Gilikson: Keyboarding Just Caught Up with Her

"After so much keying for 18 years, it just caught up with me," says Deborah Gilikson, an account specialist for UnumProvident.

Working for UnumProvident since 1982, Gilikson began to experience pains in her wrists two years ago. An ergonomics expert from the company recommended a stand-up desk to reduce the amount of time that Gilikson spent in a sitting position and ensured that her monitor was at arm's length and that her chair was the right height for those times when she needed to sit.

She started taking stretch breaks. On her doctor's recommendation, she reduced her daily keyboard work from eight hours to six, and then to 20 minutes every half hour.

Nothing helped. Gilikson, diagnosed with carpal tunnel syndrome and tendonitis, left the company on disability pay, hoping that a complete break from keyboarding would enable her to return to work. While out on disability, Gilikson went for therapy treatments and bought gym memberships to work out on machines to strengthen her upper body and arms. Although the regimen brought some relief, it was no cure.

Gilikson was determined to return to work at UnumProvident. As a young woman, she couldn't contemplate never working again. And with a serious disability, she knew her options for new employment at other companies would be extremely limited. In consultation with her workers' compensation program and the company, Gilikson did return to work in July 2001 armed with new support from UnumProvident to accommodate her disability by minimizing the amount of keyboarding she had to do. In addition, Dragon Naturally Speaking 4.0 was installed on her Microsoft Windows NT 4.0 Workstation desktop computer.

In her current position, Gilikson is responsible for coding the enrollment forms used to enroll employees of customer companies as well as for coding their insurance program changes and salary changes. Through the capabilities of the voice recognition system, combined with the knowledge that she has gained in knowing how and when to use it, Gilikson has found that having a physical disability doesn't necessarily translate into an inability to do the job. On the contrary, Gilikson is more productive than UnumProvident expects for a person in her job category. She manages 150 percent of a full case load.

Each day, Gilikson logs on to her computer system, puts on her headset microphone, logs on to Dragon, and then returns to the enrollment system. Gilikson uses the voice recognition system for input and for navigating around a screen. Instead of keying in policy numbers, termination dates, dates of hire, salaries, and other field entries, Gilikson speaks each entry and says "enter" to move to the next field. On a screen with 30 fields, the voice recognition system is 100 percent accurate on at least 27 fields without issue, says Gilikson. With navigation, she finds the system "does tabs really well," allowing her, for example, to say "five tabs" and move faster through a screen's fields than she could manually.

On the other hand, the system can mistake "four" for "for," as well as other homonyms. In addition, if Gilikson pauses while entering numbers, she finds it can insert an unwanted hyphen, which requires her to go back and make a correction either via voice commands or, as she often prefers, manually. When many users are on the system or there are other network problems, voice recognition can be prone to greater errors. To move between applications, Gilikson finds that switching manually is often more effective than speaking a custom macro that the system might misunderstand as keyboard input. In all, she credits Dragon with an 80 percent accuracy rate.

"When the system makes a mistake, you have to discipline it like a teenager," she says. "Once you do that, the remaining problems are mostly the result of network issues."

That "discipline" or training started with Gilikson's introduction to Dragon. As part of her orientation, Gilikson met with a trainer for several two-hour sessions. She spent 15 minutes training the system by reading several standard paragraphs to it so that the system could match her pronunciation to its vocabulary.

In daily use, when Dragon makes an input error, Gilikson has the option to say "correct that," which displays the Dragon correction box. She can then type or say the correct word. Once Dragon has the corrected word, she can say "train/record" to confirm the correction, and then enter the information in Dragon's vocabulary for future use. At first, Gilikson found herself correcting Dragon a frustrating 70 percent of the time. Now, that's down to about five percent.

"The first week I worked with Dragon, I thought the recognition was terrible, but I put serious time into this thing," she recalls. "It caught on to what I wanted, and the accuracy improved."

Gilikson also finds that the accuracy differs as she moves from application to application. For example, Dragon is more accurate when Gilikson is using the EMMA Easy Member Enrollment application—"it was really accurate the first time"—than when she is using the Merlin billing system. The system also works with Microsoft Outlook, which Gilikson uses for e-mail, although Gilikson acknowledges that she doesn't send many e-mail messages. If she did, she anticipates the accuracy would increase.

Boosting overall performance is also a function of knowing when to rely on Dragon and when to input instructions or corrections manually.

"I've learned when to use Dragon and when I should do something myself to get it done quicker," she says.

For example, when speaking "T-E" to enter a termination code, Dragon will sometimes insert only the "T." Gilikson says it's faster for her to enter the "E" manually than to go through the voice-based correction process for a single letter. Similarly, Gilikson has learned to rely on manual navigation between applications because they are more reliable than using macros and Dragon.

The best advice that Gilikson has for others learning and using voice recognition is to make thoughtful use of macros to enter large amounts of text.

"In coding systems for insurance, you have very long benefit IDs—a slew of letters and numbers that have to be entered to represent a specific insurance benefit," she explains. "Instead of typing or speaking a long string of letters and numbers, I can program Dragon to insert a specific string in response to my saying a simple macro name."

For example, Gilikson chose to use the phrase "Benefit One" to represent one such alphanumeric sequence. The chief downside is that any words reserved for macros are forfeited as words that can be input as spoken.

Why was it so important to Gilikson to find a way to return to productive employment at UnumProvident?

"I've worked at UnumProvident my whole life," she explains. "It's all I know. I had a good job with good pay. With the help of voice recognition, I'm earning that pay again in the place I want to work. It's demanding work, but my disability doesn't prevent me from meeting those demands and being a fully productive employee."

Elmer Pelletier: Trail-Blazing Programmer Who Likes a Challenge

Elmer Pelletier says he likes challenges, and that's a good thing because being left completely blind following a highway construction accident at age 29 certainly qualified as a challenge. Pelletier couldn't go back to the construction company he co-owned with his brothers. Instead, he went to college. It was the early 1980s, and his counselor guided him toward a career in the nascent field of personal computing. Today, Pelletier is a mainframe programming analyst for UnumProvident where he's worked for nearly 20 years, since graduating from college. Pelletier is every bit as productive as his colleagues, and he credits his employer, Microsoft, assistive technology, and his own persistence for his success.

"I'm dependent on assistive technology 100 percent," says Pelletier. "Everything I do is driven by assistive technology. It enables me to meet my goal of performing as well as my peers. I credit Microsoft for providing the leadership and the standardization that allows screen readers to work. And I credit UnumProvident for giving me the tools I need to do my job."

When Pelletier decided to embark on a career in programming, he encountered a supportive but skeptical instructor who said he'd do his best to try to teach the first blind student in the program. Pelletier didn't know computers and didn't know how to type. But a lot of nights and weekends in the lab, combined with the ingenuity to hire fellow students to read his textbooks onto tape for his playback, paid off. In nine months, he had mastered three computer languages.

He also gained experience with the first talking computer used in the state of Maine, the Total Talk computer, a mainframe terminal with a voice synthesizer interface. The computer could read aloud a line of text at a time. With the PC-based **JAWS** solution that runs on his Microsoft Windows PC, Pelletier can now read a full page or screen at a time.

"It was a tremendous challenge when I was hired; I was blazing trails," says Pelletier. In an age long before discrimination against people with disabilities was outlawed, he convinced his superiors at UnumProvident that the screen reading solution would put him fully on par with sighted programmers, similarly navigating and working through text-based screens. Now, as a programmer analyst, Pelletier is responsible for writing and maintaining programs that support the payment of commissions to the company's brokers.

The JAWS solution that Pelletier uses is software-based and runs on Windows; the PC—a 400 MHz Pentium II with 128 MB RAM—and keyboard are entirely standard. One of the biggest differences in how Pelletier navigates around the screen, compared to conventional use, is that he never uses a mouse. Instead, he uses navigation keys on the numeric keypad to move up, down, or side-to-side on the screen. Using the numeric keypad in combination with the Insert key gives him even greater flexibility: he can move the insertion point forward or back by one character, word, sentence, or paragraph at a time as he chooses.

Moving across the screen is one thing; knowing where the cursor is in relation to the text is another. To understand what's on the screen, Pelletier sets JAWS to "echo" or speak the text of every keystroke. Because he is often typing strings of alphanumeric and symbolic characters rather than English language words, it's crucial that he keys in the correct letters, numbers, and symbols. When that degree of accuracy isn't needed, Pelletier types at top speed, and the computer's recitation of the keystrokes becomes a blur. But when accuracy is needed, Pelletier slows down and listens to the machine's "echo" of his typing.

At least 90 percent of Pelletier's time is spent reading or writing alphanumeric text to the mainframe. To do so, he uses a **terminal emulator**, Attachmate, which runs on his PC. But a small and growing amount of his time is spent outside of this environment in the more graphical environment of the Microsoft Windows operating system. There, text is augmented by a variety of features about which people without visual disabilities seldom think twice: menu bars, dialog boxes, toolbar buttons, and other graphical elements. Moreover, line-by-line navigation is no longer enough; some use of the mouse is desirable if not essential.

JAWS has repeatedly enhanced its product to accommodate these features. It has special keys to open drop-down lists, and keys on the numeric pad serve as right- and left-click buttons for the mouse. Pelletier not only credits JAWS but also Microsoft for his ability to navigate in a graphical world.

"Prior to Microsoft Windows, each vendor was going its own way in speech and, without a consistent direction, the field was faltering," says Pelletier. "Microsoft took the lead and set standards on how to use buttons, dialogs, and other graphical elements, making it possible for speech vendors to follow suit and develop products that accommodated these standard elements. Microsoft also allows for multiple ways to handle most functions. The Ctrl and Alt keys usually provide alternatives to graphical input, and they're a great help to me. I feel Microsoft has been a godsend to people with visual impairment."

Not that Windows and JAWS eliminate all of Pelletier's challenges. The highly visual Internet can still be problematic. JAWS is capable of reading the tags that can accompany each visual element. But Pelletier is left to the mercy of each Web site designer or administrator, who is free to put comprehensive or obscure descriptions on visual elements, or no descriptions at all.

"I haven't needed the Internet much, so this hasn't been a real problem," says Pelletier. "But it's getting to the point where I may need the Internet for my job, so it's getting more serious."

To learn more about Internet navigation using JAWS, Pelletier attends a computer user's group at a local school for the blind and finds it helpful.

"Attending a user's group is the first avenue I'd suggest to anyone seeking to learn how to master this type of assistive technology," he says. "I find that they're a tremendous help to show people what's out there, how they can use it, and what they can do."

Pelletier also says that the company for which a person works makes a great difference as well.

"UnumProvident has been a tremendous help to me," he says. "It has given me anything I need to do my job. From the start, the company said it could help me get hardware and software, but that it wouldn't do my job for me. It's one thing to use assistive technology; it's another to do your job and program successfully. I am the only blind programmer in the state, as far as I know, and I have to keep up with my peers who can see. Whenever we change technology, going from one computer or system to another, it's a big adjustment for me to get everything to work. But UnumProvident has always been very helpful in doing everything possible to make the technology work, so I can work too."

Technology That Helps Customers

UnumProvident does far more with assistive technology than use it to attract and retain qualified employees: the company uses it in ways that help its customers retain their employees as well. Assistive technology is a key component of the company's WorkRX Return-to-Work program, which helps customers minimize the impact of employee disabilities.

For example, one UnumProvident customer, a pediatrician, developed a spinal cyst that caused neurological problems, preventing her from working at her thriving practice. The cyst was surgically removed, relieving the neurological symptoms. However, following the surgery, intense pain left her with limited use of her hands and with restrictions in her ability to stand and walk.

Despite these problems, the pediatrician told the UnumProvident Vocational Rehabilitation Consultant (VRC) that she wanted to return to work within the month.

Given the customer's limitations and pain problems, the VRC referred the case to an ergonomist, and a visit was arranged just a few days after the customer returned to her office. The ergonomist proposed a range of solutions: a more suitable office chair, stools in her examining rooms that would allow parents to hold their infants while the doctor examined them, a remote headset for the phone, and footrests so her feet would not dangle.

The VRC also arranged for the purchase of voice-activated assistive technology software, specifically designed for physicians to allow dictation of notes and charts. UnumProvident paid for the installation of the program and for modifications to meet the specific needs of the doctor's office.

As a result, the ergonomic and assistive technology solutions allowed UnumProvident's customer to perform her job in greater comfort without the appearance of impairment. They also allowed her to increase her office time and to see more patients.

Tina Davidson: The Technology "Was a Mess," but She Had to Make It Work

Tina Davidson was a new employee. She was young. She was scared. And she was in denial. That's why she kept her condition a secret for six months. It was a secret that began with pain in her elbows, pain that extended down to her fingers. Overnight, her arms would rest from the nonstop keyboarding of the call center in which she worked at UnumProvident. She would feel better the next day; that is, until she went back to work.

After a while, even the nightly rests were insufficient to stop the pain. Still, Davidson kept her secret, partly out of fear and partly out of faith that it would somehow right itself. But when she could no longer manage brushing her teeth, showering, washing her hair, or doing the laundry, she couldn't pretend any longer. She went to the doctor. The diagnosis was tendonitis and **bilateral epicondilitus**. In an attempt to restore her health and keep her job, Davidson went to an array of healthcare providers including physical and occupational therapists, an acupuncturist, and even an alternative "energy healer," but with little result.

"That started me on the process of looking for other tools to help me do my job," says Davidson. "But this was years ago, and there were few tools available. I was 26. I didn't want to finish the rest of my professional life on permanent disability. Without the tools to do my old job, I looked for a new job in the company, but I couldn't keyboard, write, or use a mouse. Every job required the use of my hands to some degree. It looked like I would have to go home and stay there."

But Davidson didn't go home. Instead, she realized that some people without any use of their arms managed to stay employed, and she set out to discover how they accomplished this. What she found were early speech recognition programs that eliminated the need to use a keyboard and a mouse. The programs were clunky and error prone during the mid-1990s, but they kept people at work.

"The technology was a mess, but I had to have it," recalls Davidson. "I was committed to making it work."

Davidson, something of a pioneer at UnumProvident, made her request for a speech recognition system before the company had much experience with the technology or a formal plan in place to adopt it. The solution, Dragon Dictate, was a forerunner to Dragon Naturally Speaking. The company gave her a sound board, a headset, and an office PC with which to use the solution. Davidson was determined to make the technology work, so she bought a home PC on which she could install and learn the solution even faster. She found it was good at command and control functions, mitigating the need for a mouse, but poor at dictation, requiring her to speak each word in a clipped fashion.

Moreover, Davidson realized that speech recognition wouldn't be enough. Although it eliminated the need for a mouse, it was a very slow replacement. If she could find a better replacement for the mouse, it would vastly improve her productivity. She tried a touch-pad mouse, which "worked like a dream" with its programmable buttons, but because Davidson was losing sensation in her fingertips, she had to stop using it. She tried other devices including a joystick mouse and a foot-pedal mouse.

She then turned to the newly introduced Dragon Naturally Speaking, which greatly improved on the dictation technology in Dragon Dictate, requiring less training and making fewer errors. Davidson found with some experimentation that a combination of the products, using Dragon Naturally Speaking for dictation and Dragon Dictate for navigation, worked well for her with a foot pedal augmenting the navigation when voice was too slow.

She also realized that she could further enhance her productivity with Dragon by relying on macros as shortcuts to the highly repetitive navigational operations she made hundreds of times each day. Her investigation led her to write hundreds of macros to simplify her computer operation, and it led her to something more. Realizing that others must be facing the same challenge, she searched for those people and found them at a user's group at the Massachusetts Institute of Technology. They all found ways to share their macros, transferring files to facilitate each other's control of applications including Microsoft Word and Microsoft Excel by voice commands.

"If I want to control Microsoft Office by voice, why should I have to write the same file/print macro that someone else has written?" asks Davidson. "Being able to share macros with others really made a huge impact on my productivity."

Today, Davidson is a computer programmer in UnumProvident's document generation department. She writes and maintains applications that create insurance-related documentation, archive and retrieve that documentation, and update contracts for policy holders.

Davidson uses Dragon on what she calls a minimum PC configuration, which consists of a 233 MHz Pentium II desktop machine with 256 MB RAM running Microsoft Windows. At home, she uses Dragon on a 400 MHz Pentium II with 256 MB RAM, which also runs Microsoft Windows. Her microphone is a VXI/Parrott, which she calls "the best microphone for this use—just so clear and well made that there's not much distortion or other noise coming through."

Davidson recognizes that accuracy and productivity with speech recognition is based on the underlying technology a person uses and on how that person uses it. Her dictation is 85 percent accurate, and her navigation 75 percent accurate. She complains that her dictation should be 95 percent and would be if she worked with the system more and trained it better. But that 85 percent is accurate enough for e-mail, which constitutes her greatest use of the software.

Her advice for others in her situation is first to be honest with their employers about their injuries. "You need to get help," she says.

About assistive technology, Davidson counsels that because of the huge variety of products available, people should talk to experts and research potential solutions themselves. If they're going to use speech recognition software,

Davidson strongly recommends a trainer to provide a good introduction to the product and to help the user customize the product to facilitate common tasks.

"Good training is as essential as having the right hardware and software," says Davidson. "It's a small investment with a big return."

Looking back on her own progress, Davidson calls herself "a success case."

"I'm not a total success. I still have my injury, and it's affected my life in a large way. But I stayed at work. And now I continue to advance in my career. I call that success."

The Fruits of a Formal Decision Tree

UnumProvident's use of assistive technology is rooted in a formal "Assistive Technology Decision Tree" process it developed in 1999. In summary form, the steps in the company's process include the following:

1. **Define the problem.** Emphasize that the problem is not the impairment. The problem is the conflict between the historical way of doing the work and the way a specific employee needs to do the work as a result of the impairment. When an employee develops an injury through repetitive typing, for example, the problem to be addressed through assistive technology is not the pain in the wrists and hands; it is the inability to perform prolonged manual tasks.

2. **Modify the work.** If a simple change in the work can suffice, that is preferred. For example, perhaps by spacing out the manual components of the job more evenly during the day, the demands on the hands will not exceed the employee's limits.

3. **Modify the work environment.** For example, perhaps there is a component of stress that aggravates an injury. If the company can offer soundproofing, it might lower the noise, the stress, and, hence the injury.

4. **Introduce technology currently in use.** Once assistive technology is indicated, the company first looks for an appropriate solution already in use within the company. Such solutions will be easy and cost-effective to deploy and maintain.

5. **Introduce a commercially available solution.** If in-house solutions don't exist, the company looks for an existing solution it can adopt from the marketplace.

6. **Create or modify a solution.** If there are no in-house or commercially available solutions, the company will consider creating or modifying a solution—possibly in partnership with an outside vendor willing to lend its expertise to create a solution with wider application.

On the CD   The full decision tree is located in Appendix B, "Identifying the Right Assistive Technology," on this book's companion CD-ROM.

The decision tree also formalizes the way the company considers assistive technology solutions for a range of disabilities including motion impairment, quadriplegia, back impairment, visual impairment, auditory impairment, speech impairment, and psychological impairment. In each case, the process calls for a determination of the level of impairment including the specific abilities that the employee has or lacks. It then specifies the range of assistive technologies appropriate for that level.

For example, a person with a visual impairment who still can see the monitor up close might only require a high-resolution or oversized monitor. Someone with more limited ability who can only see enlarged type might require a screen magnifier and an oversized keyboard. Someone with complete impairment might require a screen reader, an optical character recognition (OCR) system, and a Braille display.

The company maintains a constantly updated resource guide of its supported assistive technologies, which now includes more than 20 voice dictation systems, high-resolution monitors, alternative pointing devices, scanners, screen readers, voice synthesizers, and other products (see Table 3-1). When a recommended technology is not yet on the supported list, it must be tested and certified for compatibility with the custom systems and drivers in the UnumProvident environment. The company has not found an assistive technology that did not work in its environment, although some technologies, such as Dragon Naturally Speaking, have had to be fine-tuned to work with specific applications.

Table 3-1.   *UnumProvident assistive technology resource guide*

Item	Definition	Benefit	Need for Training	Negative Impact
Dragon Naturally Speaking	Software that recognizes and creates general text from normal continuous speech. The user speaks to a computer at a natural, conversational pace, and words, sentences, and paragraphs immediately appear on the screen. Documents are created by speaking, and are then printed and/or cut-and-pasted into other applications.	Allows full utilization of computer operation by people with an impairment but requires some hand usage.	9 to 12 hours for the average user. Typical training costs $70 to $150 per hour.	Temporary productivity costs—depending on the work type, can be a productivity enhancer.
Dragon Dictate	Software that recognizes and creates general text from discrete word pronunciations. Provides complete hands-free command and control of computer.	Allows full utilization of computer operation by people with a physical impairment.	9 to 12 hours for the average user—typical training costs $70 to $150 per hour.	Temporary productivity costs—depending on the work type, can be a productivity enhancer.
21" monitor	Enlarged viewing area allowing for more material to be viewed simultaneously or for larger text.	Can be used for clients with vision impairments or range of motion issues.	Minimal.	None.
Monitor glare guard	Shield preventing glare and reflection from overhead lights and windows.	Enables those with low vision and other visual impairments to focus on the monitor.	None.	None.
Refreshable Braille display	Peripheral with moving pins emulating the Braille translation of a line of text on the monitor.	Enables people who have low vision or who are blind to read otherwise inaccessible text.	Minimal provided the client knows Braille.	Temporary productivity costs.
IntelliMouse	Mouse with scrollable wheel between the buttons.	Allows for one-handed control of scrolling.	None.	None.

Table 3-1. *UnumProvident assistive technology resource guide (continued)*

Item	Definition	Benefit	Need for Training	Negative Impact
Joystick mouse	Upright mouse in a joystick configuration.	Allows user to rest hand on mouse and use natural grip position.	Minimal.	None.
Trackball	Roller mouse.	Allows mouse control without grip.	Minimal.	None.
Cirque Smart Cat touchpad	Touchpad mouse device.	Allows mouse control without grip.	Minimal.	None.
Microsoft Natural keyboard	Split keyboard with a soft key action.	Allows more natural approach to the keyboard; might lessen discomfort for those with cumulative trauma or static posture issues.	Minimal to none.	None.
Kinesis Maxim keyboard and numerical keypad	Split and/or sloped keyboards with a detached numerical keypad that can be moved to either side of the keyboard.	Allows more natural approach to the keyboard; might lessen discomfort for those with cumulative trauma or static posture issues. Enables those with cumulative trauma or static injury to utilize their opposite hand when keying numbers.	Minimal to none.	None.
HP scanner	Hardware that connects directly to a PC or to a PC through a network and converts paper documents into e-documents using additional software.	Allows electronic access to printed materials for those who have limited use of their hands.	2 hours.	None.
Optical character recognition system	Software that converts scanned documents into a word processing format, so the document can be "read" to the employee.	Allows electronic access to printed materials for those who have total or partial sight impairments.	4 hours.	None.

Table 3-1. *UnumProvident assistive technology resource guide (continued)*

Item	Definition	Benefit	Need for Training	Negative Impact
JAWS for Windows	Software operating as a screen reading program, reading and converting text to verbal language.	Allows full utilization by people who are blind or visually impaired of computer output and operations.	16 to 24 hours for the average user. Typical training costs are $70 to $150 per hour.	Temporary productivity costs.
MAGic for Windows NT	Software that magnifies all or part of the screen up to 20 times.	Allows those with partial sight the ability to see and interact with the visual image presented on the monitor.	8 hours for the average user. Typical training costs are $70 to $150 per hour.	None.
CentreVu Agent	Phone and software that puts the telephone console in a window within a Windows operating system.	Enables users of voice-activated software hands-free access to all phone functions.	4 hours.	Can be a productivity enhancer.
Wireless headset with wheelchair battery	An alternative to a telephone handset or a wired headset connected to a voice-activated computer system.	Allows greater mobility within the office space for those who use wheelchairs.	Minimal.	None.
VXI/Parrott Switch 60V phone/ computer toggle (with optional foot switch)	A foot-operated toggle switch enabling the operator to switch back and forth between the computer and the telephone.	Enables those with upper extremity range of motion problems to use one headset to access both the phone and a voice-activated computer.	2 hours.	None.
CCTV	A video camera placed above a desk surface to capture and enlarge printed material.	Enables those with low vision problems to absorb printed or written material.	Minimal.	None.
Articulating keyboard/mouse trays	An appliance that provides an adjustable surface for a computer keyboard or mouse.	Enables enhanced access to a keyboard or mouse for those with range of motion issues.	Minimal.	None.

It Takes a Village—of Experts

An interdisciplinary team of experts implements the assistive technology process at UnumProvident:

- **An attending physician** makes the initial medical diagnosis of an employee's disability.

- **The disability manager** coordinates the process and works with the employee, the employee's supervisor, and the IT staff to identify an appropriate solution and to secure additional resources, such as an outside trainer, if needed.

- **The IT technician** implements the solution. Software-only solutions are prepared in the company's Portland, Maine, location and distributed over the network using **Systems Management Server (SMS)**, Microsoft's solution for software distribution and management. Hardware components, if needed, are built into a PC in Portland and shipped out for local installation.

Lessons Learned

The people of UnumProvident—its disability managers, IT professionals, and its employees with disabilities—all have valuable experience with the implementation of assistive technology. The following list provides their top-level advice to other companies in the industry seeking to bolster their own assistive technology efforts:

- **Educate and motivate management.** The support of managers is crucial to the success of any assistive technology effort for their employees. Demonstrate to them how assistive technology is a cost-effective investment that boosts the productivity of their departments. Make this education part of an ongoing management education program.

- **Educate and motivate the employees who need assistive technology.** Assistive technology systems won't be effective solutions if employees refuse to use them. Let employees know as soon as possible about their options, not after they've experienced their disability for several months. Provide appropriate training so employees understand how to use the technology correctly, making it more likely that they'll use it without getting discouraged. Explain that a variety of technologies might be a better solution than just one. Help employees identify additional resources, such as user groups, that can help.

- **Ensure close cooperation between the disability and IT teams.** Each has a distinctive role to play in the assistive technology process, and each depends on the other to help deliver an appropriate solution to the employee with disabilities. Make sure the teams meet regularly to review procedures, set goals, and discuss new solutions.

- **Standardize the process of assistive technology.** Instead of repeatedly reinventing the assistive technology wheel, standardize as much of the process as possible. Standardization can include the steps to be followed in deciding on an assistive technology solution as well as the specific solutions to select based on given parameters. The result will be faster and easier implementation of assistive technology as well as more consistent and effective solutions.

- **Provide sufficient IT support.** When assistive technology is an afterthought, it's easy for it to be assigned to whomever is available, prolonging the IT learning curve and delaying the effective deployment of solutions. On the other hand, limiting assistive technology experience to a single, dedicated IT professional can leave a company's assistive technology program vulnerable if that person leaves or becomes unavailable. Instead, ensure that dedicated resources are augmented by a broader staff that is frequently trained and kept up-to-date on assistive technology issues.

Summary

UnumProvident understands that a physical disability doesn't need to mean an inability to perform a given job. That understanding has helped the company to build itself into the leading provider of disability income protection insurance as well as a pioneer in industry-leading return-to-work programs. Moreover, UnumProvident attracts and retains the best employees while preserving and leveraging its investment in those employees to maximize productivity and profitability.

UnumProvident proves that assistive technology makes great business sense—and more. As systems manager Brett Battista notes, "It's our job to support PCs, and we do it all the time, but when we implement an assistive technology solution, we're really making someone's life better. That's something we like to do."

Accessible Technology in the Financial Industry

In 1974, Mumtaz Lakhani was a young woman from East Africa who had moved to Vancouver, British Columbia, in search of a better future. She had graduated from college with a degree in business administration and accounting but shrank from pursuing jobs in her field because of a severe vision disability. Employer after employer turned her away because she couldn't use their computer systems. "You can't imagine the problems I had finding a job," she recalls.

Lakhani sought help from the Canadian National Institute for the Blind (CNIB). The Institute initially suggested that she learn how to type so she could at least work as a secretary. This she did and then drifted through a series of jobs as a receptionist, a clerical support person, a gift shop clerk, and a cafeteria worker. Her dream of a professional career seemed unattainable.

At that point, CNIB steered Lakhani to RBC Financial Group, an employer that, even 25 years ago, was trying to help people with disabilities find jobs. RBC Financial Group hired Lakhani as a typist. Although both she and the bank were anxious to make their employment relationship work, Lakhani was new to functioning in an office, and RBC Financial Group was doing its best to make its offices disability-friendly. Lakhani's assistive "technology" consisted of a handheld magnifying glass that a CNIB counselor had provided for her first day of work.

During her first 10 years at RBC Financial Group, Lakhani worked hand in hand with the company to find jobs that were suited to both her abilities and the assistive technology available at the time. In 1985, Lakhani moved into the bank's customer service area. She graduated to a device called a closed-circuit television (C.C.T.V.) made by Visualtek. This was a 13-inch television monitor attached to a tripod-mounted camera. When Lakhani put written materials under the camera, it projected enlarged pictures of the material onto the monitor. It wasn't a perfect solution, however. When someone walked by, the camera often picked up and projected shadows, making Lakhani dizzy. Still, with the bank converting all customer records to microfiche, she wouldn't have been able to do her job without the Visualtek.

Today, Lakhani is still working at RBC Financial Group. She's watched the company progress light-years beyond its early experience helping her as a young employee with a vision disability. But she's pleased with the progress she's made. Today, she uses a standard PC running Microsoft Windows and equipped with ZoomText Xtra screen magnification software (from Ai Squared at *http://www.aisquared.com*). With that solution, she can access any material her sighted colleagues can. "As more people with disabilities came on board, the support improved," Lakhani says.

Now consider the story of Eric Chiu, a customer service representative in RBC Financial Group's Card Services division. He was a baby when Lakhani began her workplace odyssey. Totally blind, Chiu joined the bank in 1998. On his first day, he was fortunate to be able to use a PC equipped with the JAWS screen reading software and a Braille display. "There were already quite a few low-vision and blind people working at the bank, even right here in my department, so the technology and the procedures were already ironed out," he says.

Because he was new to computers, Eric took some extra time to train in basic PC functions as well as JAWS. But the technology he used had been identified, tested, and approved, and was ready to be ordered (and paid for) by the bank.

A Long History of Helping People with Disabilities

RBC Financial Group has a long history—nearly 130 years. It also has a long history of removing barriers for employees and customers with disabilities. As early as 1875, the *Halifax Chronicle* publicly noted the impressive ability of the Merchants' Bank of Halifax (renamed the Royal Bank of Canada in 1901) to remain "always moving, alive, and active." Today, as one of the largest financial institutions in Canada, RBC Financial Group provides a full range of financial services to 12 million individual and business customers around the world.

It also takes seriously its commitment to provide quality customer service to all its customers and challenging employment to all its employees. To wit

- In 1992, RBC Financial Group was the first bank in Canada to provide Braille statements to customers on request.

- In 1998, RBC Financial Group became the first bank in North America to offer audio, or "talking," automated teller machines (ATMs) for people with visual impairments. Customers use a headset with a microphone to complete private banking transactions.

- In 1998, RBC Financial Group became the first financial institution in Canada to create an "Employees with Disabilities Advisory Council."

- In 1999, this same council developed the "I Make It Barrier-Free" program, which provides a budget to help managers overcome the barriers in hiring people with disabilities.

- In April 2000, RBC Financial Group cosponsored a national conference entitled "Wellsizing the Workplace," which encouraged the business community to tap into the employment potential of people with disabilities.

- More than 90 percent of RBC Financial Group's branches are accessible to people with disabilities.

- RBC Financial Group offers large-print checks and alternate format bank statements as well as other documents in Braille and large print, on audio cassette, and on computer disk. More than 13,000 customers took advantage of this service in 1999.

According to former RBC Financial Group Chairman and CEO John Cleghorn, removing barriers for customers and employees is simply good business. "If you want to be a business leader and want access to top talent and enhanced market opportunity, you should absolutely promote accessibility— it is not a regulatory issue," he says. Cleghorn is referring to Canadian government regulations that require federally regulated industries such as banking to hire certain percentages of people with disabilities (along with women, visible minorities, and aboriginal people). "As to government incentives, including favorable tax incentives and tax breaks to provide for technical and physical aids in the workplace, we don't use them," Cleghorn declares. He insists that, although such incentives might be important in the small business market where many new jobs are created, the rewards of equal employment justify themselves.

More Info   See Chapter 1, "The Business Value of Integrating Accessible Technology into Your Organization," for more information on Canadian regulations regarding the employment of people with disabilities.

RBC Financial Group Policies and Programs for People with Disabilities

RBC Financial Group has developed thoughtful, detailed policies and procedures regarding the employment of people with disabilities. The bank is committed "...to providing workplace accommodation for any individual with a disability or special need...who meets the job requirements to perform the essential duties of his or her job." These accommodations can include technical equipment: personal supports (e.g., interpreters and attendant care), renovations to premises, workstations, flexible work schedules, and the reassignment of duties.

The bank's Employees with Disabilities Advisory Council comprises 19 individuals from departments across the bank and all over the country. Its objective is to promote a better understanding of the abilities and needs of staff and clients with disabilities. The council makes recommendations to the company to eliminate barriers to marketplace and workplace opportunities. And it provides the tools and resources to support increased representation of people with disabilities.

In 1999, the council launched a program called "I Make It Barrier-Free," which empowers managers to spend up to $3,000 per employee with a disability per year. This allows managers to move quickly to outfit workspaces with the equipment necessary for a new employee to get to work as quickly as possible without special funding requests and lengthy approval chains. Funding for expenses more than $3,000 is still available but requires approval. If the cost is ongoing (e.g., interpreter services), the manager includes it in his or her yearly budget.

A Barrier-Free Workplace Is Good Business

RBC Financial Group Vice President of Information Security Diana Burke echoes former CEO Cleghorn's sentiment that removing barriers is good business. "The bank is always looking to hire top talent from all segments of the population, and people with disabilities are the least tapped segment in the population," she says. "A couple of years ago, we had to turn away certain candidates for jobs in our front-line area (customer service representatives) and call centers because we couldn't accommodate them. Those were the fastest growing areas of the bank, and we couldn't provide the technology they required."

Being able to hire the best talent is one benefit of removing barriers for people with disabilities. Another benefit is retaining valued employees who acquire disabilities over time. "The population is aging, and people are losing hearing, vision, and mobility as the years progress," says Burke. "This affects employees and customers. We have to keep up with their need for support, or we'll find ourselves in the position of not being able to serve our customers or leverage employees' talents." Adds Cleghorn, "With 58,000 employees, RBC Financial Group is like a small city. If it affects society, it affects RBC Financial Group."

Accessible and assistive technologies also help to prevent or delay disabilities such as deteriorating vision or carpal tunnel syndrome. "Everyone wants the ability to tailor their work environment to their greatest comfort, and accessible technologies let you do that," Burke says. "All employees can leverage features built into the Windows operating system and Microsoft applications to resize fonts on screen, turn off graphics on Web sites, alter colors, modify mouse and keyboard settings, and so forth. This universal design makes things simpler and boosts productivity for all."

The bank doesn't have figures on how many of its 58,000 employees make use of such built-in accessible technology features, but it's actively developing a process to capture this information. "We'd like to know what technology our employees actively use so we can develop it."

Where customers are concerned, more financial services are going virtual, and it's imperative that RBC Financial Group look beyond physical accommodations such as wheelchair ramps in branches. Customers are using computers and automated teller machines more frequently and need to be able to interact with the bank via a computer screen. Any assistive technologies the bank can offer customers or recommend helps its competitive position and allows it to better serve customers.

The bank has achieved a lot in its decades-long commitment to hiring people with disabilities and has many firsts in removing barriers for people with disabilities," Burke says. "However, our work in this area is not finished. We've invested heavily in assistive technology over the past three years, and we're just beginning to leverage it with our internal applications. Today, approximately 1,000 employees have self-identified as having a disability; that's about three percent of our Canadian workforce. Some of these newer technologies will open up many more new jobs at the bank for people with disabilities."

Brad Gillespie: "Everything Is So Much Better Today."

Along with Mumtaz Lakhani, Brad Gillespie is an assistive technology pioneer at RBC Financial Group. Gillespie had never used a computer in his life until landing a job in a photo-finishing company in the late 1980s. In 1990 he joined Royal Trust—which would become part of RBC Financial Group three years later—working in its credit card division doing telephone collections. However, officials at Royal Trust said that, "The onus was on me to figure out how to use its technology," Gillespie recalls. He used an early IBM screen reader product that was modified by an outside supplier to work with Royal Trust's software. He also had a Braille printer, a special phone setup that allowed him to listen to the customer's voice in one ear and the screen reader in the other, and a tape recorder so he could record calls. "It took about five months to get all this stuff set up, and then only a couple of software packages at Royal Trust would work with it," he says.

In 1993, RBC Financial Group acquired Royal Trust, and Gillespie continued in collections but moved into a department that used an **auto-dialer**. "A blind person had never used an auto-dialer at RBC Financial Group before," he recalls. "The bank had an outside vendor modify the dialer for use with my screen reader software, and that worked great."

When the bank standardized on JAWS for screen reading, Gillespie was able to tap into much more functionality on his desktop. "JAWS works great with all Microsoft software," he says. "And RBC Financial Group's Systems and Technology Group has written a fair number of scripts to enable JAWS to read many screens in the DOS-based application that Card Services employees use to do their jobs."

Collections and customer service people at RBC Financial Group use a custom DOS-based application called TS2 developed by Total Systems Europe PLC (*http://www.totalsystems.com*). TS2 is a scripted program that walks customer service and collections employees through conversations with customers. It consists of dozens of screens for various functions, such as displaying customer account information, credit bureau records, and so forth. Employees access TS2 in **terminal emulation mode** from their PCs. Developers in Systems and Technology write scripts that tell JAWS where everything is located on each screen. This takes time, and Gillespie has become proficient at scripting JAWS himself in order to supplement the resources available in Systems and Technology. Developers must take a snapshot of every screen in TS2 and write a "roadmap" so JAWS can find it. These scripts are invoked by keyboard commands (hot keys) that users have to memorize.

"It's a pretty involved process, to be sure, scripting JAWS commands to each and every screen in the bank's DOS-based application," Gillespie admits. "The Microsoft applications work great with JAWS without any modifications from Systems and Technology, but we need those scripts to do our jobs."

In addition to TS2, which he uses most of the day, Gillespie uses Microsoft Word, Excel, Outlook, and Internet Explorer. "I take advantage of the accessibility options in Internet Explorer to format the screen differently so it's easier for JAWS to read," he explains. "I remove the extraneous graphics and use keyboard navigation." Gillespie uses several Web sites to locate customers who have moved and to check addresses, phone numbers, and other data. He also frequently accesses RBC Financial Group's intranet to keep up-to-date on company news.

A Braille display complements his JAWS equipped PC. Gillespie uses the Braille display when he needs accuracy—to check spelling of a name or to verify account balances. The rest of the time he lets JAWS read his screen to him. He also uses a scanner to import written materials into his computer so that they can be read back to him or saved. And he uses a Braille printer and his two-way telephone headset.

"Everything is really so much better today than it was 10 years ago," Gillespie says. "People who are blind could never access the information that they can today. Only three percent of all written material is available in Braille. Now, with technology and the support of RBC Financial Group, there's virtually nothing I can't access."

Building a Company-Wide Commitment to Accessible Technology

One of the barriers that historically prevented RBC Financial Group from integrating people with sight disabilities was the non-accessibility of the bank's computer systems. RBC Financial Group has many in-house developed systems, particularly in its branch network, which are mainframe- and DOS-based. As with the TS2 application used by Card Services, the bank's IT organization must build customized bridges from these business-critical applications to assistive technologies, such as screen readers, in order for vision-impaired employees to use them. This is time-consuming, and delays the delivery of upgrades to employees with disabilities.

As the bank incorporates more Windows-based applications—and as the entire assistive technology industry matures—the amount of customization is expected to decrease. As with every other area of the computer industry, the absence of clear market standards causes difficulties for organizations and their end users when operating systems, business applications, and assistive technology products don't work together as easily as they should.

RBC Financial Group's ultimate goal is to create a universal desktop—one standard for everyone including people with disabilities. "Our goal is to make accessible technology just another technology—like the operating system or keyboard—that everyone fits into everyday business," Burke says. "We aim to incorporate accessible technology into every system we develop and every application we use. Users can leverage the features they want and ignore those they don't want. It should be mainstream, not an afterthought." As for specialized assistive technology such as screen readers and Braille displays, the bank is building a list of approved technologies that managers can easily order for employees who need them.

RBC Financial Group's Chief Information Officer, Marty Lippert, gave Diana Burke the assignment of rallying the bank's 3,000-person Systems and Technology Group around accessible technology. The first step was to get senior management to recognize technology barriers as a business problem and then to commit to removing them. Burke's team drafted an Accessible Technology Policy, which senior management and the business units endorsed.

The next task was to get rank-and-file developers to consistently implement this policy. "We needed to ensure that accessibility was built into every team's project life cycle," Burke says. "Getting Systems and Technology on board was a gradual process. Designing accessibility into applications takes extra time and thought, but it costs less to design it in up front rather than to retrofit it in later. We didn't want our IT team to embrace this just because 'HR wants it done,' but because it's necessary to provide quality customer service to internal and external customers."

Burke's team ended up developing a new position called Accessible Technology Consultant. This individual is responsible for educating IT staff about the business case for accessibility, being familiar with accessible technology standards, advocating for employee and customer needs, and establishing policies and procedures for accessibility within Systems and Technology.

Martha Johnson holds this position at RBC Financial Group today. "I set policies and standards for accessibility within Systems and Technology and work with Web and system developers to make sure they follow Web accessibility guidelines," she says. RBC Financial Group adheres to the accessibility guidelines published by the World Wide Web Consortium's Web Accessibility Initiative (*http://www.w3.org/wai*), which includes issues like making sure all Web graphics are accompanied by text, providing the ability to tab through a screen, and designing for **device independence**.

"Systems and Technology's response has been very positive," Johnson says. "The staff understands that it's not a matter of designing applications for people with disabilities but for the largest user base possible."

RBC Financial Group's Systems and Technology Group has a number of interdisciplinary steering committees and standards called *bricks* that govern the use of all key technologies in the bank. There's a PC brick, an operating system brick, an e-mail brick, and so forth, all of which work together to "build" the bank's technology infrastructure. Bricks evaluate new technologies, test and qualify technologies in the bank's environment, and do long-range planning so the bank has a technology road map.

Johnson chairs the assistive technology brick, which acts as the authoritative source on assistive technology at RBC Financial Group. If an employee needs a screen reader, the brick tells him which brands and models are certified for the bank's environment and who else in the bank uses one. "We are trying to work proactively to identify technologies for all kinds of disabilities," Johnson explains. "We want to make sure there's minimal transition for new employees."

Burke adds that by being proactive, the bank doesn't need to spend two months testing every new piece of software or hardware when an employee needs it. "Previously, a new hire with a disability would need to undergo testing to see what kind of help he or she needed," she says. "Then Systems and Technology would purchase a specialty device that might not be standard or used anywhere else in the bank. This whole approach costs more, was a support burden, and took a lot of time. By standardizing on assistive technologies, as we do with all others, we're ready for new employees the day they start their job."

Because RBC Financial Group standardized on Microsoft desktop software some years ago, all assistive technology must be Microsoft-compatible. "A Microsoft foundation allows the bank to tap into most of the assistive technology out there," Johnson says. "Because Microsoft has such a large presence in the corporate world, assistive technology vendors direct their development efforts there."

Peter Sheahan: A Typing Splint and Trackball Are All He Needs

Peter Sheahan is a personal financial advisor who serves about 300 clients in RBC Investments, a unit of RBC Financial Group. A gymnastics accident at the age of 19 left him with limited movement in his arms and no voluntary movement in his hands. Although his disability severely restricts his mobility and dexterity, it restricts his work ability only minimally if at all. He accesses the full range of RBC Investments' customer management, investment, and productivity software using nothing more specialized (or expensive) than a trackball and a typing splint.

RBC Investments hired Sheahan directly from the university in 1989 and enrolled him in a management training program in one of its larger branches. "The biggest hurdle was getting through the door my first day at work," laughs Sheahan. "There was no automatic door opener at that branch, and I couldn't open the door." The bank installed one that very week.

In his job as a personal financial advisor, Sheahan uses three different computers: one at his desk, one in a client conference room when meeting with clients, and a laptop that he takes home. All are standard issue bank PCs outfitted with a Logitech TrackMan trackball mouse. He spends most of his day in a Windows environment, using the Microsoft Office Suite, e-mail, an Outlook-based customer relationship management system, and RBC Financial Group's financial planning software. He also accesses a mainframe-based sales and service application.

He uses a typing splint, which is a rubber-tipped plastic appendage that slips over his index finger and extends it by an inch and a half, to help him accurately press the keys on his keyboard. He also makes extensive use of keyboard shortcuts, using the splint to press one key and the knuckle of his other hand to press another key. "I use the keyboard as much as possible as I find it easier than the mouse. I can do just about every function using key-board commands," he says. "The same commands work in every Windows-based application, so it's very handy."

Sheahan is a good example of a talented individual overcoming a severe disability with an inexpensive, low-tech solution. "I need to learn more about things like Microsoft's StickyKeys and other built-in features that could make me even more productive," he says. "Technology has certainly helped to level the playing field and given me the tools to be a productive team member at RBC."

Hassan Qazilbash: Progress, Yes— But Still a Long Way to Go

Hassan Qazilbash has been with RBC Financial Group since 1998, providing cus-tomer support in the Card Services division. Qazilbash is only 25 years old, but he's already traveled a long, hard road as a person with low vision in the workplace.

Qazilbash has been visually impaired since childhood and struggled through school. "Teachers would photocopy handouts with large print, and friends would type my work for me. But there wasn't much awareness of peo-ple who are blind or have low vision needing specialized software," he says. Not until 1994, when he graduated from university, did his school invest in assistive technology for sight-impaired students—too late for Qazilbash.

After school, Qazilbash began the hunt for a job, and it was frustrating. "I went through several jobs," he recalls. "One at an airport and one as a travel consultant. But I had to leave these jobs after a probationary period, simply because I couldn't use their technology. Otherwise, I was qualified." There was PC-based assistive technology on the market that would have helped Qazilbash, but neither company was committed to it.

At that point, Qazilbash went to the CNIB for help. The counselors there told him that RBC Financial Group was one of the biggest advocates of diver-sity and employment equity, and that the bank would do everything it could to meet his needs.

Sure enough, RBC Financial Group hired Qazilbash and outfitted his desk with a 21-inch monitor and Windows software customized to show large fonts and icons. That was all Qazilbash needed to do his job until his vision worsened in March 2001. "Large fonts didn't work anymore," he says. "But the bank immediately equipped my PC with JAWS, so I could do my job without even using my monitor." JAWS training for Qazilbash and writing the scripts JAWS needed to address the software he used took about three months.

"JAWS enabled me to keep my job when my vision worsened," Qazilbash says. "RBC Financial Group had a solution waiting for me when I needed it; they didn't expect me to solve the problem on my own. The bank is really committed to moving forward with assistive technologies and making people with disabilities comfortable and productive in their jobs."

Geoff Jones: "Without This Technology, I Wouldn't Be Working."

Geoff Jones immigrated to Canada from England in 1974. He learned how to read Braille and use primitive magnifiers, but functioning inside the business world was very very tough. "I tried to use personal computers when they came out, but there was no magnification software available," he says. "As a partially sighted person, it's tough getting a job as it is; assistive technology can be expensive."

Jones finally purchased a PC in 1990 and became familiar with the various assistive technologies available for people with low vision. He initially used a screen magnification program called Super Vista and in 1995 discovered ZoomText, which Jones found to be more stable and full-featured. ZoomText provides 2× to 16× magnification, color filtering for improved contrast, black-on-white or white-on-black text, fast zoom-in/out using a mouse wheel, and many other features. ZoomText Xtra also augments screen magnification with simultaneous screen reading. As the user scans a magnified document, ZoomText reads it to him.

Jones joined RBC Financial Group in the summer of 2001 and recommended ZoomText instead of the screen magnification software the bank was using at the time. Systems and Technology evaluated the product and agreed with him. Now ZoomText is the approved screen reading software for RBC Financial Group.

Jones uses the TS2 application to field customer calls about their VISA accounts. "We're constantly moving around the screen and switching screens," he says. "That's why it's important to have stable software like ZoomText." He also uses a Windows-based customer profile application and Internet Explorer to look up telephone numbers when he needs to transfer calls to other departments.

"Without this technology, I wouldn't be working. That's all there is to it," Jones says. "I was impressed at how quickly RBC Financial Group moved to accommodate me. Way back when I got my first job, it took the employer six to eight months to get everything prepared for me. RBC Financial Group took about two weeks."

Technology That Helps Customers

In the financial industry, assistive technology is just as important to customers as it is to employees. With more and more financial transactions taking place over PCs and the Internet rather than face to face, banks, investment firms, and other institutions are removing virtual as well as physical barriers.

RBC Financial Group estimates that more than 40 percent of adult Canadians have difficulty accessing financial services because of sensory and physical disabilities or low literacy skills. Reaching out to these customers is critical to attracting and keeping their business and delivering the same levels of customer service that other customers enjoy.

RBC Financial Group has long offered large-print checks and statements, Braille statements, banking guides on audio tape, check writing templates, teletype systems that allow hard-of-hearing customers to interact through a display, induction loops that allow customers to hear using a handset or hearing aid, and audio ATMs. It also makes sure its entire Web presence is accessible. All of RBC Financial Group's sites comply with the World Wide Web Consortium's Web design guidelines for accessibility including associating text with all graphics (for screen reading), allowing the user to tab throughout a page (also necessary for screen readers), and paying attention to the use of color.

Sharlyn Ayotte: She Turned Her Disability into a Business Opportunity

RBC Financial Group customer Sharlyn Ayotte of Ottawa, Ontario, makes abundant use of the bank's accessibility features. She also helped the bank create them initially. Ayotte, who calls herself *illegally* blind ("What kind of phrase is that anyway, 'legally blind?'"), has been an RBC Financial Group customer since the early 1980s. Frustrated by her inability to access not just the bank's but other companies' written documents, she confronted the bank in 1993. "I said I wanted my banking information in a format that I could use," she says.

Ayotte reasoned that if all the bank's information originated in computers, why couldn't it create an interface to those computerized systems that let customers view the information any way they wanted? The exercise did more than allow Ayotte to vent her frustrations: it gave her a great business idea.

Ayotte took it upon herself to solve the problem for RBC Financial Group as well as many other banks. She and her business partner launched their own company called T-Base Communications (*http://www.tbase.com*), a company that designs and develops interfaces between computerized content and a variety of output: Braille, computer disks, large-print text, and audio recordings. Customers call a toll-free number and navigate through a menu that offers a list of available bank documents and a list of output options. Customers simply make their selections using their telephone keypad, and the documents are mailed out that same day.

T-Base Communications is performing this service for several of the largest banks in Canada. It has just opened a U.S. office and has signed a contract with a bank in California. "RBC Financial Group is really great to work with," Ayotte says. "It is eager to do the right thing, and it has stepped out the furthest and the fastest. The accessible programs and services it has put in place to serve clients are better than any other bank I know."

When RBC Financial Group designed its audio banking machines back in 1996, Ayotte's firm designed the user interface. T-Base Communications also created the user interface for the first talking ATM in the United States in 1999.

She gives high praise to the bank's broadly accessible Web site, which she uses extensively as a consumer and commercial customer of the bank's Internet banking services. She uses the JAWS screen-reading program and the **Dragon Dictate** voice recognition software. "Screen reader software can read everything on RBC Financial Group's site," she says. "Many Web sites today are just not accessible this way. Organizations don't seem to understand that it's not about helping a few people with special needs but about reaching all consumers with more convenience and flexibility."

Ayotte admits that she sometimes gets impatient with big corporations and their archaic attitudes. "I pay taxes and fees for electronic services that aren't accessible to me. If they want to keep me as a customer, they need to make all their services available," she says. "It typically doesn't cost any more. It only requires that organizations stretch their brains just a little bit further to build in criteria that allows my technology to work with their systems."

She claims that so-called accessible and assistive technologies are more and more becoming standard elements in PCs. "Microsoft is moving many of these features into its operating system and applications, making them mainstream," she says. "The more accessibility is viewed as mainstream, the lower the costs will fall, which will remove barriers that now prevent companies from adopting it." She gets angry just thinking about the PC supplier that tried to sell her a desktop PC with JAWS and Dragon Dictate for $11,000.

"Can you believe it? That setup should have cost about $5,000 three and a half years ago. The supplier was marking it up because he presented it as 'specialized' technology. The government often picks up the tab on assistive technology, so suppliers charge as much as they can." The newest version of this same hardware/software setup cost Ayotte $3,200—$1,200 for the PC and $2,000 for the software license for both JAWS and Dragon Dictate.

"The less this technology is viewed as specialized, the more truly accessible it will become," she says. "It's not rocket science; companies don't have any excuse for ignoring it."

Dream Products for People with Disabilities

Has assistive technology come a long way in the last 10 years? You bet. Are there still improvements to be made? Of course. When asked what dream products they wish existed, blind and low-vision employees at RBC Financial Group answered in this way:

Geoff Jones: "I would love to be able to use a PDA (Personal Digital Assistant). I'm afraid some Windows-based technologies will leave us behind."

Eric Chiu: "I would love to use JAWS to access the Web on my cell phone. Moving JAWS to platforms beyond the PC will involve partnerships between Microsoft and other companies. Some capabilities that would tremendously benefit people with disabilities would be well received by everyone else too."

Rodney Tam: "I would like combined large-print and voice output. It would be nice to have one product that served both blind and low-vision employees. ZoomText is trying to do this, but the product needs refining. A low-vision person might not need to hear everything; he or she might want to zoom to small bits of the screen and listen to other areas."

Blair Jodry, Assistant Manager of Operations, Account Services, points out that as technology has improved over the past 15 years, the trend has been to make more applications graphical. This is not always a good thing for assistive technology and for people who are blind and vision-impaired. "Some assistive technology relies on ASCII characters to work," he explains. "Keyboard characters correspond to ASCII characters; having content in a somewhat standard format really helps. Even certain fonts can be a problem for technology like JAWs, which can't read anything nonstandard."

Lessons Learned

RBC Financial Group is ahead of most organizations in the financial services industry in integrating assistive technologies into its standard technology infrastructure. Here are some tips for other organizations planning to do the same:

- **It's ongoing work.** "Incorporating assistive technology is not something that you do and then are finished with," says Diana Burke. "It's just one part of providing an accessible workplace for people with disabilities."

- **It's cultural as well as technological.** Just having accessible technology doesn't solve the barriers for people with disabilities. There are cultural issues to resolve regarding overcoming discrimination against people with disabilities.

- **Treat assistive technology as mainstream technology.** RBC Financial Group decided that, wherever practical, assistive technology is just another technology to be incorporated into its standard desktop.

- **Get senior management on board.** As early in the process as possible, have management demonstrate the commitment to accessible technology.

- **Get IT on board.** Rather than have HR try to force accessible technology on IT, get the IT staff involved early on. Help developer teams understand that accessible technology is not something that benefits a relatively few employees but the entire workforce and customer base. It's critical to making the company competitive in the marketplace and in hiring.

- **Set up a center of expertise and document standards.** Set up some kind of assistive technology steering committee comprising IT staff, business users, and employees with disabilities. Have them investigate, evaluate, and select technologies that will become technology standards. RBC Financial Group's intranet lists all the technology standards the bank supports, so when a manager needs to bring in specialized software or hardware for an employee, he or she has only to look up the approved technology and order it.

- **Communicate broadly to all stakeholders.** It's easy to duplicate effort and operate at cross-purposes in an organization of RBC Financial Group's size. By corralling assistive technology responsibilities into a single, central steering committee or council, you eliminate duplicate efforts, expense, and a proliferation of incompatible technologies.

- **Provide well-trained support.** If possible, make sure there is at least one technical support person on staff who is well trained in each assistive technology used in the organization. This will greatly speed support issues, improve employee productivity, and reduce frustrations.

Summary

The vast majority of jobs in today's financial industry are PC-based, making it an ideal candidate for assistive technology. With such technologies, banks, brokerage firms, investment banks, and other financial services firms can tap into a reservoir of talented workers with disabilities who have up to this time found a barrier between their skills and the industry's information systems.

RBC Financial Group has been one of the first financial organizations to recognize this untapped asset in Canada and has moved early and aggressively to "institutionalize" accessible and assistive technologies as corporate standards. It's also made equal employment a pillar of corporate culture.

Although it may be time-consuming and challenging to incorporate assistive technology into various proprietary bank systems, RBC Financial Group has committed to building these bridges for its employees with disabilities. As more mainstream business software, proprietary software, and assistive technology embrace common standards, this work will decrease. One day, hiring an employee with a disability and getting him or her on board and productive will involve little more time and expense than hiring anyone else.

Accessible Technology in Government

David Orris is an enterprise architect with the U.S. Department of Defense (DoD) TRICARE Management Activity, the agency's worldwide healthcare and hospital system. Orris has **Multiple Sclerosis (MS)** and uses Dragon Dictate speech recognition software and a trackball to compensate for his dexterity limitations. Unable to work as a result of an operation on his shoulder, Orris was housebound for six weeks. During that time, the Computer/Electronic Accommodations Program (CAP), part of the DoD's assistive technology office, set Orris up at home with the same computer arrangement he has at work. Not only did he continue to contribute while he was recuperating, but his condition actually improved as a result of the decreased stress associated with working from home. Today, he works at home approximately 50 percent of the time.

"Assistive technology is a real equalizer for people with disabilities. It's an immense help in compensating for loss of dexterity, eyesight, or other limitations," he says. "It not only raises your productivity but also your expectations for yourself. That's a good feeling for the individual and good for the employer too."

Orris is one of many beneficiaries of a succession of federal laws passed over the last 30 years. With the passage of the first Rehabilitation Act of 1973, the federal government drove a golden stake that became the cornerstone for nearly 30 years of federal legislation and initiatives supporting increased independence and employment of people with disabilities. Today, the federal government employs approximately 120,000 individuals with disabilities. This is 7 percent of the nearly 1.8 million permanent civilian federal employee base.

An agency that's led the way in hiring, both in volume and in degree of innovation, is the DoD. The DoD is the largest federal agency and one of the largest employers in the world, employing 680,000 civilians and 1.2 million military personnel. It runs the largest school system in the world, the largest training organization, and the second largest healthcare system. It's the world's largest buyer of assistive technology and has a global, streamlined procurement system for delivering products to employees anywhere in the world.

"If assistive technology can be implemented and integrated in an organization of the DoD's size, then it can be implemented anywhere," says Dinah F. B. Cohen, Director of CAP, the DoD's assistive technology hub. CAP was established in 1990 as a centrally funded program for providing assistive technology accommodations and services to DoD employees with disabilities. Because of its success, in October 2000, Congress expanded CAP's constituency and budget (to $4.6 million), and authorized the organization to serve other federal agencies. Today, more than 45 federal agencies take advantage of CAP services, which include

- **Providing needs assessments:** A needs assessment is conducted to identify accommodations suitable for an individual's specific situation. CAP recognizes the importance of selecting the right team of people to conduct an assessment. The employee with a disability and his or her supervisor are the core team. Others who may make valuable contributions include personnel from human resources, computer support services, occupational health, procurement, facilities management, and state and community resources. The needs assessment includes a job analysis, identification of an individual's functional limitations, and selection of an assistive technology or service solution.

- **Purchasing assistive technology to make computer and telecommunications systems accessible to employees with disabilities:** CAP's purpose is to ensure that employees with disabilities get the equipment that best suits their needs, at no charge to the employer. CAP procures assistive technologies and funds sign language interpreters, readers, and personal assistants for employees attending long-term technical training (two days or more). CAP strives to provide assistive technology and accommodations to ensure that people with disabilities have equal access to information and opportunities throughout the federal government.

- **CAP Technology Evaluation Center:** CAP also maintains a Technology Evaluation Center (CAPTEC) at the Pentagon where Washington, D.C.–based workers can try out a wide range of assistive technology and meet with experts. CAPTEC contains several computer workstations equipped with a wide variety of equipment designed to accommodate people with disabilities. It provides an outstanding venue to demonstrate to senior management the impact that assistive technology has in improving access to information for employees with disabilities. Since CAPTEC's opening in 1995, it has served more than 8,000 customers.

- **Providing expertise to solve accessibility problems:** CAP's centralized approach harnesses human resource expertise to provide technical assistance to employees with disabilities and their supporting IT help desk professionals. CAP partners with vendors to ensure that the equipment is successfully installed, that proper training occurs, and that the tools have a positive impact on productivity in the workplace.

- **Customer service:** In an effort to serve customers more efficiently, CAP conducts several customer and supervisor surveys. This approach drives continuous improvements in the CAP assessment, procurement, and training process. Furthermore, it also allows CAP to learn of the real impact technology has on people's lives and to share best practices.

Other federal agencies, such as the Department of Education and the Social Security Administration, run similar centrally funded assistive technology programs, but CAP is the largest and most recognized for its efficient procurement practices and assistive technology expertise. To date, CAP has provided more than 28,000 accommodations and is able to process an assistive technology request in just 3 to 10 working days.

For serving such a vast and sprawling customer base, CAP is quite compact—just 21 people in all, a model of government efficiency. Cohen has three full-time employees and another 17 full-time and part-time contract employees. This small staff evaluates assistive technologies, processes assistive technology requests, procures the installation and training services for customers all over the world, and performs extensive follow-up to make sure customers are satisfied.

Global Customer Base

To ensure that all federal employees are aware of its services, CAP has a targeted marketing and information dissemination program. Through presentations, training seminars, and its Web site (*http://www.tricare.osd.mil/cap*), CAP is able to improve understanding of the requirements and ensure that assistive technology and related services get to the people who need them.

To meet multiple market segment requirements, CAP is active in several initiatives:

Workforce Recruitment Program (WRP) for College Students with Disabilities: Coordinated by the U.S. Department of Labor's Office of Disability Employment Policy (ODEP) and the DoD, the WRP aims to provide summer work experience, and in some cases full-time employment, to college students with disabilities. The program develops partnerships with other federal agencies, each of which makes a commitment to provide summer jobs and a staff recruiter. Each year, recruiters interview about 1,300 students with disabilities at over 150 college and university campuses across the nation and develop a database listing the qualifications of each student. As of 1996, private sector employers have been able to utilize the database. CAP provides assistive technology and accommodation services to WRP participants working with the government for the summer. The WRP and CAP work together to ensure a successful employment experience and to ensure an accessible information environment for WRP participants.

Telework: The federal government, including the Department of Transportation, the Office of Personnel Management (OPM), and the DoD, has taken measures to require policies and/or programs on telework and telecommuting. Agencies need to take a fresh look at the barriers that currently inhibit participation and offer telework options to people with disabilities. CAP purchases equipment for telework employees with disabilities to use in their homes or at other off-site locations. Items available include computer hardware and software, telephone equipment, fax machines, and assistive technology.

Healthy Work Practices Program: Because work-related injuries continue to disable employees and decrease productivity, CAP aligned with the DoD and federal programs to offer prevention and accommodation services. Via education workshops, information dissemination, and accommodations for employees with dexterity disabilities, CAP's proactive approach to disability management offers employers assistance in addressing this growing health concern.

Military Health System: CAP assists Military Treatment Facilities (MTFs) in meeting communication accessibility requirements, as well as individual requirements of MTF employees with disabilities. The DoD Directive for Patients' Rights defines a commitment to increasing communication and access for all patients. CAP has expert staff to assist in identifying and purchasing appropriate technical enhancements to ensure that DoD employees, programs, and facilities are accessible to individuals with disabilities as required by the DoD Directive 6000.14 and federal public laws.

DoD Education Activity: CAP assists the DoD Education Activity in meeting communication accessibility requirements as well as individual requirements of the students and employees with disabilities at military base schools in the continental United States and abroad. CAP works with teachers, special education directors, students, employees, and supervisory personnel to identify available solutions and provide appropriate assistive technology. The process begins at the time a student is identified as requiring related educational services or when the decision is made to hire an employee with a disability. By doing this, the equipment is available when the student is ready for the related educational services or the employee begins working.

Exceptional Family Member Program: CAP assists the Exceptional Family Member Program (EFMP), an organization that provides support to DoD employees' family members with disabilities, in meeting communication accessibility requirements as well as individual requirements of EFMP members and employees with disabilities. CAP works with the EFMP coordinator, teacher, special education directors, student, employee, supervisory personnel, and other appropriate personnel to determine equipment needs, identify solutions, and provide assistive technology when appropriate. When a family member enrolls in the EFMP, the process begins, which ensures increased accessibility for the customer.

Section 508: CAP supports accessibility efforts including the successful implementation of Section 508 electronic and information technology accessibility requirements. To assist the federal-wide Section 508 effort, CAP created a portal that points customers to appropriate information, technical assistance, and contacts.

More Info   You can find further information on Section 508 of the Rehabilitation Act in Chapter 1, "The Business Value of Integrating Accessible Technology into Your Organization."

By disseminating assistive technology through a centrally funded program, the U.S. government saves money on assistive technology through bulk purchasing and provides more efficient processing of assistive technology requests through a single knowledgeable staff. "Because we're buying in such high volume, we can negotiate great prices and great delivery times," Cohen says. "And because of our credit card procurement process, vendors get paid immediately."

Accessible Technology Slashes Workers' Compensation Costs

The DoD also encourages managers to use assistive technology to keep temporarily disabled employees working while they recuperate at home. A typical home installation of a workstation and assistive technology costs approximately $5,000 versus $28,000 for an average workers' compensation claim.

"All federal agencies, and many private companies, are spending huge amounts of money on workers' compensation," Cohen says. "It's smart business to get these people back to work, even if they're at home. With so much work today done on computers, assistive technology can keep people productive and their morale high during much of their illness or temporary disability."

CAP has filled more than 1,000 requests for assistive technology to serve temporarily disabled workers, reducing or eliminating the associated workers' compensation costs. Ironically, approximately 35 percent of workers' compensation claims today are due to technology-related injuries such as carpal tunnel syndrome. On the other hand, technology also benefits many employees by preventing some injuries and providing workarounds for many others. "As assistive technology becomes more mainstream, it will reach more people and hopefully prevent many of these disabilities," Cohen says.

Cultural Barriers Remain

Cohen states that CAP's constituency is turning out to be far larger than its founders originally envisioned. "It's not just people born with disabilities who need assistive technology," Cohen says. "More and more, we're serving people who acquire disabilities later in life through accidents or aging. We're all potential users."

Those who become disabled later in life are not only a far bigger population but also are sometimes tougher to reach with assistive technology than those born with disabilities. Seville Allen, head of CAP's blind/low-vision/cognitive team, says, "Many low-vision individuals don't want to admit they have a disability. Consequently, they are just getting by at work and not working to their full potential. Their productivity is below par, and often their managers shield them from work they can't do well. That could be something as basic as reading. If these people come to us for help, we have to do mental gymnastics to avoid using the 'B' word (blind), as it's something they just don't want to hear." Allen says such workers might request a 32-inch monitor and screen magnification software when they really need screen-reading software. "Even though the technology exists to help them, you have to use a fair amount of sensitivity in introducing it to them."

Another problem she sees is managers using assistive technology to address productivity problems that are rooted elsewhere. "We've had high-level employees request screen reading software to help them plow through large volumes of reading," Allen says, "when what they really want but couldn't get is an administrative assistant. Assistive technology doesn't solve management issues or all issues of low productivity. There may be other problems to resolve."

The Future of Accessible Technology in the U.S. Government

Early in his administration, President George W. Bush visited the Pentagon to highlight CAP and recognize the importance of individual accommodations, assistive technologies, and system accessibility. Cohen's staff used CAPTEC as a demonstration center to show President Bush the real potential of these technologies. After visiting CAPTEC, he addressed an audience in the Pentagon's auditorium, specifically noting that, "The technologies on display here have helped...Department of Defense employees enjoy greater access to communications and the computing environment."

Via his New Freedom Initiative, President Bush strives to continue the development of new assistive technologies and improved accessibility in local communities. This work, and the work of CAP, will assist the U.S. government in being a model employer of people with disabilities.

Legislative History of Accessible Technology

Over the last 30 years, the federal government has enacted a series of bills and initiatives requiring federal agencies, states, and private industry to support the employment of people with disabilities. Some of this legislation is covered in Chapter 1, "The Business Value of Integrating Accessible Technology into Your Organization"; additional milestones include

- **Rehabilitation Act of 1973:** Mandated reasonable accommodation in federally funded employment and higher education for assistive technology and services.

- **Education for All Handicapped Children Act of 1975:** Extended reasonable accommodations for students from ages 5 to 21. Assistive technology plays a more significant role in gaining access to educational programs. Created the Individual Education Plans (IEPs) to be made for all students with disabilities.

- **Handicapped Infants and Toddlers Act of 1986:** Extended the preceding Act to children ages 5 and under. Expanded emphasis on educationally related assistive technology.

- **1986 Amendment to the Rehabilitation Act of 1973:** Required all states to include a provision for assistive technology services in the rehabilitation plans of the state vocational rehab agencies.

- **Technology-Related Assistance for Individuals with Disabilities Act of 1988:** Mandated consumer-driven assistive technology services and system changes in the states. Created the development of the "Tech Act" programs throughout the country. The act was reauthorized in 1994. (*A.T. Quarterly, Volume 5, Number 2 & 3* 1994)

- **Americans with Disabilities Act (ADA) of 1990:** Prohibits discrimination based on disability in employment, transportation, and telecommunications.

- **Individuals with Disabilities Education Act (IDEA) of 1991:** Mandated that all local educational agencies provide assistive technology devices and services to benefit students with disabilities.

- **Re-authorization of the Rehabilitation Act of 1973 (1992):** Mandates rehabilitation technology to be a primary benefit to be included in the rehabilitation plan for the state rehabilitation agencies. The rehab plan was required to include how assistive technology will be used in the rehabilitation process of each individual client.

- **Assistive Technology Act of 1998:** A re-authorization of the Tech Act of 1988. Expanded outreach services of Tech Act programs throughout the country.

- **Ticket to Work and Work Incentives Improvement Act of 1999:** Provides consumer choices for the provision of vocational rehabilitation and job training and other support services.

- **New Freedom Initiative (February 2001):** Increases funding for research and development of assistive technology resources nationwide. Although not legislation, this initiative also promotes full access to the community for people with disabilities through expanded transportation options, educational opportunities, and greater integration into the workforce.

Following the lead of the federal government, all U.S. states have created vocational rehabilitation programs and assistive technology programs. Georgia has extended the effort to ensure that all its citizens have access to the assistive technology needed to lead full and productive lives. Georgia is also fortunate to have the nationally renowned Center for Assistive Technology and Environment Access (CATEA) at the Georgia Institute of Technology (Georgia Tech) as well as some outstanding medical and rehabilitative centers.

Georgia: A Leader in Accessible Technology

Like other U.S. states, Georgia's Vocational Rehabilitation Program helps citizens with disabilities function at home, at school, and in the workplace. In the 1980s, under the leadership of Joy Kniskern, manager of the State Vocational Rehabilitation Assistive Technology Services, the state initiated its first rehabilitation engineering program using a university-based engineering model. It contracted with the Georgia Institute of Technology, Mercer Engineering Research Center, and Georgia Southern University for a corps of rehabilitation engineers to help Georgians with disabilities return to work using assistive technology.

State vocational rehabilitation programs are required by law to serve only those individuals who want to go to work. Because many other individuals of all ages need assistive technology, Kniskern led the state in a successful bid for the NIDRR Tech Act grant (Tools for Life) in 1991, opening doors for the agency to provide assistive technology services to thousands of other Georgians needing them. The program maintains a strong commitment to hire qualified individuals who use assistive technology to compete success-fully in all areas of life—living, learning, working, and playing.

In the mid-1990s, Georgia made a major shift from rehabilitation as a social service to rehabilitation as a way to return people to satisfying, com-petitively paying jobs. The state strategically and symbolically removed its Vocational Rehabilitation Program from the control of the Department of Human Resources and placed it under the control of the Georgia Department of Labor.

Today, Georgia's Vocational Rehabilitation Program has developed a model Assistive Technology Unit led by Kniskern. The Assistive Technology Unit of "Voc Rehab" now consists of two branches: Assistive Work Technology Services (AWT) and Tools for Life. The two coordinated programs provide a comprehensive array of technology services to Georgians with disabilities.

"Tools for Life is Georgia's Tech Act project that provides a very broad sweep of assistive technology services to all Georgians with disabilities regard-less of age or work status," Kniskern explains. "Assistive Work Technology Services, by law, must serve only constituents of Vocational Rehabilitation Program and has the specific mandate to equip individuals with technology that will help them to work."

Assistive Work Technology Services (AWT)

The AWT organization within Georgia Vocational Rehabilitation Program is larger, more broadly skilled, and more team-oriented than similar organiza-tions in other states. Although some vocational rehab agencies either subcon-tract services or have one or two assistive technology specialists to serve the entire state, Georgia has a full-time staff of 30 professionals dedicated to matching citizens with assistive technology to return them to the workplace. Furthermore, these specialists are located at four regional offices around the state rather than in one central location, better serving the entire population.

Each region offers the skills of four different specialists:

- **Rehabilitation technologists.** These professionals receive referrals from state vocational rehab counselors in the field and develop vocational plans for individuals that can include assistive technology. Rehabilitation technologists evaluate the individual's home needs, vehicle modification needs, and workplace needs. Once the individual obtains a job, the technologists survey his or her work site and modify it for accessibility. This can include products ranging from specialized furniture to voice synthesis software and Braille printers.

- **Occupational therapists.** These professionals get involved if there are physical conditions that involve special considerations in seating, reaching, and moving.

- **Rehabilitation engineers.** Engineers get involved in cases requiring the design of specialized equipment such as customized technology or furniture. They work closely with the occupational therapist to understand what the client can do, and then they figure out how to help him do it. Again, this covers home, vehicle, workplace, and computer modifications.

- **Rehabilitation technicians.** These are the builders who create whatever the rehabilitation engineer designs. They have backgrounds in general contracting, computer integration, and other building skills.

Joy Kniskern and Frank Coombs provide team building, coordination, and technical and programmatic assistance to the statewide team.

"About six years ago, the Georgia Vocational Rehabilitation Program looked at its entire operation and identified several core values for its services, one of which was assistive technology," says Tony Langton, a consultant who has worked with the state of Georgia and other states on developing assistive technology programs and training. "It committed a large number of staff to this effort, more than any other state," he says. "Plus, it has worked hard at integrating the technology services into its day-to-day activities."

"I think what distinguishes the Georgia Department of Labor's AWT organization, besides the sheer number, talent, and diversity of our professionals, is our tremendous teamwork," Kniskern says. "We are not passing a client's file over the proverbial partition from one desk to the next. Rather, we are very proud of our team's ability to work together, and with vocational rehab counselors, to help our clients." Georgia recruited nationally to fill its AWT posts and has a number of masters-level engineers and occupational therapists—quality as well as quantity. "Too often, people think of the assistive technology device but not the assistive technology services that are the foundation for making good decisions about assistive technology," Kniskern continues. "Assessing a person's unique needs for assistive technology is critical in making a successful match. Our AWT team excels at this."

Hunter Ramseur, manager of Technology Access Services at Georgia Tech's CATEA says, "I attend a lot of national conferences and have become familiar with the way other states have set up their assistive technology programs. Georgia has a much more organized and sophisticated approach to providing assistive technology resources. What's unique is the degree of intensity and commitment and the degree to which it has incorporated its assistive technology team into the whole rehabilitation process."

For example, the State Department of Labor has 53 career centers throughout the state that provide job leads and skills training for all citizens. Virtually all of these centers are equipped with at least one assistive technology workstation for people with disabilities. These computers are raised to accommodate wheelchairs, are accompanied by trackballs and keyguards, and are loaded with screen-reading and magnification software—some even have voice recognition software. There are also talking calculators, talking dictionaries, scanners, and other assistive technologies at these stations.

"The Georgia Department of Labor, under the leadership of Commissioner Michael L. Thurmond, is way ahead in this area," Kniskern says. "Our assistive technology unit works very closely with Vocational Rehabilitation and with our career centers to reach every citizen with the technology they need to find work and perform that work."

In its first year of operation (1999), the AWT had 1,000 referrals from vocational rehabilitation field counselors throughout the state. During its second year, that number increased to 2,000. It is actively pursuing ways to reach more citizens. "We're exploring the principles and equipment behind **telemedicine**, which will allow our 30 assistive technology specialists to serve even more individuals in the state, especially in rural areas," Kniskern continues. "We are already using video conferencing for AWT team meetings in North Georgia, and we see tremendous potential to extend this reach by using more conferencing technologies."

The AWT is also preparing a Web site to make its services more accessible, exploring a refined tracking system to document and study outcomes, and staying abreast of the latest technological innovations.

Christopher Lee: "The Computer Is My Right Arm"

If words were big sturdy objects that Christopher Lee could touch, heft, and climb over, he might have a lot easier time reading. But as flat symbols on a page, they confound him. A severe learning disability called a **cognitive processing deficit** affects his ability to read, write, and sound out words. As a child growing up in Florida in the 1960s and 1970s, the experts were just starting to understand dyslexia. They had no idea what the source of young Christopher's problem was.

He was labeled retarded. Mildly brain damaged, said some specialists, where his parents sought help. His teachers moved him quietly to "special" classes in a trailer behind the school. Christopher didn't feel dumb, just baffled and frustrated.

"Anything that I could do with my hands I was very good at," he says. "But anything dealing with reading and writing was a problem." Luckily, Christopher was a likeable kid who had the social skills to finagle his way through the system. He would volunteer to help in the office when the class was reading aloud. He would feign illness when he knew of an upcoming spelling bee. He learned to read his teacher's body language to tell which questions were most important. He faked and cajoled his way to a high school diploma—but inside he was worn out and angry.

In the fifth grade, Christopher discovered sports. "Swimming saved me," says Lee of his middle and high school years. "I finally found something I could excel in, something that made me feel good about myself." The University of Georgia accepted him on a swimming scholarship. But he was reading at a fourth-grade level.

He received help in the school's Developmental Studies Program, which provided tutoring in basic reading, writing, and math. But the rule was if you couldn't move out of Developmental Studies in four quarters, you were kicked out of school. Christopher flunked Developmental Studies English four times. It was then that one of his professors steered him to the university's Learning Disabilities Center. There, he was tested, pronounced learning disabled, and given a second chance.

"That was a turning point for me," Lee recalls. "I had heard the term learning disability before, but I didn't want to admit that's what I had."

The folks in the Learning Disabilities Center taught Christopher Lee how his brain worked. A worker at the center, Rosemary Jackson, was invaluable to Lee. "She figured out how I learned," he says. "She saw that I wrote best when I was walking around and dictating. She saw that I needed smaller classes and more one-on-one instruction. She told me to use a tape recorder in class to take notes. She helped me communicate my needs to my professors—to tell them I needed time and a half to take tests, for instance, and sometimes to have tests taped rather than written." Lee spent hundreds of hours at the Learning Disabilities Center getting basic tutoring and having the workers there translate his assignments into a format he could understand.

In his junior year of college, early 1989, Lee had another turning point: he discovered computers. "I loved the keyboard; it took away that dreaded piece of dead wood—the pencil or pen. The keyboard was tactile; I could feel it. I could connect letters with physical action," he says. When letters appear on the monitor, they're far clearer to him than when he writes them down on a piece of paper. Spelling checkers cleaned up his frequent misspellings, and grammar checkers flagged muddled word distinctions such as "pull," "pole," and "pearl," all of which sound the same to Lee.

He became a crackerjack typist and developed a love of writing. "The computer made a huge difference in my ability to learn," he says. "Ever since then, the computer has been my right arm."

During his fifth and last year of college, however, a lifetime of frustration boiled over. Lee had learned well how to communicate his disability and became a vocal and prolific advocate of people with learning disabilities. However, he was angry at the system, angry at the ignorance, angry at his own limitations. He sat down and wrote a book with Rosemary Jackson called *Faking It: A Look Into the Mind of a Creative Learner.* (Heinemann 1992) The book elevated him to prominence in the cognitive community, the press picked up his story, and Lee had a brief stint as a national speaker.

However, when he left school, reality set in, and he failed at job after job. "I left my support system behind at school," he says. "The people at the Learning Disabilities Center, the computers, the accommodating professors were all gone."

In 1994, through a University of Georgia connection, Lee landed a job at the Roosevelt Warm Springs Institute for Rehabilitation as training director for a learning disability, research, and training grant. "It was my first real job, and I was lucky to get it," he says. "That's when I really began learning how the state helped accommodate people with disabilities."

Once inside the Georgia state system, Lee met another life-changing person, Gene Spalding. He worked in Georgia's Tech Act project called Tools for Life, which is funded under the National Institute on Disability and Rehabilitation Research (NIDRR) and is one of 56 projects operated in each state and U.S. territory. Tools for Life and its sister programs are increasing access to assistive technology for Georgia's 1,700,000 citizens with disabilities. (See the section "Tools for Life" later in this chapter for more information.)

Spalding is paralyzed and uses the Dragon Dictate speech recognition software to facilitate communication. This software was a revelation to Lee who saw it as a way to bypass the troublesome writing and spelling steps and go directly from thought to printed expression. Spalding also introduced Lee to other assistive technologies such as word prediction programs, word abbreviation programs, voice organizers, and screen readers.

"These products were a huge help to me, especially after the Internet came along," Lee says. Today, Lee uses a standard Windows-based PC outfitted with textHELP! Read & Write (*http://www.texthelp.com*), which combines a screen reader, phonetic spelling checker, homonym color coder, word prediction program, word abbreviation program, and thesaurus. He also uses Dragon Naturally Speaking for speech input, the ZoomText screen enlarger, and Inspiration Software's Inspiration visual thinking and learning software (*http://www.inspiration.com*), a program that lets him draw his way to clear expression.

When he needs to read a lot of scanned documents, Lee uses the Kurzweil 3000 screen reading program, a high-end optical character recognition program that reads typed text and will even read definitions using a built-in dictionary. He uses the Soothsayer on-screen keyboard, which aids him in navigating his way to correct word choices and spelling. As Lee types the word "cat," for example, the keyboard eliminates all letters of the alphabet that would not follow the letter "c," simplifying his choice from 26 letters to nine.

He uses the accessibility options in Microsoft Windows 2000 and the Microsoft Office 2000 suite, taking advantage of the enlarged icons and color features. For some reason, brown text on a white background is easier for Lee to read than black text on white.

"Assistive technologies for cognitive disabilities usually come from other physical disabilities, although this is slowly changing," Lee says. "Vendors are starting to see that there is a huge market for individuals with learning disabilities in addition to sensory disabilities. Because cognitive disabilities are invisible, it's easier for individuals to fake it or deny the existence of the disability. They end up falling into the welfare system because they don't understand their challenge, and they don't know what technology exists to help them."

Tools for Life

In 1994, Christopher Lee joined Tools for Life as project director. (Gene Spalding became an AWT rehabilitation engineer.) Tools for Life is Georgia's Assistive Technology Project mandated by the federal Tech Act of 1988 (re-authorized and expanded in 1998). However, far from just fulfilling its legal duties, Tools for Life, like its work-focused partner, the AWT, provides the citizens of Georgia with many beneficial services.

Focused on the entire citizenry rather than just those trying to reenter the workforce, Tools for Life maintains four Assistive Technology Resource Centers, one of which is home to a nationally renowned computer recycling program for people with disabilities. Tools for Life offers the following services to all Georgia citizens:

- **Assistive Technology Resource Centers.** These regional centers provide outreach for citizens all over the state. They work with children who need assistive technology at school or during the summer months when schools are closed. They loan specialized, expensive equipment such as closed-circuit TV magnification systems, and they help locate funding sources.

- **ReBoot Computer Recycling Program.** This nonprofit effort recycles used computers from corporations and state agencies into the hands of citizens with disabilities. ReBoot is associated with the National Cristina Foundation, which provides computer recycling services nationally. To date, ReBoot has placed more than 4,500 recycled computers with people throughout Georgia and the southeast.

- **Gtrade.** This is an equipment loan library and online equipment exchange for used and donated assistive technology. It functions much like classified advertising, providing individuals opportunities to sell or purchase assistive technology.

- **Georgia Statewide Funding Guide.** On its Web site (*http://www.gatfl.org*), Tools for Life provides a wealth of nonprofit and public resources to help with the cost of assistive technology.

- **Microsoft Lifelong Learning Lab.** With a grant from Microsoft, Tools for Life established a lab where any citizen can try various assistive technologies or receive training in programs such as screen readers.

- **Cognitive Disabilities Guide.** Because of Christopher Lee's wealth of experience, Tools for Life offers a comprehensive guide of assistive technology for individuals with learning disabilities. It includes an online screening tool to provide early diagnoses of learning disabilities and matches various types of cognitive disabilities with available technology aids.

- **Assistive Technology Conference.** This annual conference (Touch the Future Expo) draws citizens with disabilities, suppliers of assistive technology products, and service providers from state agencies and private rehabilitation organizations to see the latest assistive technology and learn about advances.

Separate from the AWT and Tools for Life, both of which reside within the Georgia Department of Labor, is the State Department of Education's Georgia Project for Assistive Technology. This program helps school-age individuals and special education personnel access assistive technology so kids with exceptional needs can benefit from a free public education. Tools for Life also works cooperatively with the Georgia Advocacy Project regarding assistive technology issues (e.g., getting Medicaid to pay for assistive technology devices).

Jamie Cahill: "I've Been Given Back My Arms and Hands"

All through the 1970s, Mike and Jamie Cahill were on the move and in the spotlight. Mike was on the professional tennis circuit, traveling with the likes of John McEnroe, Jimmy Connors, and Stan Smith. At Wimbledon, in 1979, Jamie's leg suddenly and mysteriously went numb. The diagnosis: MS.

Jamie Cahill, then age 27, was one of the most active, people-oriented persons in the world and claims, "I never sat still." It was inconceivable to her that she would spend the rest of her life in a wheelchair. The MS symptoms came and went, worsening with each reoccurrence. After the initial bout of numbness in her limbs and loss of balance and strength, her body actually returned to normal, and Jamie became pregnant with her first child. Exactly one year later, however, the numbness returned.

"I went through the denial, the anger, the whole bit," Cahill says. "I had a double major in speech therapy and education and had taught school for a year before joining Mike on his tour. It never crossed my mind that I couldn't go back to work."

After a second daughter was born to the Cahills, Jamie's strength waned further, and she began using a wheelchair around the house to save her strength. "No one told me that once you get in, you never get out," she says ruefully. She first lost all use of her legs, and then her arms and hands.

The Cahills' local doctors didn't know how to alleviate the constant fatigue, stiffness, and other annoying side effects of MS. Ten years passed, and Jamie grew progressively worse each year.

At this point, Mike took a job in Atlanta, where Jamie discovered the Shepherd Center. She fell into a support network that changed her life. Her doctor, Dr. William Stuart, put her on drugs that alleviated her fatigue, stiffness, and other medical symptoms. During her five-day evaluation at Shepherd, Cahill met what she calls, "an unbelievable group of people who helped me get my life back."

A nutritionist designed an eating plan that would boost Cahill's energy. A recreational therapist told her that white water rafting, scuba diving, horseback riding, and many other activities were possible. A vocational rehabilitation counselor listened to Jamie say that, more than anything else, she wanted to go back to work.

"I couldn't imagine that I could be of any use to any business without the use of my arms or legs. But my girls were in school all day, and I was going crazy," Cahill says. "Plus, everything accompanying my illness was very expensive—home health care, the van, special lifts, treatments. I wanted to be able to contribute financially to our family."

The Shepherd Center connected Cahill with Georgia State's Vocational Rehabilitation Program. These professionals gave her a complete vocational evaluation. The counselors proclaimed Jamie Cahill an excellent candidate to return to work and promised to help her get there.

The state's AWT team immediately recommended a voice-activated computer. The team configured (and the state paid for) a Windows-based PC equipped with the Dragon Dictate speech recognition software, the Microsoft

Office suite, and a standard mouse. A voice-activated tape recorder hooks into both her phone and her computer so she can record phone conversations. When off the phone, she rewinds, listens to the conversation again, and speaks important points into her computer. She uses a mouth stick to press the buttons on the tape recorder and turn pages in her notebook. Occasionally, she uses the Magnifier program built into Microsoft applications to ease eye strain and the on-screen keyboard program as a substitute for voice recognition when there is too much background noise.

Operating this setup is tedious and takes a lot of time, but "I don't care," Jamie says. "When I got this computer I thought, 'I've been given back my arms and hands.' I was on it 24 hours a day; I taught myself a lot."

To help her configure her computer for easiest access and use, a Georgia state vocational rehabilitation counselor put Jamie in touch with CATEA at Georgia Tech. The team analyzed her abilities and built her a customized computer table that allows her to drive her wheelchair into position under a platform that contains her mouse. The engineers built a stand that holds her mouth stick in position; the phone she keeps in her lap. CATEA even designed a special wheelchair-accessible shelf in the Cahills' kitchen that allows Jamie to feed and take medicine herself during the day when no one else is at home. "Little things like this that give me back my independence mean the world to me," she says.

Empowered by assistive technology and her new support network, Jamie Cahill bravely and excitedly confronted the job market. Through a series of events that started with Jamie demonstrating her computer to a class of Georgia Tech graduate students with CNN present, Jamie landed a job with Hartford Insurance Company's Benefits Management Division in Atlanta, dealing with claimant disability claims. Ironically, she was the only employee in that office to come to work in a wheelchair.

The journey from her bed to her desk every day was an arduous one that involved the help of her family, friends, and a home healthcare professional, but Jamie was thrilled to put in the effort. In her job, Cahill called physicians' offices and followed up on insurance claimants' medical status. She used much the same computer setup at work that she had at home, which was designed by CATEA and paid for by Hartford. Unfortunately, this job ended after two and a half years due to Hartford restructuring its office.

Since then, she has had several part-time, home-based jobs that pay little more than minimum wage. She teaches English as a second language to

Koreans in her community and is helping a doctoral student at Georgia Tech defend his dissertation in English. She uses her computer to prepare her lesson plans and search the Internet for resources. But more than anything, she wants another professional job with benefits.

CATEA—A Georgia Assistive Technology Asset

One of the jewels in the crown of Georgia's assistive technology resources is the Georgia Institute of Technology's CATEA. In operation for more than 20 years, CATEA evolved from a class project for industrial design students in the school's College of Architecture. Their assignment was to create playground equipment for children with different disabilities. From that humble start, CATEA was established and today receives approximately $4 million in grant funding each year. In fact, CATEA receives more funding from the NIDRR than any other organization in the country. It was one of the three contractors that helped the Georgia Vocational Rehabilitation Program establish its rehabilitation engineering services.

Hunter Ramseur, manager of Technology Access Services at CATEA, says that professionals at CATEA look at what individuals *can* do rather than what they cannot. "We have tremendous assessment capability and have been able to place people with very severe disabilities into work situations," Ramseur says. "In the past, if the assistive technology consumers needed didn't exist, we would invent it. Now, our main focus is on researching technology that already exists because chances are, it does somewhere in the world. And we're not just focused on work issues: if someone wants to climb a mountain, we'll help them figure out how to do it."

CATEA has a staff of approximately 30 professionals, several of whom are masters-level rehabilitation engineers recruited from all over North America. CATEA collaborates with other schools and departments within Georgia Tech, such as the Industrial Design Department within the College of Architecture and the Computer Science College, to support custom design and modification of products for consumers with disabilities. To date, CATEA has worked on more than 3,000 cases, many of which involved designing first-of-a-kind assistive technology products for people with disabilities.

Although most Rehabilitative Engineering Research Centers focus on one topic, such as hearing enhancement, prosthetics, or telecommunications access, CATEA takes a more comprehensive approach. (Visit *http://www.ncddr.org/rpp/techaf/techdfdw/rerc* for information on federally funded

Rehabilitation Engineering Research Centers and their work.) CATEA currently has four separate national grants that focus on

- Developing training support for rehabilitation professionals
- Consumer-driven assistive technology resources
- Americans with Disabilities Act (ADA) resources for consumers and businesses
- Telecommunications and information technology accessibility

CATEA also has ongoing research in anthropometrics (body measurements of individuals), computer-driven furniture manufacturing, and assistive technology resource development for science in the schools. CATEA collaborates with Emory Healthcare to provide assessments through the Advanced Assistive Technology Lab (AATL) housed at the Center for Rehabilitation Medicine at Emory University Hospital.

Before the state of Georgia formed its own assistive technology unit—the AWT—CATEA provided these services to the state under contract. Thus, CATEA helped lay the groundwork for Georgia's current assistive technology program. Today, CATEA provides assistive technology services through fee-for-service referrals that come through Emory's Center for Rehabilitation Medicine. Individuals, insurance representatives, and employers from all over the southeast make these referrals.

CATEA also maintains a Web site (*http://www.catea.org*) that describes its programs and a toll-free number (800-726-9119) to field consumer questions about assistive technology. CATEA freely shares its large database of assistive technology products, funding resources, and work-related training resources.

Glenn Moscoso: Speaking Up

One of the Web sites CATEA maintains under grant is called assistivetech.net (*http://www.assistivetech.net*). It provides consumers and vendors with online access to a comprehensive database of assistive technology products for various disability types. A young man named Glenn Moscoso maintains the resource section of this site. Glenn has cerebral palsy and uses an augmentative and alternative communication (AAC) device to help him circumvent his own erratic speech patterns and communicate more freely.

"I'm a real people person, but it's difficult for me to get words out," Moscoso says. "This device has opened up public speaking for me." Glenn is pursuing a career in marketing and public relations, which requires him to frequently speak and give presentations. His speech synthesis device, the hand-held Portable IMPACT made by Enkidu Research (*http://www.enkidu.net*), gives him the clear voice to do that. Moscoso types what he wants to say into the device—or selects from a library of phrase icons—and the IMPACT speaks what he types.

In the office, Moscoso is on his computer all the time. He uses a standard PC equipped with the Windows 98 operating system, the Microsoft Office suite, Internet Explorer, and Microsoft FrontPage. He looks forward to improvements in speech recognition software so it can recognize his erratic speech patterns. Today's products force you to say words the same way every time, which Moscoso can't do. "More and more telephone-based services such as directory assistance, computer support, and even getting airline schedules require you to speak words plainly into your handset. That's difficult for me," Moscoso says.

Wil Morales: "Don't Take No for an Answer"

Wil Morales has expanded his arsenal of assistive technology as his condition—spinal muscular atrophy, a variant of muscular dystrophy—has worsened. Morales has very limited strength in his contracted muscles and limited dexterity in his arms. He uses a motorized wheelchair for mobility and a modified workstation that allows him to position his trackball for easy access.

Morales works at CATEA, on its Southeast Disability and Business Technical Assistance Centers and Tech Connections grant projects. He is an audio conference coordinator and training manager, putting together Web-based training on various assistive technology topics and offering training in CATEA's ADA disability resource center.

When Morales joined CATEA in 1999, the experts there performed an informal technology assessment of both his home and work environments. A big problem at home was securing his apartment door. Morales couldn't manage the keys and therefore always left his apartment unlocked. He had previously located an automatic door opener from an assistive technology vendor, but it cost $1,500 and had to be permanently installed. A technology specialist at CATEA found a Black & Decker PowerLock for $99 that works via radio frequency signals and a remote control.

CATEA introduced Morales to voice recognition software, but he didn't like wearing a headset and microphone all day, and depending on others to put it on and take it off him. "I also had to talk louder than normal for it to recognize my speech, and that was obnoxious in a busy office," he says. So, he uses a virtual keyboard called My-T-Soft (Innovative Management Group) that costs only $99 and is fully compatible with all his Windows products. He positions the virtual keyboard in the upper-right corner of his screen and uses a trackball pointer to click letters and command keys. He's been clocked at 25 words per minute. Morales also uses a wrist glide, which supports his hands and arms while typing and prevents them from tiring.

Morales urges others with disabilities to be proactive. "Figure out what you want to do. There are great resources out there, like State Vocational Rehabilitation Program and CATEA. Don't take no for an answer. Do your own research, and push the limits."

Lessons Learned

Joy Kniskern, Assistive Technology Unit Manager for Georgia's Vocational Rehabilitation Program, offers these tips to other governmental agencies trying to strengthen their focus on assistive technology in rehabilitative efforts:

- **Make assistive technology a core value of your vocational rehabilitation organization.** Commit adequate resources to support it.

- **Involve key people from all levels of the vocational rehabilitation program (counselors, managers, account representatives, work preparation technicians, and any existing assistive technology staff) in the planning process.** Identify needs and determine staffing requirements, service areas, and scope of services. This will ensure that all stakeholders have a voice in design, will improve program acceptance, and make implementation much smoother.

- **Include interdisciplinary professionals such as rehabilitation engineers, occupational therapists, rehabilitation technologists, and rehabilitation technicians.** This way you can address a wide array of assistive technology needs.

- **Advertise widely for these assistive technology professionals.** Leverage professional associations at the national and state levels (e.g., the Rehabilitation Engineering and Assistive Technology

Society of North America [RESNA], the American Occupational Therapy Association [AOTA], and the American Speech-Language-Hearing Association [ASHA]).

- **Design a thorough in-service orientation and training program for new staff.** Expose them as fully as possible to all the roles of key vocational rehabilitation staff, policies, procedures, practices, and decision-making protocol.

- **Develop a process for keeping abreast of new technologies.** The field of assistive technology is in its infancy, with vendors producing new technologies in many fields. No one has yet developed a thorough process for consumer product reporting for these technologies. Georgia's AWT is considering several ways to keep informed about new products including a Web site with links to product sites, in-service training, talent pools among its staff, active participation at national assistive technology conferences, and participation in assistive technology credentialing bodies such as RESNA.

- **Consider resources available within each state to provide AAC services by licensed speech and language therapists.** Consider how your service delivery design will address needs of customers who might require AAC interventions to reach their work goal. Georgia experiences a shortage of providers in this important area of highly specialized assistive technology services.

Summary

The U.S. DoD is not only the largest employer in the world but the world's largest buyer of assistive technology. CAP provides assistive technology to thousands of DoD employees all over the world and, as of two years ago, to the employees of more than 45 other federal agencies as well. If an organization of the DoD's size can implement assistive technology, it can be implemented anywhere.

As a model implementation of federal policies, the state of Georgia shines. The State Vocational Rehabilitation Program within the Georgia Department of Labor has made assistive technologies a core value of its effort to provide work opportunities to all citizens who want to work.

A major role for state government is getting the word out to citizens that assistive technologies exist and are available to them, often at no charge. Georgia does this by integrating its AWT team into the entire vocational rehabilitation organization and networking widely. It also provides public Tools for Life Resource Centers, a solution-based assistive technology Web site, and works with leading private assistive technology organizations like Georgia Tech's CATEA and the Shepherd Center.

Hunter Ramseur of CATEA observes, "One of the most interesting aspects of the growth of assistive technology is the gradual shift from government-supported initiatives to private sector/commercial initiatives. In the last several years, the industry has seen the beginnings of a market-driven approach to the creation and delivery of assistive technology appliances, devices, and services." The aging population and the "bulge" of the baby boomers have driven this, like many other areas of the economy. As the individuals in this group age, they are requiring more and more convenience products to provide them with the independence they desire. This group has significant buying power and therefore presents an economic incentive for companies to provide products the people in this group can use. As competition increases, choices will improve and prices will fall. Consumers with and without disabilities will both benefit.

CHAPTER

6

Accessible Technology in the Retail Industry

Less than two years after Tony Norris ran in the 1984 Chicago Marathon, doctors discovered a tumor wrapped around his spinal cord. Norris underwent surgery, knowing full well that removing the tumor was likely to result in paralysis. The operation—the first of a dozen during a 20-month hospital stay—left him quadriplegic.

Norris was released from rehab in fall of 1987 "feeling rotten" and resigned to life in a wheelchair at age 42. He was recuperating at home and learning to deal with the extent of his disability when he got a call from his former supervisor at Sears, Roebuck and Co., where he'd worked for 18 years.

"What will it take to bring you back?" the supervisor asked.

The answer was not simple, but it was clearly workable. It took a determined employee who was unwilling to give up all his training and skills along with the use of his arms and legs; a retailer whose business philosophy has long embraced workforce diversity; and an evolving set of physical accommodations and assistive technologies that empower Norris and other people with disabilities to keep their careers on track and to have fulfilling, productive lives.

"Part of the problem with being disabled is having low self-esteem," says Norris, now a veteran of more than three decades in the retail industry. "And I really believe that working brought me back to my full potential."

Norris celebrates 34 years of employment at Sears in 2002, as well as his 58th birthday. Before becoming disabled, he held various positions within the company, starting out in the field as a management trainee and department manager. Later, he moved to the retailer's corporate headquarters in Hoffman Estates, Illinois, a suburb of Chicago, and was promoted from merchandising assistant to sales promotion manager to shoe buyer.

Today, his job title is senior systems specialist for Sears. But Sears store employees in shoe departments all over the country know Norris as the help desk guru who can answer almost any question imaginable about women's boots or the next shipment of cross-trainers from Nike. Norris receives thousands of such queries each month via phone or e-mail. He answers many of these questions by drawing from the store of information that he's accumulated over the years and forwards the balance to merchandise assistants.

Assistive technology makes Norris a productive and valued employee in the eyes of his managers. He relies chiefly on the Dragon Naturally Speaking speech recognition system and the Dragon Dictate dictation system, which run on his Microsoft Windows 2000–based computer at Sears headquarters. Along with a microphone and speakers, these technologies enable Norris's PC to respond to the sound of his voice. Norris also uses a CINTEX3 dialing system from NanoPac Inc. (*http://www.nanopac.com*), which allows him to make outgoing calls and answer the phone using just his voice. This hardware/software environment is replicated at his home office so Norris can extend support beyond the Chicago business day to associates (the company's preferred term for employees) at stores in other time zones, such as Puerto Rico and Hawaii.

Having a voice-controlled PC has enabled Norris to become adept at using e-mail as well as off-the-shelf applications including Microsoft Word, Microsoft Excel, Microsoft PowerPoint, and Microsoft Internet Explorer. He considers it a remarkable turnabout for a man who had no computer experience prior to returning to work in 1988 with a disability so severe that he can move little more than his head.

Norris gives Sears credit for his long and fulfilling career, pointing out that the company has been a leader in recruiting, hiring, and accommodating people with disabilities since 1948. The company's track record, which originated with a post-war commitment to employ veterans returning with disabilities, is well known throughout the retail industry. Indeed, Sears was miles ahead of many other companies and industries, modeling the principles of the Americans with Disabilities Act (ADA) decades before its 1990 passage.

Norris had been back at work for two years when the federal law was enacted. To accommodate his sophisticated, motorized wheelchair, all the furniture was removed from his work cubicle at Sears headquarters, and the counter that holds his computer equipment was raised.

"I hear so many people say they're afraid to hire the disabled because it takes so much to accommodate them," Norris says. "But it's not rocket science. Sometimes it's just a matter of getting access so you can drive your wheelchair in. And frankly, all the things I need are simple, not insurmountable."

Assistive technologies and physical accommodations have done more than just make Norris a trusted and reliable employee. He routinely joins other Sears volunteers at a Chicago area school where 98 percent of the students are from families whose incomes are below the poverty level. He serves on the advisory board of the Illinois Center for Rehabilitation and Education in Chicago, a live-in school for children with severe disabilities. He mentors high school students with disabilities, often inviting them to work beside him at his PC all day and then showing them how he maneuvers at home, too, so he can be a role model for independent living. He teaches youngsters at the retailer's on-site childcare facility not to be afraid of someone in a wheelchair. And, he serves as co-chair of a corporate-wide diversity network for Sears associates with disabilities, whose mission includes community outreach and education. Norris considers such efforts small payback for his rewarding career.

"It wasn't so long ago that people like me would sit in a room and look out the window," Norris says. "But the computer, and especially the Internet, is a tremendous doorway to us. Assistive technology has changed my whole life."

A History of Commitment to Workforce Diversity

Richard Sears and Alvah C. Roebuck launched more than a business partnership when they joined forces in 1886. They started a tradition of providing U.S. families with top-quality products and services, and they planted the seed for a retail presence that became pervasive in the nation's communities. The Sears, Roebuck and Co. mail-order catalog, which grew from selling watches and jewelry to purveying entire homes, was a fixture in every American household for many years.

Today, Sears has a customer base of more than 60 million households, approximately 3,000 retail locations, and annual revenues of more than $40 billion. And, with 300,000 employees, Sears typifies the American workplace. Consequently, Sears customers—and in fact, the population at large—expect Sears to reflect the values of the communities it serves. The company's long-held philosophy on workforce diversity derived in large part from this consumer expectation.

"Our organization strives to focus on the inclusiveness of all individuals because we want to be representative of the people we serve," explains Peggy Sledge, vice president of diversity at Sears. "We want to make sure that the perspectives and opinions of Sears associates—regardless of race, age, gender, physical ability, or what have you—reflect those of our customers."

Sears CEO Alan J. Lacy mirrors that sentiment in a statement posted on the company's Web site (*http://www.sears.com*): "Diversity is not just the right thing to do at Sears," Lacy says. "It is a business imperative."

The retailer's decades-long history of integrating people with disabilities into the workforce is punctuated by some specific milestones:

- In 1947, Sears was a founding member of a group that later became known as the President's Committee on Employment of People with Disabilities.

- Beginning around 1948 and continuing through the post-war period, Sears made a conscious effort to recruit and hire returning veterans who were disabled during their World War II service.

- Sears established a formal Program for the Employment of the Physically Handicapped in 1954 to provide a set of guidelines for integrating people with disabilities into its workforce.

- In 1972, Sears established a Selective Placement Program that actively encouraged people with disabilities to apply for employment and matched their skills with job requirements.

- In 1976, Sears became a founding member of the Industry Labor Council, now the National Business and Disability Council (NBDC), a resource for businesses that hire, work with, and market to Americans with disabilities. Sears continues to support the organization financially and serves on the NBDC's Executive Leadership Team.

- Following the passage of the ADA in 1990, Sears established a policy that allows employees with disabilities to work from home. The company equips them with and supports the assistive technologies they need.

- In 2001, Sears established the disAbled Associate Network to build connections among employees with disabilities, encourage discussion about their needs, offer them support, and remove any obstacles from their career paths.

Today, Sears continues to actively recruit employees in various venues that afford the company opportunities to hire people with disabilities. In a report issued subsequent to the ADA, researchers who examined the pre- and post-ADA employment practices at Sears estimated that the company employed approximately 20,000 people with physical or mental disabilities. (Blanck 1994) This statistic reflected a workforce of 300,000—roughly the same as it is today.

Sears does not track the types of disabilities represented within its ranks, but they clearly run the gamut, from employees who bring guide dogs to work and associates who are hard-of-hearing to people who are physically disabled by polio and cerebral palsy. The company recognizes that it can accommodate employees with disabilities more easily in an office setting than it can at a retail store because nonstore employees perform their jobs largely by interacting with a computer and a phone. Thus, although a number of people with disabilities work at Sears stores around the country, Sears employees who have serious visual or hearing disabilities or who use wheelchairs are typically matched to positions at one of the retailer's 10 nationwide service centers or at the suburban Chicago campus. In the field sites, employees with disabilities take calls from customers, dispatch repair services, authorize credit card purchases, make collection calls, or resolve problems that customers experience at Sears.com, the company's online business. Sears also has two processing centers in Ohio, where employees with disabilities mail statements and perform other types of clerical work. Sears management is adamant, however, that fair treatment of employees with disabilities means not congregating them in a particular building, wing, or office, or setting them up differently in any way.

"Our associates with disabilities are integrated within the organization and the associates population, just as anyone else would be," Sledge says. "They are not singled out because of their differences. We optimize on their differences. Through the means of technology, we can enhance whatever expertise they may not be able to use fully."

Making a Case for Business Value When Every Dollar Counts

Retail is legendary as a low-margin business. Even the industry's largest and most successful businesses claim that they keep only a couple of cents out of every dollar of revenue. How then can retailers justify the costs of assistive technologies and other accommodations that make employing people with disabilities feasible—especially during economic downturns, when they must fight even harder for discretionary dollars?

' At Sears, the rationale is not governed by any sort of formal cost/benefit analysis. Conventional business wisdom, of course, holds that it costs more to bring in a new employee than it does to hold on to an existing one. But that falls short of explaining how Sears can afford to actively recruit people with disabilities and integrate them into its workforce.

Jan Drummond, the senior director of external communications at Sears, says it amounts to a corporate mind-set. Accommodating disabilities is simply "a smart thing to do," even if many of the benefits aren't manifested on the balance sheet.

"Whether you accommodate someone already in your employ or you accommodate a new hire, it adds an element of loyalty," Drummond says. "And it's good for the morale of a company to see an employer running on all cylinders, working on all phases of diversity, including disability."

Sears also takes pride in its reputation as a good place to work. Providing jobs and assistive technologies for people with disabilities—like all of its efforts to encourage associate diversity—is part of a package that also includes competitive salaries, flexible work hours, and tuition reimbursement. Sears sees such incentives as ways to enhance its position as the retail industry's employer of choice.

Anecdotal evidence suggests that Sears gains in other ways as well. For example, employees with disabilities at Sears boast that they have a better than average attendance record because they value their jobs so highly. Fully sighted coworkers talk of blind associates whose keyboarding speed outperforms their own. And Tony Norris says that, using his speech recognition system, he can produce a letter faster than anyone. Jim Frank, a Sears IT coordinator who over-sees the engineering of software and hardware solutions for associates with special needs, acknowledges that an extra measure of motivation seems consistent with the company's implementation of assistive technologies.

"From a legal standpoint, if a job is available and we can make a reasonable accommodation with assistive technology for a disabled person who has the skills to qualify, we must consider hiring him or her the same way we would consider hiring any other individual," Frank says. "But as it turns out, many associates who need accommodation turn out to be the more productive associates."

Sears does not appear to have paid a penalty for refusing to let cost stand in the way of providing employment opportunities to people with disabilities.

The company has weathered many economic storms in its 115-plus-year history and emerged intact, due largely to smart management. Even during the recessionary period that began in late 2001, Sears beat industry odds by ending the fiscal year ahead of expectations despite declining revenues. Although some parts of the company suffered as a result of the recent downturn, Sears increased its market share in some segments (such as major appliances) and made supply chain improvements that upped productivity. Other retailers did not fare as well in this lean climate.

Bradley H. Shorser: "Assistive Technology Is My Equalizer"

Like Tony Norris, Bradley H. Shorser goes back a long way with assistive technology and its role in enabling workplace equity. Early in life, Shorser developed retinitis pigmentosa, a genetic disorder in which the retina of the eye progressively deteriorates, ultimately causing blindness. By age 20, Shorser could no longer read, and by his mid-20s, he could navigate only with the aid of a guide dog.

A New Yorker, Shorser initially went to work in his father's firm on Wall Street, but because Wall Street is notoriously cyclical, he saw his income as a broker dwindle to nothing. The realization that his sighted friends could subsidize their income, whereas he couldn't due to his disability, spurred Shorser to seek more self-sufficient employment. His quest took him to rehab for counseling, and then back to school for a bachelor's degree in marketing. But despite graduating nineteenth out of a class of 400, Shorser met with a cool reception from potential employers. One New York area retailer was especially glacial.

"I walked into my interview with my dog and they said, 'Don't even bother sitting down,'" Shorser recalls.

Not long after, in 1974, Sears sent a recruiter from Chicago to call on Shorser. After three interviews, Sears offered him a job as a retail management trainee. Twenty-seven years later, Shorser is a respected and valued Sears executive. As customs compliance manager, he's responsible for ensuring that all Sears direct imports comply with U.S. Customs regulations. He also serves in a government liaison role, representing Sears at an international trade association, and on occasion, he is involved in lobbying efforts. He travels routinely in both capacities, always accompanied by his guide dog.

The assistive technologies that make Shorser's demanding position possible include a Braille display from ALVA Access Group Inc. (*http://www.aagi.com*);

the JAWS screen reader software from Freedom Scientific; DECTalk, a stand-alone speech synthesis machine made by Digital Equipment Corp. (now Compaq); and a Kurzweil scanning interface (by Kurzweil Educational Systems, Inc.) that lets him use a scanner as a text reader.

Shorser finds his ALVA Braille display extremely useful because it enables him to navigate around the screen of his Windows NT 4.0 Workstation–based PC, not just listen to words. The display supports 80 characters across (Shorser's portable ALVA display supports only 40 characters across), making it easy for him to scroll across spreadsheets, and it interfaces transparently with the JAWS software and his DECTalk machine.

Shorser also has a Companion Note Taker (produced by Pulse Data International Ltd.) that he brings to meetings and conferences; a printer that allows him to convert meeting agendas and other documents from text to Braille; and a 6-key Braille writer that enables him to take notes while on the phone so he can keep track of commitments that emerge from business conversations.

Shorser's current technology accommodations are a far cry from what awaited him when he joined Sears in 1974. Back then, there just wasn't much in terms of assistive technology, he recalls. True, Kurzweil offered a scanner/reader device that converted the printed word into speech, but at approximately $30,000 per machine, it was beyond what Shorser considered reasonable accommodation. So, another employee was pressed into service, reading aloud anything that Shorser needed to learn, understand, or get done.

As Shorser worked his way up at Sears, assistive technologies improved. Early in his career, Shorser insisted on paying for his own equipment, arguing that the responsibility for his disability rested with him, not his employer. His attitude softened as his expertise and his longevity with the company grew. Today, he points out, the new Kurzweil scanner on his credenza costs Sears around $2,900, a reasonable investment in a 30-year employee.

"Once scanning, speech synthesis, voice recognition systems, and telecom became integrated in business applications, the cost of the equipment [came down] and products using that technology grew to include a wider customer base," Shorser explains. "The disabled population has benefited from that dramatically."

In the past, he adds, one of the biggest problems facing people who are blind was getting access to material and being able to read it quickly. Today, Shorser scans periodicals each day for news on the world of international trade so he can make senior management aware of its impact on Sears. He accesses the *Wall Street Journal*, *The New York Times*, *The Washington Post*, and the *Journal of Commerce* via the Web, using his Braille display to read the content and using JAWS to identify links on a page and zero in on particular areas of interest. He also searches the U.S. Customs Web site for rulings and regulations that affect Sears's import business.

"Assistive technology today is my equalizer," Shorser says. "When I sit at a meeting, I am up to speed as much as I can be on issues. I can pull my own weight. It puts me on a level with the able-bodied community."

Shorser recalls reading a national report on employment statistics several years ago, which held that 79 percent of the people who are blind were unemployed. What that report didn't address, he points out, is how many of the remaining 21 percent were underemployed.

"How many of them were doing things commensurate with their ability?" he asks. "That's what makes Sears's policies especially meaningful: what Sears has given me the opportunity to do is aspire to the level that I could accomplish with my capability. It's a policy that transcends mere window dressing."

A Commonsense Approach to Accommodations

Sears has learned over the years that the cost and effort of accommodating employees with disabilities is generally reasonable. In some instances, the price is nothing more than a little time. In one case, after Sears relocated a building at its Des Moines customer service center, a handful of employees with visual impairments no longer had convenient access by public bus. An HR employee took note of the situation, called the bus company, and asked whether those employees could be dropped off closer to the door. Within days, a transit authority manager altered the route to accommodate them.

Sears has taken a similar commonsense approach to complying with ADA requirements. Depending on the nature of the work, the company feels it can be creative about accommodating a person's disability, physical health needs, or mental health needs. Drummond notes from experience that this doesn't have to be expensive or complicated.

"It could be as simple as changing work hours for an employee with a disability because he wants to attend a support group or needs to see a specialist for treatment," Drummond explains. "And it may not even rise to the level of a disability. Because many of our locations are staffed by part-time people, Sears has the flexibility to accommodate personal needs at little or no cost."

She cites an example of someone in a sales position who, for whatever reason, experiences pain due to past injury to her knee joints, making it difficult to stand for long periods of time. Drummond says Sears might provide that associate with a $40 stool so she can lean against it and occasionally get her feet up off the floor.

Technology solutions also run the spectrum, from upgrading to a new version of an e-business application or Windows operating system to buying a special keyboard for someone with arthritis or providing a specialized computer and software to accommodate a blind employee who reads Braille. The assistive technologies commonly implemented for people with disabilities at Sears include the following:

- To accommodate employees with visual impairments—the JAWS screen reader software, the Duxbury system (a Braille translator), a Kurzweil scanning interface that lets employees use their scanner as a text reader, and the ZoomText or MAGic screen magnification software (from Ai Squared and Freedom Scientific, respectively). Hardware solutions include an ALVA Braille display or a PowerBraille 40 display.

- To accommodate employees with hearing impairments—the KeyPlus TTY, a keyboard with a built-in phone interface that allows employees to talk on the phone while typing on a computer and the Dialog 3 display TTY, described as a "telephone on steroids." At call centers, employees who are hard-of-hearing use dual headsets with or without amplifiers.

- To accommodate employees with mobility impairments—the Dragon Naturally Speaking and Dragon Dictate software, which allow a user to control his or her PC via voice.

According to Kay Hackwell, who is involved with making technology accommodations for associates with disabilities throughout the company's national network of call centers, there's essentially no disability that can't be addressed by means of technology. Hackwell, the IT manager in Sears's Louisville Customer Care Network site, has been working with Sears in the disability environment since 1986, when Discover Card, then owned by Sears, began looking for innovative ways to enable individuals with disabilities to own and manage retail establishments without the aid of a sighted assistant.

"There's nothing they've presented that we haven't been able to adapt technology for," says Hackwell, who works predominantly with people who have visual impairments. She estimates that 10 to 15 of the roughly 850 employees at the Louisville site have disabilities, ranging from loss of hearing and low vision to a woman with cerebral palsy who has no use of her right arm but can still perform her job.

The imperative for IT, Hackwell says, is not being afraid of the technology—and knowing where to look for a solution if you can't find one. She says the Internet is an excellent resource for locating the appropriate hardware and software assistive technologies, noting in particular the Web site *http://www.abilityhub.com*. This site provides an extensive list of adaptive solutions and alternative methods available for accessing computers, as well as technical information, articles, online links, and frequently asked questions (FAQs) about assistive technologies.

Hackwell's IT colleague, Jim Frank, adds that assistive technologies sometimes come disguised as off-the-shelf solutions aimed at mass-market users and offer fixes for employees who don't identify as having a disability or who don't seek out special IT services. Frank cites the case of one Sears employee who had no fingers on one hand. Because the man insisted that he did not have a disability—though he clearly had difficulty working a standard-issue mouse with only his thumb—IT technicians sought an ergonomic design that would allow him the same access and ability as any other user. Their recommended solution, a Logitech Trackball, designed with both mouse buttons near the thumb, proved not only cost-effective but also acceptable to the user.

In another instance, an employee at Sears headquarters had developed a reputation for failing to return e-mail. Although she insisted she didn't need assistance, discreet inquiries determined that she was having trouble reading her messages. IT technicians responded by modifying the screen settings within Windows to give her a higher contrast color scheme and extra large type. That simple change solved the problem at no cost.

Sears has discovered other forms of solutions within Windows as well. Frank notes, for example, that IT technicians are actively migrating users with disabilities from Windows NT to Windows 2000 because they've found that the Windows 2000 interface is easier to use with assistive technology. And, some Sears users with limited mobility are taking advantage of the accessibility features built into Windows, such as StickyKeys functionality and MouseKeys. Many other Sears associates with disabilities are set up with keyboard short-cuts that are built into the Windows operating system. One consultant who contracts with Sears to provide technology solutions for people with disabilities notes that blind employees use keystroke alternatives to menu commands on a regular basis because they're easier than using the mouse.

At the Des Moines call center, the Sears HR staff found a valuable use for Notepad, a text editor application that comes with Windows. In the past, training manuals had been converted into Braille for employees with visual impairments. For users, looking through three binders of Braille material proved time-consuming and cumbersome; for staff, replacing outdated information was difficult and inefficient. The HR group came up with a plan, in cooperation with the IT staff and the local Department for the Blind, to get the information from the training source on disk or as an electronic file, and then convert it into Notepad format. (Any tables or charts within the document must be rekeyed as text so they can be read by the JAWS software and output via the ALVA board in Braille.) The file is then saved to a password-protected shared drive, where employees with visual impairments can access it directly from their PCs.

"Vision-impaired associates can consult the procedure log online, even while talking to a customer," says Wanda Conway, an HR generalist at Sears in Des Moines. Conway notes that HR materials at the site—company procedures, attendance manuals, brochures on harassment, and drug-free workplace policies—are now handled in the same manner so resources are constantly fresh and accessible. "It's ideal for orientation for new associates with vision impairments," she says. "Some of the other associates are envious because they still have to page through a binder."

The retailer's approach to accommodating employees with disabilities also takes its cue from the employees themselves. In 2001, Sears established the disAbled Associate Network, the newest of seven diversity groups, to encourage awareness of disability issues and facilitate discussion about ongoing challenges in the workplace and beyond. (Other Sears associate networks link African-Americans, Asians, gay and lesbian employees, Hispanics, parents, and women.) The disAbled Associate Network hosts monthly meetings at the headquarters campus; associates at other sites can participate by teleconference. The group also sponsors an intranet site, where members post information such as the World Wide Web Consortium's (W3C) Web content accessibility guidelines and links to the ADA's Web site. Members of the network are encouraged to bring their concerns forward so Sears can move to implement any needed changes. For example, the council recommended adding Braille signage to building elevators. The network has an executive liaison who reports any issues directly to the company's CEO. Sledge, the diversity vice president, says the network is still small because it's new, but she counts on members to help Sears "recognize any misses throughout the company where we're not meeting the needs of disabled individuals."

"These are people who may be in wheelchairs, but through the implementation of technology or some other means of accommodation to help them do their jobs, they're able to excel," Sledge says. "When you can build offices and environments so that the disabled can function, you will learn that their contribution to the organization is as normal as normal can be."

Tim Needham: Without Assistive Technology, He Wouldn't Have a Job

When Tim Needham graduated from the University of Illinois Champaign in 1985 armed with a bachelor's degree in math/computer science, he had a tough time finding a job. Needham had been diagnosed with cerebral palsy shortly after birth, and potential employers did not look kindly on him because the disability impaired his speech and left him with limited use of his hands and arms.

To overcome these challenges and boost his chances of finding meaningful work, Needham enrolled in Program Able, an effort sponsored by a number of large corporations in the Chicago area, including Sears. Program Able's mission lay in teaching programming skills to people with disabilities so they could become productively employed.

The program opened the way for Needham to find gainful employment in the retail industry. He accepted a position at Sears in 1988, working at the corporate headquarters in Illinois as a mainframe programmer for his first 11 years with the company. In 1999, he transferred to the Sears intranet team because he wanted to gain skills in Web technology. Three years later, at age 42, Needham has a rewarding job as a quality assurance specialist for Web-based applications. Once he arrives at work, he can navigate essentially everywhere on the Sears campus in his electric wheelchair.

A variety of assistive technologies help accommodate the limited dexterity Needham has in his hands and arms. One of the simplest elements of his mobility solution is a keyguard that covers the keyboard of Needham's Windows 2000–based PC to help prevent mistyping. Manufactured by a non-profit organization in Conyers, Georgia, called Tech-Able (reached by phone at 770-922-6768 or e-mail at *techable@america.net*), the keyguard allows Needham to move his hand over the keyboard until he comes to the key he wants to press; he then presses that key through a circular cut-out.

Needham is also a longtime user of the accessibility features in Windows including StickyKeys and MouseKeys. According to Jim Frank, a Sears IT specialist who coordinates the engineering of software and hardware solutions for individuals with special needs, Needham really needs the StickyKeys functionality to log on and off his PC.

"Before Sears had Windows, we usually had OS/2, and I had to use a trackball; I could not use the mouse," Needham adds. "The features in Windows made it much easier for me to use the mouse around the screen as more and more programs utilize the mouse. I use these features very often in my work."

Needham has also used a program called Macro Magic from Iolo Technologies, which can be found at *http://www.iolo.com/support*. Macro Magic allows him to create macros—essentially, keyboard shortcuts—for longer items that he must type often, which can be an effective time-saver for someone who has limited mobility.

Because Needham's disability also makes answering the phone difficult, IT specialists at Sears have modified his PC so he can answer calls more easily. The solution is based on the Creative Labs Modem Blaster speaker phone, a 56K modem that has analog functionality built in. By using this technology with his computer, microphone, and speakers, Needham can answer the phone without having to turn away from his PC.

Although Needham's disability does affect his speech, he has found that after a short time working with other Sears associates, it is not a problem. He did discover early on, however, that his speech disability did not lend itself well to the voice-activated computer that Sears provided him. Those technologies required him to speak the same all the time. For many of his daily communications, the technology that works best is e-mail. But the technologies that have had the most impact for Needham are clearly those that enable him to effectively access a computer.

"Assistive technology allows me to be a productive employee at Sears," he says. "If it wasn't for all the assistive technology, I could not operate the computer, and I would not have a job."

Gay Norton: All It Takes Is an Inexpensive Headset and Amp

Before joining Sears in 1999, Gay Norton had spent the better part of 20 years in jobs where she worked essentially on her own. She operated a press for eight years at a ceramic tile plant, and before that had driven semi trucks for a dozen years. The noise level of both work environments, combined with sinus problems and recurrent ear infections, left her hard-of-hearing more than a decade ago. Norton didn't need special equipment at her earlier jobs to compensate for her hearing loss because she hadn't had contact with people to the extent where communications were difficult. Plus, she'd learned that she could get by as long as she watched faces closely and read lips.

That changed when Norton, at age 58, came to work as an accounts services representative at a Sears call center in Des Moines, Iowa. Although her disability wasn't severe enough to require a hearing aid, Norton couldn't hear well enough over the phone to handle incoming calls in a timely fashion. When customers would call with a question about a credit card statement, for example, she often had to ask them to repeat key information.

The assistive technology that Sears initially implemented to accommodate Norton consisted of a dual headset. Unlike the single-ear headset that most call center employees use—which leaves one ear free to hear conversations on the department floor—Norton's model covered both ears. It helped, but not enough, prompting Sears to order her a more sophisticated solution. The dual headset Norton uses now plugs into an amplifier, which in turn plugs into the phone and allows Norton to control call volume through the amplifier.

Sears purchased Norton's dual Supra Binaura headset from its regular headset supplier, Call One Inc., at a cost of just $77. The Universal M-12 amplifier that allows Norton to control volume, also available from Call One, cost $80. An HR manager in Des Moines notes that a tip from the assistive technology manager at the Iowa Division of Vocational Rehab Services initially led Sears to the proper equipment to order for employees with hearing disabilities.

This simple technology solution not only shortened Norton's call handling time, but also empowered her to move up the job ladder. Approved to become an account services specialist, she now handles escalated customer concerns and technical issues. And as a member of a "transition team," she helps out with new hires in the period between their initial training and the time they go out on the floor.

"Sears goes the extra mile to make sure we have the equipment we need for the different types of disabilities people have," Norton says. "The assistive technology and the training Sears provides enable people to have jobs who might otherwise not be able to have jobs at all, or at least not in this line of work. And on a personal level, it means that I have been able to advance in my job to meet company standards so that I was eligible for promotions and pay raises."

Room to Improve: Building IT Policies on Proven Practices

Despite Sears's longstanding practice of accommodating employees with disabilities, the company has no formal policies for doing so in its overall technology plan. Jim Frank, the IT coordinator based at Chicago headquarters, and Mike McMahon, the company's ADA coordinator, are reviewing the company's policies. Frank and McMahon are two members of a committee drawn from various business areas to get Sears onto a policy path that will bring more consistency and legitimacy to the implementation of assistive technologies. Launched in 2002, the committee aims among other things to create a structure for technology accommodations, devise a plan for managing equipment, and consolidate support for disability-related accommodations from many remote IT sites into one organization. One of the first steps in this effort is establishing some corporate standards.

"My plan going forward, and I've discussed this with several of my IT partners, is if there's any programming that needs to be done here, we need to take it through a certification process designed specifically for accommodation," Frank explains. "And any software we decide to purchase or use enterprise-wide also needs to go through that same certification."

Frank concedes that corporate standards can be difficult to achieve when you're accommodating the varied needs of employees with disabilities. But they are imperative if the organization hopes to move beyond a process that to date has been essentially reactionary. The typical scenario at Sears today goes something like this: An associate is hired. He lets his HR manager know that he has a disability, for example, a visual impairment. The HR manager puts in a call to action to engineering, which must determine how to assist the user to interface the same way as anyone else. Engineering analyzes the situation, defines the user's needs, determines which technology is best suited to the individual, and then proceeds with an action plan to develop an appropriate solution. A solution can include a screen magnifier, JAWS software, or a Braille display, for example. (Some users, of course, choose not to request special services. In those cases, engineering doesn't get involved. Instead, the employee might approach the help center and ask for ergonomic design changes.)

Frank has learned from experience that IT can use the same processes repeatedly to accommodate certain disabilities. For example, he says, Sears doesn't have to buy a different Braille terminal for every employee with a visual impairment. As long as a person can read Braille, IT can standardize on a specific terminal or specific software.

"But we need to keep those groups that are programming in the loop so that as they write their programs, they write them in such a way that the software will work with them," he adds. "In fact, Microsoft provides some guidelines for writing programs, and as long as you follow the guidelines, the assistive technology interface is easier. You don't have to do any radical programming or scripting changes within the product."

Frank says Sears's field IT locations have built up sufficient expertise over the years to recommend appropriate technology solutions for people with disabilities employed at those sites. In cases where field technicians are stumped, they call him. If he in turn encounters a problem, he calls a consultant who specializes in helping organizations make computer-related accommodations for people with disabilities.

One initiative that has helped bring structure and uniformity to Sears's efforts is an online tool that outlines the process of accommodating associates with disabilities. Created internally and in effect since mid-2000, the corporate process aims to ensure that HR managers throughout the company know how to react when such situations arise, whether with new recruits or existing employees. It clearly spells out the information that managers need and the steps they should follow, from the nature of the dialogue with the affected employee to the types of technologies available.

"Having something online that people at Sears's retail stores and product services units can go in and work with is very effective, especially with a company as large as Sears," says McMahon, who oversees the online accommodations program. "It helps make sure we cover all the bases from an ADA and legal standpoint."

After making an accommodation—or in some cases, deciding that they can't—HR managers at Sears close the loop by reporting back to an online ID at headquarters. McMahon's team looks at every determination to review what sorts of assistive technologies are being implemented and to make sure that all steps in the process have been followed. The online program will come under review as part of the company's IT policy development effort, but in the interim, it seems to be well received and well used. Another resource that will soon be available to Sears's HR managers and employees with disabilities is a guide book of organizations that provide certain kinds of assistance for individuals who are blind or deaf. The book will include contact information for groups that will work with companies on technology accommodations.

Jannet Laughrey: "The Opportunity to Be a Real Person"

If your Kenmore clothes dryer starts acting up and gives you cause to call Sears for service, you may well find yourself on the phone with Jannet Laughrey. Laughrey, a customer service representative in the retailer's Louisville, Kentucky, Customer Care Network site, will schedule a service technician to come to your home to repair the faulty appliance. And, if you call back later to confirm the time of service or to ask for a heads-up call from the technician, Laughrey can handle those requests as well.

A Sears associate since 1999, Laughrey, 47, is also training to be an authorization representative. That means, in addition to her service dispatch duties, she'll field calls from Sears associates at stores nationwide who need to verify, for example, a customer's credit availability before approving a credit card purchase.

Like the rest of her 850 or so coworkers in Louisville, Laughrey routinely handles hundreds of such incoming calls every day, each lasting an average of three minutes. But unlike the bulk of her colleagues, she does so with virtually no eyesight. At age 8, she was diagnosed with a disease that by age 15 had progressed to the point where she was reading Braille—Laughrey can only barely perceive light and shadows.

Assistive technologies help compensate for Laughrey's negligible vision. She uses the JAWS software, which runs on her Microsoft Windows NT 4.0 Workstation–based PC, in conjunction with Freedom Scientific's Blazie PowerBraille 40 display, which interfaces with her PC and sits under her keyboard for easy access.

The JAWS software, which runs constantly, essentially reads the printed text on Laughrey's screen to her. When she has gleaned enough information by that method to move on, Laughrey taps a button on her PC to silence JAWS and shifts to her Braille display. She's learned that she can do her job much more quickly by reading text on her own in Braille than she can by listening to the speech program. Another quick keystroke starts JAWS talking again at Laughrey's command.

Sears IT technicians have also modified JAWS to interface with another application called **HotKeys**, which will help Laughrey and other blind associates who work as authorization representatives. HotKeys, a shareware utility developed by H2 Software, can be scripted to allow Laughrey to determine, for example, the balance of an account with a single keystroke. Thus, if the F1 key were programmed for "balance," pressing it would take JAWS to that exact line and read it to her.

Laughrey's workspace also includes a Perkins Brailler machine (made by Quantum Technology) that allows her to write notes. For example, she can manually key in information such as a customer's name and phone number, and then send the information (essentially as an e-mail message) to a field service technician's handheld computer.

To further accommodate employees with visual impairments, the Louisville center has a Braille printer on site. When Laughrey recently asked for the company's attendance policy in Braille format, she had it in hand a couple of hours later.

"That's a plus for Sears as a whole, and it impressed me and my colleagues," says Laughrey, who is one of five people with visual impairments working at the Louisville site. "Even the Lighthouse for the Blind in Louisiana, where I worked as a receptionist, didn't have the accessibility products or the technology that I find here."

Training sessions on new technologies have also made a difference for Laughrey in terms of equipping her to work in a busy retail environment. She notes that Sears training classes typically consist of a whole team of people, but the teleservice training sessions she's participated in were limited to small groups of associates with visual impairments. Trainers do a lot of reading and explaining, but they also have the computer read to trainees, and they provide many of the materials in Braille. Moreover, Laughrey says, the hands-on component of training and the opportunity to ask questions run longer as a rule than in the standardized training classes. Asked what assistive technology overall means to her, Laughrey is quick to reply.

"It makes it possible to be independent, and working on my own and making a living," she says. "I don't have to depend on the system. I can get out, I can do the job."

Laughrey also polled several of her coworkers with visual impairments, asking what they'd gained from Sears's practices and policies on accommodating people with disabilities through technology. The consensus: the opportunity to be a real person.

Removing Barriers for Customers

Sears does more on the accommodations front than deploy assistive technologies to recruit and retain employees. The retailer is also clearing obstacles to make its stores—real and virtual—more accessible to customers with disabilities.

At the company's 3,000 retail locations, counters are being lowered as remodeling proceeds and as new structures are built so that a person with a disability or in a wheelchair has better and easier access. Customer service areas are also growing roomier, and physical accommodations such as drinking fountains, elevators, restrooms, and lighting fixtures are being improved in terms of accessibility. Much of this effort today is in response to and in compliance with ADA guidelines, but Sears was arguably one of the few retailers that took the initiative early on to make sure those pathways were clear.

In terms of technology implementations for customers with disabilities, Sears has installed two types of solutions that make it easy for people with hearing impairments to interact with Sears. Specified call centers, including those in Louisville and Des Moines, have phone devices equipped with a **Telecommunications Device for the Deaf (TDD)** on site, and Sears plans to install similar equipment at other call centers over time on an as-needed basis. A TDD device is essentially a telephone with the capability to display spoken words as text, allowing a person with a hearing impairment to carry on a conversation by phone.

TDD devices are used primarily to provide Sears customer service functions. For example, a Sears customer with little or no hearing might take advantage of this technology if she wanted to request an increase in her credit line or if she discovered a questionable charge on her Sears statement. As another example, a customer with a hearing impairment who encountered problems while trying to make an online purchase at Sears.com might have reason to call Sears via a TDD device.

Some Sears sites also have **teletypewriter (TTY)** capability in addition to TDD devices. TTY technology provides essentially the same functionality as TDD, but it involves the use of a PC-based program rather than a physical telephone. Kay Hackwell, the IT manager at the Louisville call center, says that it's easier to use a PC-based solution in a call center than a stand-alone device. However, some call centers have both TDD and TTY capabilities. Because the solutions are not in constant use by customers, associates who are hard-of-hearing can make phone calls from home and talk to other associates using these technologies.

To determine whether Sears has TDD equipment in place, Hackwell adds that any hard-of-hearing Sears customers nationwide can dial 711 from any phone and reach the relay service for that state. Operators there have TDD devices that allow them to "relay" the voice message across the phone to the toll-free Sears customer service number (or any other number for that matter) and translate the reply into text. This enables a two-way conversation between customers and the companies they do business with.

Lessons Learned

Sears has found that patience, persistence, and a sound grasp of an individual's needs are imperative to the successful implementation of assistive technologies in the workplace. On a more practical plane, the retailer outlines some tips and practices that can serve as a blueprint for organizations looking to follow its lead.

- **Establish corporate standards.** Because every employee's situation is different, assistive technologies don't generally allow for a "cookie-cutter" solution. But processes can be repeated across work sites to accommodate certain disabilities. Having a standardized suite of hardware and software products that have proven effective in your organization will make implementation proceed more quickly and smoothly. This approach should include clear instructions on implementing any request that will be fulfilled with a standard action or item.

- **Analyze the situation and define the user's needs before seeking a solution.** Keep in mind that many people don't seek out assistive technologies because they feel they'll be singled out. Others need only slight modifications to their PC, phone, or workspace. Tact and sensitivity to an individual's needs are critical. Remember that simple changes can be the best form of accommodation.

- **Call on external IT resources.** Sears IT manager Kay Hackwell notes that the companies developing assistive technologies will usually "bend over backward" if you need help interfacing their solutions into your organization. Most also provide evaluation software at no charge. Service providers that specialize in the disability access field are also good resources. Sears relies on Houston-based Ability Consulting (*http://www.abilityconsulting.com*).

- **Forge alliances with organizations that serve people with disabilities.** The Sears call centers in several U.S. locations, for example, connect their IT staff with the IT staff at state departments for the blind and get in touch with the state divisions of vocational rehab services for suggestions on assistive technology for the hard-of-hearing. These and other regional and national groups, including the Lighthouse for the Blind, are available to other organizations seeking technology solutions. Some groups also offer technology training for managers, tips on coaching and interviewing people with disabilities, and awareness training.

- **Bring in-house programmers into the loop.** IT coordinator Jim Frank recommends making sure that any software developed internally follows industry programming guidelines so that it interfaces easily with off-the-shelf assistive technology products.

- **Train the trainers.** To effectively train employees on using assistive technologies, you must learn how to use them as if you have a disability. In other words, if you're training employees who are blind on new hardware or software, learn the material and the technology with your eyes closed. If you're an IT manager working with an employee who is deaf, learn sign language and use it.

- **Get implementation information and resources online.** Compile a list of assistive technologies that are available for specific disabilities. Don't rely on program rollouts and packets of paper to communicate your organization's implementation policies and practices. Post the guidelines on an intranet or other online location where they can be standardized, updated, and accessible to managers and employees.

Summary

The practices and technology solutions that Sears has put in place to meet the needs of people with disabilities demonstrate that the retail industry is well positioned to gain from their contributions. Granted, there are limitations when a person with a disability comes to work at Sears, but the company knows it has the ability to adapt.

"Once you define what those disabilities are, what your needs are, what the individual needs are, and you install the assistive technology, you'll find that the work disabled individuals deliver is of equal or better quality," says Sledge, the diversity vice president.

Kay Hackwell points out that today's employment opportunities in retail are a far cry from the legacy created by the U.S. government's Randolf Sheppard Act. Enacted in 1936, the federal law guaranteed that job preference would be given to a person with a disability if a retail vending facility was located in a federal building. In plain words, if a man who was blind was lucky back then, he could go to school and study and be allowed to run the cigar stand in the courthouse.

"That was their future for many years," says Hackwell. "But we've given them the ability to go out and make a living, to have as much equal opportunity as anyone else. Assistive technology affords those who in the past were kept at home and shut in the opportunity to live a normal life."

Accessible Technology in the Manufacturing Industry

Rick Burgos says he's probably a better listener than you are, even though he has an 80 percent hearing loss. "My hearing loss has forced me to be an aggressive listener," says Burgos, an advisory support specialist in one of Compaq Computer Corporation's Global Customer Support Centers. Listening is a crucial part of Burgos's job, which itself is crucial to Compaq and to many of its largest customers. Burgos supports Compaq's NonStop Himalaya computers, dubbed "the Fort Knox for moving money." The Himalaya computers are used by major financial institutions for automated teller machine (ATM) systems and securities transfers, by major telecommunications companies to handle most of the United States' wireless calls, and by public safety systems to handle half of the nation's 911 calls.

Given the mission-critical nature of the Himalaya computers, Burgos's ability to rapidly understand and respond to customer issues is mission-critical as well. He backs up his aggressive listening with a range of Microsoft products including Microsoft Outlook, Microsoft Windows Messenger, and Microsoft NetMeeting plus a Phonak HandyMic TX3 wireless microphone and a Plantronics M10 amplifier and headset.

"Outlook is my main tool," says Burgos. "For certain types of information, it's more useful to me than a phone call. For example, if a customer rattles off a detailed error message to me, he may only repeat the parts he thinks are relevant, missing important information. Or I may not hear it correctly. My ability to capture lengthy and detailed information through e-mail is greater than over the phone."

Beyond communicating with customers, Burgos finds Outlook an ideal solution for calendaring, scheduling, and tracking tasks—one he relies on to capture information even more than do his peers, who are also avid Outlook users. Of course, Burgos recognizes that many Himalaya customers might prefer to contact Compaq via phone, and when that's the case, Burgos tries to accommodate them. But when phone communication with a customer is difficult, he'll inform the customer of his disability and suggest that the customer switch to Outlook or Windows Messenger. Most customers are happy to oblige, and the interaction generally concludes successfully.

Instant Messaging, the other text-based communications tool Burgos uses, is helpful to him in a variety of ways. "I was one of the first in our group to try Instant Messaging when it became available," Burgos recalls. "I saw the value in it to make my work go faster, better, easier."

In addition to holding an Instant Messaging conversation with customers, Burgos uses the technology to consult with Compaq colleagues from coast to coast. He has also enrolled in masters' degree classes in science and technology commercialization at the University of Texas, and he finds Instant Messaging the best way to have exchanges with fellow students in Mexico, Australia, and Russia. Electronic conversations—whether via e-mail or Instant Messaging—are also ideal workarounds for understanding customers, colleagues, or fellow students with accented English that is especially difficult to hear and understand for someone with a hearing disability such as Burgos. To make these applications even more helpful, Burgos configures them—using their standard options—to provide pop-up visual cues in addition to audio cues when, for example, a new message arrives.

NetMeeting, which is widely used as a training tool, is even more helpful for Burgos because he can plug his headset into the PC and hear the audio component of the training sessions perfectly. And, amazingly to him, Burgos says that colleagues who speak with heavy accents, which are always a challenge for him, for some reason now sound "like they were born in the U.S.A." when they speak through NetMeeting.

All of these applications run on Burgos's standard Windows-based Compaq Deskpro PC with the only extra component being a sound card to accommodate his headset. The wireless amplifier and headset both boost the volume and clarity of telephonic conversations and filter out the background noise of his support center environment, which can otherwise make conversations difficult to hear. As an added bonus, Burgos—unlike his colleagues—knows when he has an incoming call even when he's 50 feet away from his phone, engaged in conversation with a colleague.

"It enables me to excuse myself from another conversation when I know I have an incoming call back at my desk," says Burgos.

Burgos' assistive technology may be so effective and so seamless that he doesn't have to think much about it, but he does recall that it hasn't always been that way. Burgos's hearing loss stems from nerve damage in both ears caused by measles and a high fever when he was a young child. At first, he relied solely on hearing aids. But the technology wasn't well developed. It increased background noise as well as the sounds Burgos wanted to hear, and it failed to support Burgos's use of the phone and computer.

Burgos joined Tandem Computer in 1983, which was acquired by Compaq in 1996. Both Tandem and, later, Compaq were completely supportive of Burgos's need for accommodation. Those first accommodations included office space that had less of the disturbing background noise he couldn't filter out of his hearing aids, and included a flashing light to indicate when he had incoming phone calls. As technology has advanced, Burgos has alerted his supervisors to products that can help, and they've supported his use of them.

"I'm a technologist; I'm really curious about technology around the corner," says Burgos. "When I learn about something that can help, I get it and give it a try. Self-discovery of solutions is important. For example, no one told me about Instant Messaging—I came across it myself. I think that's a carryover from the New York survival skills I learned growing up in the Bronx."

For those with disabilities who didn't grow up in the Bronx, Burgos urges them to "give new assistive technology products a try, to hang in there," and to think about not only how products will help them as an employee with a disability, but also how they'll help them build communications with customers, friends, and colleagues.

"The bottom line to success, in work and in life, is building and maintaining relationships," says Burgos in a particularly philosophical moment. "And that requires a good level of communication. I can't think of better motivation than that for taking advantage of all the great assistive technology products out there."

Broad-Based Commitments from a Broad Range of Manufacturers

Compaq, Burgos's employer, exemplifies a commitment to people with disabilities that is similarly evident in a broad range of manufacturers. General Motors (GM), an even larger company, has been a major force on the economic landscape for a century. Cingular Wireless is a one-year-old company formed through the merged interests of two regional carriers. All these manufacturing companies not only share a record of utilizing assistive technology to grant broader access to employees, customers, and others, but also a conviction that doing so is more than the morally right thing to do—it's the sound, productive, business-oriented thing to do.

We discuss GM and Cingular later in this chapter. First, let's look at Compaq Computer.

What It Takes to Be an Employer of Choice

Compaq's workforce includes a full range of disabilities: impairments of hearing, sight, mobility, and cognition. But don't ask Equal Employment Opportunity Commission (EEOC) and Affirmative Action manager Bob Brintz or Accessibility Program Office director Michael Takemura how many Compaq employees have disabilities—they don't know. And the reason they don't know is revealing.

"We know an employee has a disability when he or she self-identifies and tells us," says Brintz. "And that number is incredibly low—far lower than the number of employees who probably do have disabilities. I think it's so low because having a disability simply is not an issue here. We have a culture that's inclusive, open. We have occupational nurses on staff and physician consultants to assist managers, human resources professionals, and employees in working out accommodations. It's exceedingly rare that accommodating an employee with a disability becomes an issue."

That "inclusive, open" culture is no accident. According to Compaq, it's good business.

"We don't try to make fine distinctions between what accommodation is legally required and what accommodation goes beyond that," says Brintz. "We are an employer of choice, and we want to be perceived that way. To the extent that we can accommodate our employees, we do so. It's as simple as that."

Takemura explains why this is so important to Compaq. "We have an extremely talented pool of employees throughout the company—in engineering, marketing, information management, Web development, human resources, and so on," says Takemura. "We would suffer without these people. Even when the labor market is loose, it's difficult to replace good people.

So we want to ensure that these people stay with us and stay effective on their jobs. If assistive technology helps them to do that—and it does—it's a modest investment for us to make. From our vantage point, assistive technology is just another productivity tool for those employees who can benefit from it."

How does Takemura know that an emphasis on accessibility, including assistive technology, translates into attracting and retaining people of quality?

"When we established our Accessibility Program Office last year, we were flooded with resumes of people who wanted to work for us, simply because of what that initiative said about our commitment in this area," he says.

Hardly a New Commitment

Compaq might continue to make news—and collect resumes—by its focus on accessibility and assistive technology, but it's hardly a new commitment for the company. Compaq has always been at the forefront of developing and promoting technology solutions that are accessible to people with disabilities. Among major computer manufacturers, Compaq was

- First to use the Voluntary Product Accessibility Template (VPAT) online to assist federal agency efforts to locate accessible products.

- First to provide accessible product information on the Section 508 "Buy Accessible" Web site.

- First to develop a third-party Assistive Technologies Partner Program— the Compaq Solutions Alliance (CSA) Program.

- First to offer the option of audible rather than peripheral output.

- First to provide matching funds (of $100,000) to support scholarships for people with disabilities seeking technical certification through the industry association **CompTIA**.

- One of the first to produce an online safety guide and keyboard warnings.

Compaq has long invested in diversity training for all of its employees. That training is broad-based, eschewing a focus on any single group of employees and instead making all employees aware of their own attitudes and biases and how they affect those around them. That training is consistent with the legacy from Digital Equipment Corporation, which Compaq acquired in

1998. That company, too, was a leader in diversity promotion dating back to the 1980s.

Accessibility: Another Name for Usability

Both employees and customers use Compaq's products, so building accessibility into those products is a win-win situation for the company. To achieve that success, the company begins to consider accessibility early in the product development process.

"If we think about accessibility right from the start, we can do a better job—and it costs less," says Takemura.

At times, making a computer accessible might seem to require screen readers, speech synthesizers, and other assistive technology products discussed throughout this book. Sometimes it does, but sometimes, according to Takemura, "accessibility is just another name for usability."

"That's consistent with our view of the computer," says Takemura. "It's less about computing per se, and more about providing access to information and entertainment. Making our products more usable for all increases the accessibility of information for all—including people with disabilities. In this way, we address accessibility in our products as a mainstream part of product design, not as something segregated off on the side for a small group of users."

For example, the easy-open lids on Compaq Armada and Evo notebooks can be operated with just one hand. That makes them more usable for everyone and accessible for those with mobility impairments.

"One of our vice presidents lost several fingers in an accident," notes Takemura. "He's ecstatic about the ability to open and operate his Compaq notebook with just one hand."

Similarly, the **universal serial bus (USB)** ports on Compaq desktop computers are located on the front of the machine, where they're easy to reach, rather than in their more traditional spot on the back of the machine. Keyboards are easily identifiable by touch and include color-coding and status lights to make their use clearer to all, especially to people with vision or hearing impairments. Grouped function keys are easier for all users to find, especially people with visual disabilities. And batteries and other devices that can be ejected from notebook PCs with a single hand are more convenient for all, especially users with mobility issues.

Compaq Accessibility Program Office

In March 2001, Compaq expanded and focused its commitment to accessible products and assistive technology through the creation of its Compaq Accessibility Program Office. The program is tasked to

- Design and engineer products, services, and programs with improved usability and accessibility for all customers with or without a disability.

- Improve Web sites, user documentation, and information accessibility for employees, customers, and persons with disabilities.

- Partner with assistive technology vendors (ATVs) and industry leaders, like Microsoft, to develop and test accessible products and solutions.

- Conduct human factors research and testing with the help of the disability community in a continual process to improve usability and accessibility.

- Support national and community disability organizations through financial assistance and equipment donation, technical expertise, and volunteers.

Partnering with ATVs is a key aspect of the program. It enables Compaq to ensure that its technology works seamlessly with the full range of assistive technology devices including screen readers and magnifiers, keyboard enhancement utilities, and voice and speech input devices as well as alternative input devices.

Vendors and products participating in the program include

- **Freedom Scientific JAWS screen reader.** Discussed frequently throughout this book, JAWS allows people with complete visual disabilities to work with their PCs.

- **Ai Squared ZoomText low-vision solution.** This solution combines a screen magnifier and screen reader, supporting users with significant visual disabilities.

- **Madentec Tracker 2000 head mouse.** This device sits on top of a PC and tracks a tiny reflective dot worn by the user on his or her forehead or glasses, allowing the user to move the cursor simply by moving his or her head.

- **Interactive Solutions iCommunicator system.** This speech-to-text and speech-to-sign language technology is a multisensory tool for persons with hearing or learning disabilities.

- **Quad Media Portable Interactive Kiosk.** This product allows users with a variety of disabilities to access all features of a kiosk.

- **GW Micro Window-Eyes.** This screen reader enables PC use by people with visual disabilities.

Compaq's close working relationship with Microsoft is a key component of its accessibility program. Because there is inconsistent awareness of the accessibility features in the Windows operating system, the Microsoft Office productivity suite, and related products, Compaq promotes these features to its customers. In addition, it works to ensure that Compaq hardware and Microsoft software work well together.

The iCommunicator: A Fruit of the Compaq Accessibility Program

At the Florida Department of Law Enforcement (FDLE), iCommunicator software from Interactive Solutions—a Compaq ATV—running on a Compaq notebook computer is helping employee Abbey Drigot, who is deaf, learn the job skills she needs to contribute to the agency and succeed in her career.

Hired as a photography forensic technologist at the FDLE, Drigot knew she had a lot to learn. It's why she jumped at the chance to attend a two-week training class about fingerprints. But familiar questions about Drigot's participation in the class arose quickly. Could a sign language interpreter be located in time? Was there enough money in the budget for the interpreter? From elementary school through college, the answers to these questions too often left Drigot reading lips, which experts say is accurate only about 30 percent of the time.

FDLE wanted better for Drigot and the department. Coworkers took sign language classes. The department arranged for signing interpreters for scheduled meetings. Together, Drigot and the department investigated other options, knowing the agency would not provide an interpreter forever.

Drigot's Internet browsing paid off. She discovered the iCommunicator software, which is designed to translate voice into text and sign language and to generate a computer voice from text. The solution fit Drigot's needs. Soon, Drigot was in her training class using iCommunicator software on a Compaq notebook computer. Drigot understood the instructor. She asked questions in class, she answered questions from the instructor, and she passed the course.

The solution combines off-the-shelf speech recognition software with iCommunicator custom software. The user speaks into a wireless microphone and that speech is then translated into text the user sees on the screen. In a screen window, the user sees video of a signing interpreter translating the speech into American Sign Language—without any language shortcuts.

"American Sign Language includes about 8,500 words, but as a society we use about 60,000 words," says Michael Dorety, president of Interactive solutions. "Words for which there are no signs must be finger spelled. American Sign Language was intended as a shortcut to keep the communication at a level that allows the interpreter to physically complete the task. With iCommunicator, the user sees every word signed in exact English order, so she gets the message and learns language skills, grammar, and composition the way they are taught to hearing students."

"The third thing the software does is the most exciting," Dorety says. "The text is transmitted into a computer-generated voice that can be plugged directly into a hearing aid or cochlear implant."

That eliminates ambient crowd noise, laughter, and other sounds. Some people who are hard-of-hearing hear words distinctly for the first time. That new information can improve their ability to speak clearly. The software can also save the text translation of speech for later display. That means a student can replay a lecture to help her study for an exam.

Dorety cautions that the software isn't right for every deaf or hard-of-hearing person or useful in every situation. Nor is iCommunicator intended to replace signing interpreters. "We don't have enough interpreters as it is," he says. "In fact, we hope iCommunicator encourages more people to become signing interpreters."

"We've been in conversations with Compaq for about 18 months," says Dorety. "We did a lot of development work in hopes that Compaq would come to market with a notebook computer running at least a 700 MHz Pentium processor. They did. We found out that the Compaq product delivers speed, accuracy, and efficiency. As the speed goes up, our software runs much smoother and better, and the speaker training time goes down. We've continued to migrate with Compaq up the Pentium trail."

The other key part of the iCommunicator's migration trail is the Windows operating system.

"We run on Windows 98 and Windows XP, but we really recommend Windows XP to our customers," says Dorety. "Windows XP delivers even more speed, for even smoother software performance. Windows XP is very stable and doesn't seem to lock up, which is very important when someone is trying to capture a live presentation."

The iCommunicator is now enhancing accessibility for users throughout the country including Drigot.

"We hope iCommunicator will afford Drigot the same opportunities that everyone else has in terms of learning and career advancement," says FDLE's Steve Balunan, a crime laboratory analyst responsible for training Drigot. "It wouldn't surprise me for Drigot to become one of the first nonhearing forensic experts in the country."

Anders Johansson: Sometimes, a Screen Reader That Speaks American English Is Weird

Anders Johansson sees the problem of accommodating a visual disability on the job from a different perspective than that of most of his fellow Compaq employees. He sees it from his vantage point in Stockholm, Sweden, where he's a software developer for Compaq's VMS operating system.

Johansson, 38, joined Digital Equipment in 1987 as a software support engineer and became a Compaq employee when the company was acquired. He moved on within Compaq to become a business-critical consultant and then, last year, became a software developer. In that capacity, he creates debugging tools for operating system engineers. He's one of 1,500 employees that Compaq has in three major offices plus more than 20 service and support offices in that large but sparsely populated country.

Johansson was born with slightly less than 10 percent vision, which, according to official Swedish designations, puts him in between *low* and *seriously low* vision. Until the summer of 2000, he had never used any form of assistive technology for the 16 years he worked with computers. Then he began to suffer from persistent headaches and neck problems, which were traced to his frequently leaning forward to better see the computer screen.

For two months, he was confined to bed rest, and he used the time to contemplate how he could return to work. As a first step, he obtained new glasses. Then he sought advice from one of Sweden's low-vision help centers. Several of the center's proposed solutions involved hardware products and specialized PC graphics cards. Because Johansson needed a solution that would work on the various PCs he used—including those at work, at home, and on the road—he preferred a more cost-effective, software-only solution. The solution he now uses is exactly that: the accessibility features in Windows, combined with ZoomText screen magnification software from Ai Squared.

Johansson uses the standard accessibility options in Windows to set the character sets to extra-large size. He uses audio cues such as pings rather than visual cues such as pop-up boxes—not because he can't see the visual indicators, but because, with the many windows he typically has open on his screen, it's often difficult for him to know which window is connected to the indicator.

He also uses Windows to reverse the display to show white text on a dark background. Like many people with low vision, Johansson is sensitive to strong light. The reverse text and background is more "relaxing" for him to use—when he can use it. On the Web, for example, he's at the mercy of the Web designers of the sites he visits. The background colors they choose are the ones he must attempt to use and, with color blindness a part of his disability, that can be a problem. Some color combinations are "useless" to him, presenting contrast that's too low for him to perceive. But perhaps the biggest complaint he has about the Web sites he visits is that they frequently hard-code the font sizes, making it difficult for him to magnify them to a readable size.

Beyond these features built into Windows, Johansson uses the ZoomText magnifier for smooth magnification of the fonts on his screen. ZoomText also includes a screen reader, which Johansson uses most frequently for reading e-mail messages. Although he reports that it works "fairly well," one of the inevitable oddities of his situation is that the reader assumes that it is reading American English. Indeed, for about 80 percent of Johansson's computer use in a typical day, that's perfectly true. Most of his e-mail exchanges are with colleagues back in the United States, and all of Compaq's documentation and official communication is in English. But when Johansson communicates with local colleagues or customers, it's in Swedish.

"When the screen reader tries to read Swedish thinking it's English, the results can be very weird," says Johansson. "I can usually imagine what word it is supposed to be, so it's not a big problem. And there is a Swedish engine I could use, but for most of what I do, I prefer the American English speech synthesis better."

Part of Johansson's comfort with ZoomText comes from knowing when and how best to use it. Because he finds it easy to switch magnification on and off, Johansson frequently flips between the two modes based on what he's doing. For example, when he's concentrating on the lines of code that he's writing, he generally keeps the magnification on. When he wants to see "the full picture" of what he's written, he switches magnification off. And when his eyes are particularly tired, he tends to rely on magnification more steadily.

During his recent excursion through the world of assistive technology, Johansson says that Compaq "has been very supportive."

"Compaq has been very helpful by understanding the problems I have and working with me to factor in these issues when I'm upgrading my computer or acquiring a new piece of technology," he says. For example, Johansson points to Compaq's willingness to deploy a relatively large, 18-inch, Compaq Professional Series monitor for him despite its extra cost.

For others facing his situation, Johansson advises them to turn to advocacy groups with information about products and services that can be of help, and that their employers encourage them to do so.

"No one should think that they're in this alone," Johansson cautions. "I couldn't have done this by myself, and no one should have to. People with disabilities should go to knowledgeable sources and let others provide the information that can help them. No one should try to solve this themselves."

Laurie Simpson: Telecommuting across the Country

Together, telecommuting and assistive technology make support engineer Laurie Simpson a full member of Compaq's language support team. Even though she's in Atlanta and her group is in Colorado Springs and she is blind with only the slightest perception of light, Compaq and its customers are able to benefit from her expertise in the relatively arcane field of complex computer languages.

Simpson's disability is a congenital condition, resulting from the failure of her optic nerve to fully develop. Yet she has taken an active role in building her success in concert with her employer, Compaq, which has been "very supportive" in providing the assistive technology she needs.

Simpson joined Digital Equipment in 1983, started in PC product support, and became a Compaq employee after the merger. She used assistive technology from the start although, nearly 20 years ago, the available options were a far cry from today's highly effective choices. One of her first assistive technology products was a device into which she inserted her left hand while she used her right hand to pass a screen-reading lens over material she wanted to read. The shapes of letters would form via pins in her left hand.

In 1985, she began using a tool that remains part of her assistive technology arsenal to this day: a Braille display developed within Compaq by Alpha systems engineer Tim Litt. Litt had seen the difficulty a visually impaired colleague had in tracking calls, knew there were several other company employees with the same problem, and stepped in to help. His solution, first created as a terminal for mainframe access, eventually became PC-compatible as well. Unlike commercially available Braille displays, Litt's homegrown solution includes a buffer so users can scroll back up a page to review previously read material. It looks like a giant pizza box, says Simpson, and 40 solenoid pins provide the Braille output.

Since 1998, Simpson has also used the JAWS screen reader, connecting the Braille display to it for output. The combination allows her to toggle between speech and Braille output, and knowing when to use each one helps to make her highly effective.

"For example," explains Simpson, "there are times when I'm not sure what the word is that JAWS is trying to speak or spell. There are ways to go into the program and get it to repeat the word phonetically, but because the Braille output is there, I don't have to do that." Similarly, when she is at a Run command and presses Enter to go to the C prompt, JAWS doesn't say "C:\>"— but it does send that data to the Braille display, which it then outputs. On the other hand, in most of her customer interactions, she finds the JAWS speech output to be the fastest way to record information while taking a call.

Simpson begins her day by starting her communications program, dialing into Compaq customer support systems in Colorado, and making a **telnet** connection. She connects to the call-tracking system and assesses the queue of calls. She reviews an open call, reads the customer's ID number, name, phone number, and a description of the problem and then calls the customer to get more detail and to attempt to solve the problem.

"It's interesting having the customer speaking to me in one ear and JAWS speaking to me in the other as I take down the customer's information," says Simpson.

When she contacts the customer, she marks the call *contacted* in the Compaq database, and the call appears in a second screen in the call-tracking system. Simpson enters information about the customer while she speaks with him, and JAWS repeats it to her and sends it to the Braille display for output. If she can resolve the incident during the call, she does so. She then concludes the call and continues to enter information in the database so other support engineers can use it to assist customers with similar issues. If she can't resolve the issue during the call, she opens another telnet session to get to another system, one with databases of technical issues, problems, and documented solutions. If she still can't solve the problem, she opens an **Internet Relay Chat (IRC)** session to other members of her group and consults with them.

When she's not using a telnet session to connect with Colorado Springs, Simpson's primary computer use is searching for solutions on the Internet. She finds the combination of JAWS and Internet Explorer on her Windows 2000 PC to be "pretty effective."

"There are few sites where I can't maneuver," she says. "Occasionally, I find a site with lots of graphics, and JAWS doesn't deal well with that—there's nothing for it to hold onto. You get the equivalent of a blank screen. But in most cases, I find the tags to be sufficient. I think it's a combination of things: tags are more complete, so I can read them, and JAWS has gotten better, particularly on Windows 2000."

Still, there are some problems. Large spreadsheets can be difficult for Simpson to understand via JAWS as well as documents produced with fancy fonts. At least Simpson isn't facing the situation of a colleague, who also has a visual disability and whose call center is moving to a terminal server solution using a Citrix mainframe client. In this solution, information is sent rapidly from the mainframe to a dumb terminal, but what appears on the screen is a *snapshot* image of the data, not an actual download of the data. The data and the application to manipulate it remain at the mainframe. The problem for Simpson's colleague is that JAWS can't read *snapshots* of data, which are, after all, pictures.

"No screen reader can do anything with that; it's like asking us to read a photograph," says Simpson. "There are no underlying programming hooks for JAWS to get a hold of."

Simpson got a taste of the problem first-hand when a colleague sent her a Word document in a text box. JAWS read the text box as a graphic and presented her with a blank screen. To address this problem, Simpson searched the Internet and found a workaround that places text from the screen into the title bar of the screen's window in 50-character chunks—inelegant, perhaps, but functional.

Simpson praises Compaq's support for her assistive technology over the years. The company has generally asked her what she needed and what it would cost, and it then went about acquiring it. For example, when the company migrated to Windows NT as a standard several years ago, Simpson and several colleagues got together and asked for what they saw as the best assistive technology solution for Windows NT: JAWS. They also asked for appropriate training time and resources. The company obliged. Since then, says Simpson, when she's asked for upgrades and maintenance agreements, the company has provided them as well.

Having used a variety of tools over the years, Simpson's advice to others in her situation is to be clear about what they're trying to do with the technology.

"Understand what you need it for," she says. "Be as aware as you can be about the available technology. Try alternatives. See if vendors will allow you or your company to purchase a demonstration trial version so you can try before you buy. But if you don't have a clear understanding of what you need the technology for, you may end up with a solution that's not good for the way you want to use it."

Matthew C. Montelongo: "Being Aware of What You Have Is the First Step"

Apparently, Matthew C. Montelongo had the mumps when he was five or six years old. That case of the mumps, undiagnosed at the time, was deduced only in retrospect when Montelongo began to lose his hearing. The hearing loss came on suddenly—"one day I had 100 percent hearing, and a month later it was gone"—and it continues today. Montelongo, 35, has 100 percent nerve deafness in one ear and 25 percent nerve deafness in the other for less than 50 percent total hearing. In five years, the doctors tell him, his functional hearing will be gone.

Montelongo gave up on hearing aids long ago. Like Compaq colleague Rick Burgos (mentioned earlier), he found that hearing aids contributed to the problem, not the solution.

"They were functioning as nothing more than a speaker," he says. "They didn't provide the assistance I needed. They weren't giving me depth of sound or access to frequencies I couldn't hear anyway. They only amplified what I could already hear."

So, he turned to visual technologies including phone systems with paper printouts. In meetings, he positions himself with his "good" ear to as many people as possible. He has learned to read lips. "You learn to adapt," he says, simply.

Adapting is something that Compaq has supported him in doing, starting with his recruitment by the company. After his initial interview by telephone, Montelongo went to Compaq's Houston headquarters for an onsite interview with 30 people. He mentioned his disability to explain why he was positioning himself in what otherwise might seem an odd position in the room. Like his colleague Burgos, he also pitched his disability as a selling point for the job.

"I said my hearing loss was a positive because it makes me a very good listener," recalls Montelongo. "I watch for visual cues, I make eye contact with people. Other people don't have to do that because they can hear. But for me, it's a necessity. I have to look someone in the face."

Compaq invited Montelongo to join the company and he accepted. Only then was his disability, and potential accommodation for it, discussed.

"They brought it up and asked what they could do to accommodate me," says Montelongo. "I was pleased. I told them I was going to buy an earpiece to plug directly into my phone. And I asked for a mobile device I could plug in to participate in conference calls."

He makes a point to arrange his office so that he can always see his computer and the incoming call light on his telephone. He doesn't set his phone ringer on high because any sound loud enough to attract his attention will be loud enough to disturb those around him. Montelongo's desktop setup is a standard Windows PC with nothing added. But Montelongo does get tremendous mileage from carefully configuring his Windows options to compensate for his hearing loss.

"Being aware of what you have, what you can use, and what your options are within the technologies in front of you—that's the first step in assistive technology," he says.

For Montelongo, those options include configuring warnings and reminders in Outlook, Word, and other Office programs to provide visual cues rather than auditory ones. He also makes considerable use of the Office Assistant—Montelongo is partial to the Albert Einstein cartoon figure—to give him visual feedback about his use of the software.

To Montelongo, one of the most important options in Windows is the ability to set color preferences. Montelongo sets notifications in a blinking red with low-priority items set in blue.

"I also try to minimize colors around me so I'm not confused," he says. For example, he avoids screensaver choices with gyrating, brightly colored designs in favor of static images that change periodically. "If I have a lot of bright colors moving around the screen, I'm more liable to miss an important notification when it pops up."

Most people use their Pocket PCs to remind them of meetings and other scheduled events, and Montelongo is no exception. But no matter how brightly colored a reminder is, it's unlikely to be seen if the Personal Digital Assistant (PDA) is tucked in a jacket pocket. So, Montelongo uses a Compaq iPAQ Pocket PC with a vibrator function—much like the vibrators on silent cell phones—to alert him to preset events. He's also trying out the unreleased product as a member of Compaq's Assistive Technology committee. This version of the Compaq iPAQ Pocket PC is expected to be available soon as part of Compaq's continuing effort to increase the accessibility of its products to the public at large.

"Access Makes Good Business Sense" at Cingular Wireless

Access for people with disabilities would seem to be no big deal at Cingular Wireless, the nation's second largest wireless company with 35,000 employees nationwide and revenues of $12.6 billion in 2000. For example, there's no single individual or department where information on assistive technology is maintained.

But, in fact, such access for people with disabilities is a *very* big deal at Cingular Wireless; it is fully integrated into the company's workforce diversity program. A Wireless Access Task Force encourages Cingular employees and vendors to develop products that are accessible. Its Web site meets the Web Access Initiative guidelines of the World Wide Web Consortium (W3C). The company regularly meets with advocacy groups for guidance, and every employee is trained in diversity issues.

The only reason there's no single assistive technology department or expert at Cingular, according to Gloria Johnson, vice president for diversity at Cingular, is that accommodating people with disabilities is *everyone's* business at the company.

"We make sure that our workforce is reflective of the communities in which we do business—that we're looking for talent wherever it exists," says Johnson. "And we extend the concept of diversity beyond our workforce to embrace our suppliers, our communities, and our multicultural marketing.

Every employee and everyone with whom we come into contact is part of our diversity program. We do everything possible to make every person with whom we interact—employee, customer, supplier, community member—as comfortable as possible."

Living up to that commitment "requires a team approach that extends from product development to customer care, and everything in between," says Susan K. Palmer, director of Federal Regulatory Affairs for Cingular. But Cingular doesn't make this major effort solely out of philanthropic sentiments.

"It's safe to say that accessibility for people with disabilities makes good business sense, whether you're developing accessible products and services for customers or making the tools of the job accessible to employees," says Palmer. "It benefits the company. While it is not legal to discriminate in hiring against people with disabilities, the disabled population has a 70 percent unemployment rate, so it is almost certain that some companies may not consider such a person for employment. However, in addition to having the skill sets needed for a job, people with disabilities are often highly motivated and highly skilled problem solvers and we can benefit greatly from their contributions."

Providing that accessibility can involve very subtle modifications, such as extending the timeout in voice dialing services to support customers who require a little extra time to respond. It involves providing bills, on request, in large print and in Braille for customers with visual disabilities. And it involves training every customer-care representative to better serve customers with disabilities, setting up a specialized center able to provide direct **teletypewriter (TTY)** access, and training every product development specialist to keep in mind the needs of people with disabilities.

Federal and state regulations require basic accessibility, but Cingular's commitment goes far beyond the requirements. Its determination to make a strength of diversity and accessibility comes from top leadership—who regularly communicate this commitment as one more way to serve all customers. "Cingular understands that assistive technology is another productivity tool," according to Palmer. That determination also extends beyond Cingular's one-year history to the corporate parents—SBC and BellSouth—behind the company. It translates into the crucial, personal dedication of Cingular employees, according to Palmer.

"You can require people to act in certain ways, but to act with passion, more is necessary," says Palmer. "You need direction from the top, and you need the best employees in the world. We have both."

The company's Wireless Access Task Force, for example—"one of the exemplary things we do," according to Palmer—is six years old and originated in Pacific Bell Wireless, then an SBC subsidiary. Its 13 to 15 disability community leaders meet regularly with Cingular and its vendors to focus on the needs of people with disabilities. Discussion on a handset, for example, can include the need for people with mobility issues to hold the product in a certain way, the need to provide TTY access for people who have hearing and speech disabilities, the need for people with visual disabilities to have voice output to supplement visual displays, and the need for people with cognitive disabilities to have handsets that allow callers to use shortcuts such as one-touch or speed dialing.

Vendor manuals are one concern of Cingular and its task force. Braille and large-print manuals promote accessibility, but they are not always enough. Cingular's vendors also promote electronic manuals as a way to increase accessibility. For customers with visual disabilities, an electronic manual is more easily searchable than a Braille version, and it can be far easier to handle because Braille documents tend to be much larger than standard print versions. Electronic manuals also promote accessibility for people with other disabilities, such as motor disabilities. Such customers might be able to read a printed manual but not flip its pages or hold the material still. For them, manipulating the manual on screen enables equal access to its contents.

Palmer's interest in accessibility is both professional and personal. In addition to her role as director of Federal Regulatory Affairs—in which capacity she works on issues related to consumer and disability interests—Palmer has used assistive technology for 16 years to accommodate a visual disability. Although she can see light and large contrasts, Palmer has limited vision. To compensate, she uses the JAWS screen reader, a scanner, and a Braille embosser for printed output.

"There's been real improvement in assistive technology over the time I've been using it," says Palmer. "I'm so accustomed to using these products, and they've gotten so much better that I don't think of them as anything special, anything disability-related."

In fact, many of the technologies that Palmer uses to accommodate her disability aren't anything special by anyone's definition. For example, keyboard shortcuts possible with Windows are "crucial" in enabling her to navigate through and work with documents without having to manage drop-down menus. Auditory cues rather than visual ones guide her software use. And she appreciates the fact that she uses the same Office applications that her colleagues use without the need for specialized software and "horrible translation" procedures. Palmer also recently learned to use Windows Messenger—not because she needs it to accommodate her visual disability, but to communicate effectively with colleagues who are deaf.

"I'm fortunate; my supervisors have been excellent examples of how to accommodate people with disabilities in the workplace," Palmer says. "This has by far been the best experience I've had in the workplace, and not only because it's the first place I ever interviewed where I was not asked an illegal question about disability accommodation. It didn't come up at all during the hiring process. After I was hired, the people who set up computers called and asked me what I needed to do my job, and we worked it out that way."

"Cingular likes to think outside the box," sums up Palmer. "That's worked out well for me, for our employees and customers with disabilities, and for our company."

Willie Jones: Just a Guy Who Likes Cars

Willie Jones is a guy who really likes cars—who's always liked cars. He's restored a variety of old cars himself, researching and finding parts on the Internet when necessary. And he's one of those lucky people whose profession reflects his preferences: he works as technical liaison in the Technical Assistance Center for General Motors Corporation, supporting the service departments of GM dealerships nationwide in their repair of customer vehicles. He's been in that position for four years, has been with GM for 17 years and, before that, worked in the service department of a Chevrolet dealership.

Jones, 43, does just about everything you can do with a car except drive one because he's blind and has been blind from birth.

"I'm a nuts and bolts person, a car person," Jones explains. "I grew up around cars my whole life. I relate to them the way people who can't play the piano sometimes have one in their living room—for looks and for the enjoyment of company. I enjoy it when someone comes over and enjoys one of my restorations. Half the fun is working on it. The other half is going cruising in a car I've restored with a friend at the wheel. I wouldn't be able to enjoy those things I do in my personal life if it weren't for assistive technology."

Assistive technology makes it possible for Jones to be fully productive on the job, where he serves as a liaison between the frontline GM consultants to dealers and GM's own engineering community. When the consultants can't solve a dealer's question, Jones provides his expertise or involves an engineer in the issue as needed. He's one of 18 technical liaison staff members in GM's Pontiac, Michigan, facility, directly supporting 180 GM consultants for GM van products.

Although the assistive technology Jones uses is effective, it's not intrusive. Jones's desktop computer is the same Windows Compaq Pentium 233 MHz computer he's been using since 1997, with only 64 MB of RAM. Among the key assistive technology products Jones uses is the JAWS screen reader and voice synthesizer, and a Kurzweil scanning interface by Kurzweil Educational Systems, Inc., that lets him use a scanner as a text reader.

A key part of Jones's assistive technology solution is Windows. Given the way Windows and Windows applications work, he can do virtually everything he needs to do with keystrokes on the keyboard and the numeric keypad, eliminating the need for the mouse and thus making it much easier to use his other assistive technology products. Jones uses hot keys to bypass the mouse and facilitate a variety of functions including printing, copying, cutting, and pasting.

JAWS starts automatically when Jones turns on his PC, and he uses it for virtually all of his applications: sending and receiving e-mail messages, accessing the in-house knowledge base for engineering solutions, utilizing Office, and browsing the Internet.

"JAWS is very user-friendly," says Jones. "When I'm navigating, I don't use the mouse. To navigate, I use the arrow keys on the keypad or on the numeric pad to move word by word or line by line as I prefer. JAWS can be programmed to give me error messages spoken in different tones of voice from the default for text, so I can distinguish it easily from the document I'm working with. It can read punctuation or not as I prefer. It can even use a different voice to distinguish capital letters. And I can control the rate and pitch of the voice as well."

Jones also uses JAWS to read back his typing letter by letter as he works. The faster he types, the more the readback becomes a blur, which allows Jones to pay more or less attention to the readback by varying the speed with which he types. To further illustrate the simplicity of his desktop configuration, JAWS works without external speakers or a voice synthesizer card. Jones is currently running JAWS 4.0 and generally acquires every other update.

JAWS also works with Internet Explorer to facilitate Jones's Web browsing on the job for GM specifications and other documents as well as in his off hours when he's researching an auto restoration project. He uses the arrow and Tab keys to move from link to link, to learn how many links are on the page, and to hear the tagged descriptions of Web graphics. This solution eliminates the need for a separate program to assist in Web browsing—something he needed before adopting JAWS—and also allows him to print Web pages for the first time.

"I've noticed a big difference in JAWS 4.0," he says. "It's my second upgrade, and it makes quite a difference. For example, the software has gotten much better at reading an entire page without any trouble."

Jones's increased facility with Web pages mirrors GM's own increasing implementation of Web support for people with visual disabilities. GM consulted with the experts at iCan, a leading Web site for people with disabilities, to ensure that its public, e-commerce Web site was as accessible as possible.

"Everything on the GM site is tagged for accessibility," says Jones. "When GM does Web sites, we have people whose sole job is to ensure that the site is accessible, so there aren't many navigational problems. Sometimes, they use me as a guinea pig!"

Most of the documents with which Jones works come digitally—as e-mail messages or from GM's intranet—but about 10 documents, such as service and parts bulletins, come each week the old-fashioned way: on paper. To read them, Jones uses his Kurzweil scanner. He puts the document in the scanner and has the option to display the document on screen with auditory output. Or, he can output the document—or any electronic document for that matter—to his Braille embosser, a type of printer that produces Braille output on paper.

When Jones has meetings with colleagues, he takes notes using Braille and Speak, a small handheld device that includes a Braille keyboard for input and a speech interface for output. Like anyone else with a PDA, Jones uses this device for storing addresses and phone numbers.

Taken together, Jones says that his various assistive technology aids compensate at least 95 percent for his inability to see. Among the few areas where he still sees a gap is in his ability to work with some specialized in-house databases at GM with which JAWS sometimes has difficulty.

Jones's disability posed no obstacle to landing the job that began his GM career 17 years ago in the Customer Assistance Center at GM's Pontiac division. But it was an impediment to landing the first GM job he tried to get, directly out of college, as a district service manager. For that position, traveling by car from dealership to dealership was a necessity that Jones couldn't accomplish. Instead, he worked in the service department of a Chevrolet dealership until a friend told him about the Pontiac division opening. This time, Jones was determined to make the leap to GM.

He had heard a commercial for a talking, voice-activated computer. He gathered as much information as he could on that solution and called Pontiac to set up the interview. After hammering home his credentials, Jones was able to explain how, with the assistive technology solution, he could do his job as well as any person without his disability. He got the job and used that solution, which included a terminal connected to the mainframe, to access database records for 12 years until moving with his division to a PC-based solution in 1997.

"I came in with something I thought would work, and GM's in-house technology staff took it from there," says Jones. "They worked with me and my supervisor to decide on the best solution and the way to implement it. And that's the way it's worked ever since. I let my supervisor know what I think I need, I have the business case and the information ready, and we take it to the IT department."

Willie Jones sees nothing odd in focusing so much of his life around the cars he cannot drive. And who knows, given his ingenuity and determination to succeed, combined with continuing advances in assistive technology, the day might yet come when he takes one of his vintage cars out for a spin without needing a friend behind the wheel.

Lessons Learned

The experiences of manufacturing companies including Compaq Computer Corporation, Cingular Wireless, and GM provide a variety of key learnings for business decision makers contemplating or enhancing their own assistive technology efforts:

- **Start with the basics.** Standard options in products such as Windows and Office allow users to vary screen magnification, font size and colors, visual notifications, and backgrounds as well as to use keystroke alternatives to mouse input. For many users, these features will provide significant accessibility. Think of assistive technology as starting in the same place as broader usability issues.

- **Mainstream assistive technology.** Make assistive technology products routinely available just as you would provide any other productivity tool. Do not set the bar at what the law requires, but at what it takes to become an employer of choice.

- **Involve as many audiences as possible in your assistive technology effort.** This includes not only employees and customers, but also partners, suppliers, distributors, and others. Similarly, use assistive technology to make more than your office PCs accessible—use it to bring accessibility to product manuals, customer service, invoices, and product design as well.

- **Seek the advice of outside consumer and advocacy groups.** Search for groups with a special interest in issues related to accessible technology for people with disabilities.

- **Encourage employees with disabilities to explore and learn about a variety of potential solutions to identify the one, or the combination, that's best for them.** Urge them to think about the context in which they would use each tool so they can choose the optimal solutions.

Summary

Manufacturers as large and well established as GM, as young as Cingular Wireless, and as involved in cutting-edge technology as Compaq all understand the value of assistive technology. It is not merely the *right* thing to do, but is the right business decision, one that empowers and motivates employees, enabling the corporation to attract and retain the best talent.

At the same time, these companies see assistive technology as a tool to be extended beyond its workforce to enable broader access for customers and other audiences as well. Again, the result is the *right* thing as well as broader market reach and penetration. To reach customers with accessible products, these companies don't go it alone. Instead, they actively collaborate with suppliers, designers, technology partners, and others to create a rich, seamless infrastructure for their products, guaranteeing customer success.

And although their assistive technology solutions may include the latest products, these companies have also discovered that assistive technology can start with simple usability features designed into telephone handsets, notebook PC cases, and other products. From simple features to complex solutions, what these components of accessibility have in common is that they're backed by a commitment that starts with top corporate leadership and extends throughout the company. Manufacturing that commitment is as much a key to the success of these companies as is manufacturing any of their products.

Accessible Technology and Your Business

Developing an Accessible Technology Plan

Now that we have discussed the business value of accessible technology and presented experiences of multiple organizations, this chapter outlines the best practices you should consider when making accessible technology a reality in your organization. The goal of this chapter is to provide you with the framework and resources you need to develop and execute an accessible technology strategy.

Although each organization is unique and has unique requirements, common steps in developing a good accessible technology plan are presented in this chapter. This chapter is organized into a five-step plan (shown in Figure 8-1 on the next page). These are the same proven steps used in many technology development plans. In this context, the five strategic planning steps are simply applied to accessible technology. Many of the themes throughout this chapter are based on the steps in Susan Conway's and Char Sligar's book *Unlocking Knowledge Assets*. (Conway, Sligar 2002)

Admittedly, many organizations adopt accessible technology without thinking through the early stages of strategy and requirements; instead, they jump right into implementation. Although some may be successful with such an approach, carefully thinking through the strategy and requirements will reduce costs and increase efficiency—reducing false starts, ensuring compatibility with existing technology, and accurately addressing your organization's unique situation and needs.

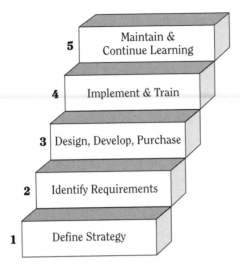

Figure 8-1.   *Five steps of developing an accessible technology plan*

The five steps are

1. **Define the accessible technology strategy.** In this critical first step, you define how accessible technology fits into your business by identifying a vision and objectives that set the groundwork for the next steps.

2. **Identify requirements.** In this step, you develop a comprehensive set of requirements by describing the scope of the accessibility needs of your organization and evaluating the current technology being used.

3. **Design, develop, and purchase technology.** This next step involves the design and development of technology based on the requirements outlined in Step 2. This step might also include purchasing accessible technology and assistive technology products and identifying internal technology systems that need to be updated to increase accessibility.

4. **Implement and Train.** Once the accessible technology is in place, including new technology, it is rolled out to the organization. This step also involves increasing awareness among employees about the availability of accessible technology and training employees on how to use the accessibility features.

5. **Maintain technology and continue learning.** In the last step, you increase awareness of the accessible technology vision in your organization, support employees in their use of technology, and evaluate success and opportunities for improvement.

Step 1: Define the Accessible Technology Strategy

In this important first step, you describe how accessible technology fits within your organization—specifically, how it fits with your business and competitive strategies, objectives, and measures of success. This information will help you integrate accessible technology into your business plan and ensure that your accessible technology strategy is aligned with your business needs. What you produce in this first step provides the framework for the rest of the planning process.

Elements of an Accessible Technology Strategy

An accessible technology strategy should both stand alone and reinforce your organization's overall technology plan. The two plans should be complementary. If your organization has an overall technology plan, review that plan as you begin outlining your accessible technology strategy to make sure there are no conflicts and to strengthen how these two plans can work together.

An accessible technology strategy should include the following elements:

Vision statement. Create a unique vision statement that defines the role of accessible technology in your organization and how it will support the organization's overall vision of accessible technology objectives. If your organization's overall vision statement already provides the proper foundation for creating accessible technology objectives, restate that vision statement. This was the case for UnumProvident, whose vision statement reads, "Be the number one provider of services that help our employees and our customers' employees get back to work when they become injured or ill."

Objectives. Define success metrics and clarify the specifics of the vision. Using the vision statement, create accessible technology objectives that also align with business objectives. You'll use these objectives to measure success in Step 5. For example, RBC Financial Group estimates that 40 percent or more of Canadians have trouble using financial services because of disabilities such as mobility impairments or low literacy skills. In order to be a leading financial institute in Canada, RBC Financial Group wanted to improve the accessibility of its branches to ensure it was reaching these customers. Therefore, a sample business objective for the bank might be,

"Ensure that 90 percent of branches are accessible to customers with disabilities such as mobility impairments or low literacy."

Expenses and budget. Clarify how expenses will be covered and describe funding sources. For example, determine which expenses are part of the overall technology purchases of the organization versus which expenses should be part of a separate budget that might be used only for assistive technology products. Some organizations choose to have all assistive technology product purchases come out of a centralized accommodation budget, whereas other organizations deduct these expenses from the individual technology budgets of each department. It is important to clarify these budget decisions at the outset and to allocate funds appropriately.

Ownership and next steps. Clarify responsibilities and plan execution. For example, outline who or which groups will be responsible for completing the next steps of the plan, which are to identify requirements (Step 2); design, develop, and purchase (Step 3); implement and train (Step 4); and maintain technology and continue learning (Step 5). This will require strong partnerships among various groups. One technique is to form a council or committee that meets regularly to ensure that the plan is moving forward and that the next steps and responsibilities are clear. You might even find it helpful to assign a person within the organization to project manage the accessible technology plan. RBC Financial Group developed such a position called the Accessible Technology Consultant. Responsibilities of this position include educating IT staff about the business value of accessibility, selecting assistive technology products, and advocating employee accessibility needs.

Whichever unique approach your organization takes, two elements are critical to success: support from senior management and alignment with business objectives and the organization-wide technology plan.

As with any strategic planning process, the leaders and senior management in your organization must clearly understand the business value of accessible technology. Only then can they stand behind the plan, be spokespersons for the strategy, and help ensure support from other key stakeholders.

It is important to gain the support of those responsible for executing the plan and other key stakeholders including those who manage the budget. Although some resistance is normal with any change or new idea that has not yet been implemented, one key to success is ensuring that stakeholders fully understand and embrace the strategy because these stakeholders will be responsible for carrying out the next four steps.

With a number of steering committees that oversee the use of technologies within the bank, RBC Financial Group also created an accessible technology committee headed by its Accessible Technology Consultant. This provided a natural way for the accessible technology strategy to be integrated with the rest of the technology planning. Each committee head advocates for his or her technology area when evaluating new products, testing, and doing long-term planning. This process ensures that key stakeholders are more informed about the importance of accessible technology when making decisions.

Step 2: Identify Requirements

In this step, the owners and stakeholders identified in the accessible technology strategy are asked to do a needs assessment, evaluate the current state of technology, and create success measures.

The needs assessment involves outlining the accessibility requirements from the perspectives of employees, your organization's processes, and current technology. Ideally, you should integrate the requirements you outline in the needs assessment with your organization's existing technology plan so that technology evaluations, purchase decisions, and development of new technology will take accessibility needs into consideration.

Also in this step, it is important to gather information about the current state of technology and prioritize needs if your current technology is out of date. In addition, at this stage you determine success measures to help your organization clearly evaluate and measure results. The outcome of this step is a document that includes a comprehensive set of accessibility requirements and measures of success that owners can use to execute the design, development, and implementation steps.

Needs Assessment

The needs assessment task identifies the organization-wide accessibility needs, which include specifying collaboration and communication needs among all employees—regardless of abilities—and identifying the assistive technology needs of individuals with specific disabilities. Even if your organization does not currently employ people with visible disabilities, you should still define your accessibility requirements. In the future, you might find much greater use and desire for accessible technology than is initially apparent. As discussed in Chapter 1, a proactive accessible technology plan can offer

- Increased performance and productivity through enhanced process flow

- Reinforcement of your organization's diversity vision

- Accommodations that will expedite employees' return to work after injuries and illness

- Organization-wide ergonomic (or human factors) benefits by reducing the impact of repetitive stress injuries

As part of your needs assessment, list the specific accessibility needs employees have, the processes in your organization, and the technologies you want to support. Ask how your employees and customers use technology. For example, if most employees in your organization need to use a sales data entry application, that application needs to work well with a variety of assistive technology products. That way, an employee who is blind, for example, can access the application with a screen reader and keyboard (rather than a mouse), and an employee who has a mobility impairment can access the application with voice recognition software.

To gather your list of requirements, consider conducting surveys of employees. During this process it might also prove helpful to provide lists of possible needs or requirements because many individuals won't understand what you mean if you simply ask them to list their accessibility needs.

On the CD   Appendix A, "Determining Your Organization's Accessible Technology Requirements," includes a sample list of accessibility requirements.

Evaluate the State of Current Technology

As part of identifying requirements, it is important to describe your current technology and compare it to the information gathered in your needs assessment. This evaluation will help establish priorities and show where changes can have the greatest impact.

Plan to evaluate the following:

- **Operating system(s).** Do operating systems used in your organization have built-in accessibility options that allow individuals with visual, hearing, mobility, learning, and language impairments to adjust options to their needs? Is the operating system compatible with a wide range of assistive technology products?

- **Office productivity and communication software.** Is office productivity software such as e-mail, word processing, and presentation applications accessible? Are accessibility options available consistently among these applications?

- **Assistive technology.** Are compatible assistive technology products available for your current operating systems and office productivity software?

- **Proprietary or legacy systems.** Consider whether you have overlooked accessibility options you already have. Are you utilizing built-in accessibility options, features, shortcuts, and toolbars in your current systems? Consider the state of your proprietary and legacy systems. Do you have legacy systems that employees with disabilities have difficulty accessing? Can all employees use your proprietary systems?

- **Internal systems.** Are internal technology systems, such as intranet sites and internal purchase applications, accessible to all employees?

- **Customer systems.** Are the systems your customers use, such as your organization's Web site/e-commerce site, touch screens, or automated teller machines, accessible?

As part of your technology evaluation, ask the following questions about your current technology:

- How does your present technology meet your employees' and customers' accessibility needs?

- Can employees effectively collaborate and communicate regardless of their abilities?

- Is the technology flexible and does it allow customization so that individuals can be more productive?

At the end of this evaluation, you should have an understanding of the current state of your technology as measured against needs.

On the CD   Appendix A, "Determining Your Organization's Accessible Technology Requirements," includes a sample list of technology assessment questions.

Leveraging Legacy Technology

Most organizations will want to take advantage of the improved accessibility in the most recent releases of products including Microsoft Windows XP and Microsoft Office XP. But many organizations are not able to upgrade every employee simultaneously to the latest operating system and software, so they need to plan for scalable solutions.

In recent years, software and operating system upgrades have become more streamlined, and today, employees using different versions of products can continue to collaborate effectively. For example, if the majority of employees in an organization use Windows 2000 Professional, and an employee develops a disability that requires the use of a screen reader that works best on Windows XP Professional, that employee can be upgraded to Windows XP Professional and still effectively work with his coworkers who all use Windows 2000 Professional. Or, if an employee simply needs to change his or her font settings and sound options, Windows 98, Windows 2000 Professional, and Windows XP all provide these options.

Each organization needs to set its own priorities and, with the help of an accessible technology consultant, make the most of the accessibility in legacy technology.

On the CD   Product accessibility comparison charts for Windows and Office are available in the Technology Planning section on the companion CD provided with this book. These charts show you the accessibility features and options available in different versions of Windows and Office.

Success Measures

At this point in the process, you should create success measures based on the objectives outlined in Step 1 and the baseline information gathered in the needs assessment and evaluation of current technology. In Step 5, you'll use these success measures to evaluate progress and highlight areas of improvement.

Examples of success measures include

- Increase the retention rate of employees who develop impairments by 15 percent in two years
- Increase the employees' awareness of accessibility by 25 percent within 12 months of implementation
- Increase reported improved collaborations and communication among employees to 50 percent within 18 months
- Increase the job satisfaction of employees with accessibility needs by 35 percent in 24 months
- Increase the satisfaction of customers with accessibility needs by 25 percent in 12 months
- Broaden the customer segment that includes a disability demographic within two fiscal years

Step 3: Design, Develop, and Purchase Accessible Technology

In this third step, the focus is on designing and developing the technology based on the accessibility requirements outlined in Step 2. This step includes identifying and purchasing accessible technology and assistive technology products, updating internal technology systems to be more accessible, and determining how to make use of legacy systems.

Select an Accessible Technology "Foundation"

The standard operating system and office productivity software used by your organization is the foundation for accessible and assistive technology. Therefore, it is critical that the operating system and office productivity software be accessible.

Choose products that allow employees to customize the system to their preferences as well as those products that address the requirements outlined in the needs assessment. Be sure that the operating system and all office productivity software chosen are compatible with a wide variety of assistive technology products for specific disabilities. To check compatibility, contact assistive technology manufacturers to learn if products are compatible and if settings can be adjusted to optimize compatibility.

> **More Info**   A catalog of assistive technology products that are compatible with Windows is available at *http://www.microsoft.com/enable*.

An Accessible Operating System

Windows XP Professional provides better integration with assistive technology than any other operating system, and it offers a high level of accessibility for specific visual, hearing, mobility, learning, and language needs. Built-in accessibility utilities include **Magnifier**, **Narrator**, On-Screen Keyboard, and **Utility Manager**. A wide range of assistive technology products are also compatible with Windows XP Professional.

An Accessible Office Productivity Suite

Microsoft Office XP makes productivity simple, provides collaboration, and provides flexibility to address business and accessibility needs. Microsoft Office XP accessibility improvements help people with accessibility needs quickly and easily customize their workspace to further improve their productivity. Office XP is also compatible with a range of assistive technology products.

An Accessible Browser

Microsoft Internet Explorer 6 offers accessibility enhancements that provide flexibility for users with differing needs. Internet Explorer 6 includes adjustable text size and style, formatting, colors, and extensive keyboard shortcuts. Customizable toolbar options used to personalize toolbars to specific user needs and preferences include showing or hiding text labels, changing the size of buttons, and adding, removing, and rearranging buttons on toolbars. A wide selection of assistive technology products are compatible with Internet Explorer 6.

> **More Info**   For details about accessibility in these Microsoft products and others, see the Product Resources section of this book's companion CD or the Microsoft Accessibility Web site at *http://www.microsoft.com/enable*.

Identify and Select Assistive Technology for Individuals

Many employees with disabilities need to use assistive technology products to fully access their computers. In the next two sections, we discuss two approaches to providing assistive technology to employees as well as how the partnership between human resources (HR), employees, managers, and assistive technology experts might work.

Two Approaches to Selecting Assistive Technology

As discussed in the case studies that precede this chapter, organizations generally take one of two approaches to identify and provide employees with assistive technology. One approach is to custom select assistive technology product(s) for each employee with a need. Another approach is to provide an approved list of assistive technology products that are tested, evaluated, and selected as the standard assistive technology products for an organization. Each approach has its own advantages and challenges.

Microsoft Corporation does not have a standardized list of assistive technology products. Instead, employees partner with their manager, a human resources representative, and an assistive technology consultant to identify the appropriate assistive technology products for their business and personal accessibility needs. For Microsoft, this makes sense because, as a technology company, it has a broader mission to ensure that technology works for everyone using all types of assistive technology products.

For organizations such as RBC Financial Group, a standard list of assistive technology products is more efficient because the assistive technology products are evaluated and tested to ensure that they work properly with RBC Financial Group's systems. This makes providing technical support easier and getting new employees up to speed faster.

Whether your organization provides a standard list of selected assistive technology products or not, it is still important to accurately identify which type of product works best for an individual's needs and to partner with HR and assistive technology experts to work through the process of selecting assistive technology.

Partnering with Human Resources and Assistive Technology Experts

The need for accommodation arises for various reasons. Employers often ask new employees when they are hired if they need any accommodation. For existing employees, when new accommodation needs arise, an HR representative is often one of the first to know. This makes HR a pivotal resource for learning about accommodation needs of employees.

HR representatives are at the forefront for identifying employees who will benefit from accessible technology. Because accessible technology is part of providing accommodation and involves health and privacy issues, it is important to consult with HR and an assistive technology consultant to identify and select assistive technology for individuals.

HR representatives usually manage worker compensation claims, ergonomics evaluations, and accident reports. They should be contacted directly by employees and managers with inquiries about accessibility. An accident report or even a change in an employee's productivity might be a sign of a need for accommodation. HR representatives can be trained to identify these signs.

Do not assume that individuals who are technology experts are also knowledgeable about accessible and assistive technology. Expert consultants who understand disabilities and the latest assistive technology products can provide valuable guidance to organizations. If your organization is large, it might be beneficial to develop one of your own IT professionals into an accessibility expert. In this way, you can avoid relying on outside consultation if you prefer.

More Info   See the "Consultants and Resources" section at the end of this chapter for more information about how to find accessible technology consultants in your area or to find training.

In order to accurately identify an individual's needs and provide insight into assistive technology, a strong partnership needs to be formed between the employee, the manager, a human resources representative, and a consultant.

On the CD   See Appendix B, "Identifying the Right Assistive Technology," for two examples of tools used by organizations to select technology for employees.

Clarify the roles and responsibilities in this partnership for a better understanding of who makes decisions and how the partnership will work. The following five lists are a sample of how one organization outlines this partnership.

Employee

- Provides medical documentation of need through HR and manager
- Meets with ergonomics team if required
- Meets with assistive technology consultant to review work and work processes
- Reviews assistive technology proposal
- Participates in education and training as required
- Reports any concerns or issues to HR or manager if necessary
- Provides an update on accommodation needs if necessary
- Responds to surveys to help measure success of program

Manager(s)

- Partners with HR to ensure employee is supported and aware of resources and accommodation process
- Provides clarification on job requirements and business needs if needed
- Reviews assistive technology proposal to see if the proposal will address the business needs and job requirements
- Supports employee in getting training and education on the assistive technology if needed

HR Representative

- Provides or coordinates ergonomic assessment
- Defines and coordinates accommodation and assistive technology process with employee and manager
- Requests medical documentation from employee
- Coordinates assistive technology consultant
- Reviews assistive technology proposal with employee
- Prepares assistive technology proposal for manager review and sends a copy to manager
- Provides training and additional information for manager and employee as needed

Assistive Technology Consultant

- Meets with employee to assess assistive technology needs
- Creates a needs assessment or assistive technology proposal
- Recommends assistive technology product(s)—from a standard list, if applicable—that meet medical accommodation and business needs
- Sets up products and training on products as required

Medical and Rehabilitation Professionals

- Provide medical recommendations
- Provide additional or updated accommodation information for employee as needed or required

---

Ergonomics Evaluations and Accessible Technology Recommendations

A number of organizations, including Microsoft, train their ergonomics specialists to look for situations in which accessible technology will benefit an employee. At Microsoft, all employees can request an ergonomics evaluation, which involves a 30-minute one-on-one consultation with an ergonomics specialist who works in the HR department. This HR representative's role in this case might be as simple as educating employees about changing their font sizes or using different mouse devices, or it might involve a discussion about assistive technology. According to Ellen Meyer, an HR lead at Microsoft Corporation, "Employees who would benefit from accessible technology have been identified through an ergonomics evaluation. Through a coordinated process of review, implementation, and education, these technologies are in place. Ergonomics and accessible technology go hand in hand, so it makes sense for Microsoft to combine the two."

Evaluating and Updating Internal Systems

As part of the design and development step, your organization will need to evaluate, and possibly update, internal systems based on requirements and success measures outlined in Step 2. Integrating the task of checking for accessibility criteria into the update and development processes for all your internal systems will help eliminate the need for reengineering later.

For example, a requirement identified in Step 2 might be to provide access to a legacy sales application for employees who are blind. This step determines how you will accomplish that requirement. One approach might be to use a tool that your IT professionals develop to allow access by a screen reader. Other approaches might be to change settings on existing software or acquire another product that makes access possible.

For new systems that are currently being planned, evaluate accessibility needs and requirements and make necessary changes in the design to ensure that your new systems are accessible. To do this, it is necessary to modify design specifications and add accessibility testing into test plans. For example, design specifications can be modified to include keyboard access for all features. Similarly, test cases can be modified or added to test without a mouse to ensure that keyboard access is fully implemented.

For existing systems, evaluate and measure the system against the accessibility needs and requirements. Next assess the impact based on systems used by the most people, identify the frequency the system is used, and determine if there is an alternative that is accessible. (See the sample list of technology assessment questions in Appendix A, "Determining Your Organization's Accessible Technology Requirements," on this book's CD.) Once you've analyzed the impact, prioritize the systems that must be updated for better accessibility. For those that are a lower priority, document the issues and make them requirements for the next scheduled update of the system.

Step 4: Implement and Train

After you have developed, purchased, and updated technology, it is time to deploy technology, and train employees how to use it. This step involves setting up the systems, communicating the change to your organization, and providing training. It is important to align these efforts with the original strategy and success measures to make sure you are on target as the implementation stage unfolds.

Implementation

The implementation step includes a range of projects such as setting up one computer for a single employee with a disability who is using a new assistive technology product, launching a more accessible intranet site, and deploying a new operating system and office productivity suite across the entire organization.

Deploying Microsoft Products and Adjusting Accessibility Options

For organizations that choose Microsoft products, **Microsoft TechNet** is a central information and community resource for IT professionals and is one source of assistance. TechNet is designed to meet the technical information needs of anyone who plans, evaluates, deploys, maintains, or supports Microsoft business products.

Microsoft TechNet information is available either online at *http:// www.microsoft.com/technet* or through the Microsoft TechNet CD/DVD Subscription service. The subscription saves time and increases productivity by providing 12 monthly issues with the latest technical information, service packs, resource kits, tools, utilities, Microsoft Knowledge Base articles, and other information useful for IT professionals.

Once the business products are set up, accessibility options in the products need to be adjusted for people with accessibility needs. Information about accessibility features and options is available in select resource kits available on Microsoft TechNet as well as on the Microsoft Accessibility Web site. Tutorials for accessibility and guides by disability are discussed in the sections "Step by Step Tutorials for Accessibility" and "Guides by Disability" later in this chapter. Although these materials were originally written for trainers and users with disabilities, IT professionals who are new to accessibility might find these resources helpful.

Deploying Assistive Technology Products

IT professionals within an organization will likely be the ones called upon to help individuals set up new assistive technology products. Most importantly, whoever helps set up assistive technology should first contact the assistive technology manufacturer to check compatibility with the operating systems and applications that will be running with the assistive technology product. The assistive technology manufacturer should also provide information about settings that need to be adjusted to optimize compatibility.

Deploying Your Internal Systems

As identified in the accessible technology plan, you'll need to roll out any modified or new internal systems. These systems might be newly accessible updated applications that should be rolled out to all employees, or add-ons or new applications for a specific employee's access needs.

Training

Just providing accessible technology doesn't mean employees will automatically know about new accessibility options or how to use them. As part of this step, educate and train employees on how to make full use of the accessible technology available to them. Accessible technology benefits everyone, so be sure to educate everyone about the availability of accessible technology, not just those with disabilities.

Although some organizations choose to offer classroom-style training, another option is to provide self-paced training materials on intranet sites. This is an inexpensive and efficient option.

Microsoft publishes a variety of training resources helpful to trainers, IT professionals, and people with disabilities. The next two sections highlight specific training resources available to help customize a computer for people with disabilities and people with accessibility needs.

Step by Step Tutorials for Accessibility

Microsoft publishes a series of free step by step tutorials to introduce the most commonly used accessibility features in Microsoft products and to educate people on how to adjust the accessibility options and features to best meet their needs. The instructions demonstrate how to use the mouse or keyboard to navigate, select options, and change settings. This information is presented in a side-by-side format so that users can see at a glance how to use the mouse, the keyboard, or a combination of both. Tutorials are available free at *http://www.microsoft.com/enable/training*. Tutorials are available for products including

- Windows XP
- Windows 2000
- Windows Millennium
- Windows 98
- Outlook 2002
- Word 2002
- Outlook 2000
- Word 2000
- Internet Explorer 6
- Internet Explorer 5

On the CD   The Guides by Disability and Step by Step Tutorials are available on the CD provided with this book and on *http://www.microsoft.com/enable*.

Guides by Disability

Microsoft produces a series of free guides called Guides by Disability on this book's companion CD and on the Microsoft Accessibility Web site at *http://www.microsoft.com/enable/guides*. These guides organize information into helpful resources by each specific type of disability. Each guide provides a list of assistive technology and links to step by step tutorials that can be used to customize computers to accommodate an individual with a specific disability. Guides are available for

- Visual impairments
- Hearing impairments
- Mobility impairments
- Cognitive and language impairments

Step 5: Maintain Technology and Continue Learning

The last step in the accessibility technology planning process involves increasing awareness and sustaining your accessible technology strategy. In this step, you promote the accessible technology vision statement in your organization, support employees' use of the technology, and evaluate the success. This ongoing step is critical—accessible technology is a fundamental part of your business, and true success is measured by how well your employees can collaborate and communicate with one another and how productive individuals will be. It is important that your effort does not result in a big launch with little follow-up. The outcome of this step is continued feedback and synergy that will help you improve your accessible technology strategy over time and make accessibility part of your organization's culture.

Increase Awareness

Successfully building and implementing an accessible technology strategy isn't the end of the work. A measure of success for the strategy is having high awareness among employees that accessible technology is available and for employees to understand where to go for information. Another measure of success is for all employees to accept accessibility as a part of the business culture.

Although the saying, "If you build it, they will come," might have worked for Kevin Costner's character in *Field of Dreams*, your organization will likely need to increase awareness through various communication strategies. The following sections contain techniques that many organizations use to educate their employees about the availability of accessible technology.

Educate HR and Managers First

It is important that HR representatives and managers be aware of the accessible technology your organization provides, and that they know whom to contact for information.

Consider educating your HR representatives first, and then asking HR to educate managers about the accessible technology. Be sure to hold this meeting or training session for human resource representatives and managers first so that when the program is rolled out to employees, they know where to get more information. Reeducate your HR and management staff periodically at regularly scheduled management and HR-sponsored training sessions.

Educate New Employees at Employee Orientation

Most organizations have some form of orientation for new employees. This is an ideal opportunity to provide information about the availability of accessible technology. Because many people might not even know what accessibility means or what accessible technology can do for them, you might sponsor a presentation by an expert in this area that explains accessible technology and where to go for more information. However, if resources are tight, a simple handout that explains that accessible technology is available and provides a confidential contact person will suffice.

Educate Current Employees through Newsletters, E-Mail, and Web Sites

Just because an employee is already on the job and hasn't notified you about his or her accessibility needs doesn't mean there are none. As discussed in Chapter 2, many people do not self-identify as having an impairment, or they might not realize the accommodations available to them. Employees' needs change also as they age or if they are involved in an accident. Be sure to educate all employees about the availability of accessible technology through employee newsletters and flyers, e-mail, and Web sites that explain employee benefits and ergonomics resources. Plan ongoing communication sessions. Although it might seem like the communication is redundant at times, an employee who recently had an accident would welcome a reminder about the assistance that is available.

Provide Support

Once accessible technology is up and running, it is important to keep the gears oiled and running smoothly. Here are a few ideas on how to provide support:

- **Assign contact(s) in the IT department responsible for helping individuals with accessible technology issues.** Although this isn't necessarily a full-time position, it is important that employees have a point of contact for technical issues. This contact should be aligned with HR to ensure that only technical support is being provided and that no recommendations about needed technology are being made. Such contacts might be consultants hired by the IT department because of their expertise in the area of accessible technology.

- **If you have a technical support center to assist employees using technology, educate them on assistive technology products.** Train technical support personnel to know when to contact the accessible technology expert to assist an employee with problems related to assistive technology products or accessibility issues. Also, train support personnel to know how to adjust the way they work with an employee for general technical issues when the employee is using assistive technology or uses different access techniques. For example, if an employee indicates he or she is using keyboard-only access, support personnel should know how to translate the step by step mouse instructions they normally use into keyboard instructions.

- **Host an accessibility Web site as part of your IT department's Web site.** Information on the site should include links to the e-mail support alias, a newsletter, and names of people to contact for specific questions.

- **Create an e-mail alias for employees to discuss and troubleshoot problems.** Such an alias provides employees with an opportunity to share problems and determine solutions. Choose a moderator (preferably the same person assigned to accessible technology in the IT department if the alias is specifically about technology, or an HR representative if the alias is for broad accommodation issues) to make sure the discussion stays on topic and to identify important issues that require additional assistance. Sears encourages its employees to use the disAbled Associate Network to facilitate discussion about ongoing challenges facing its employees with disabilities.

- **Publish a newsletter for employees who use assistive technology.** This newsletter can include solutions to issues, information about available product upgrades, and new resources available. Individuals should be able to subscribe to the newsletter anonymously, giving them the option to maintain privacy of their accommodation needs or impairment.

- **Form a committee that addresses accommodation and accessible technology issues.** This committee can meet on an as-needed basis to talk about accommodations, exchange advice, and discuss improvements to the accessible technology strategy.

Evaluate Success and Areas of Improvement

To evaluate success and identify areas of improvement, review the original success measures created in Step 2 and evaluate progress against those original success measures. Many organizations gather data through follow-up surveys and interviews of employees, managers, and IT professionals.

Because integrating accessible technology is a long-term goal, recognize and reward success and follow through on feedback received by outlining next steps and areas of improvement, assigning owners to follow up with the next steps, and determining when you will next evaluate success.

Consultants and Resources

There are many Web sites and other resources available to help you learn more before implementing your accessible technology plan. As mentioned earlier, seeking consultation from an expert in the field is well worth the investment. This section contains more information on consultants and resources.

Finding Consultants

The Alliance for Technology Access, *http://www.ataccess.org*, has a network of community-based resource centers, developers and vendors, affiliates, and associates dedicated to providing information and support services to people with disabilities and increasing their use of standard, assistive, and information technologies. Find a center in your local area to visit and learn more, or ask for recommendations for local consultants.

The National Business and Disability Council (NBDC), *http://www.nbdc.org*, provides a full range of services to assist corporations in successfully integrating people with disabilities into the workplace and marketplace. The NBDC offers services such as customized training and support, informational mailings, an information hotline, and job postings.

The Sierra Group, Inc., *http://www.thesierragroup.com*, is a rehabilitation engineering consulting firm that works with organizations, educators, individuals, and rehabilitation professionals in the area of assistive technology to help increase employability of people with disabilities. Sierra Group consultants evaluate the needs of clients, compare those needs with the diverse talents of individuals with disabilities, and integrate systems and procedures that create successful employment for all.

On the CD   In Appendix C, "Interview with Michael Fiore of the Sierra Group," Fiore provides insights based on his 10 years of experience working with organizations as an accessibility consultant and rehabilitation engineer.

Resources for More Information

If you are interested in additional information about disabilities and assistive technology products, we recommend the following resources and conferences:

- **The companion CD** at the back of this book contains information about the accessibility of Microsoft products, step by step tutorials for accessibility options in Microsoft products, information about assistive technology compatible with Microsoft products, resource guides organized by disability, and articles about people with disabilities who successfully use computers. If the CD is missing from your copy of this book, the majority of the resources are also available at *http://www.microsoft.com/enable*.

- **The Assistive Technology Industry Association (ATIA)**, *http://www.atia.org*, is a not-for-profit membership group of organizations that manufacture or sell technology-based assistive devices for people with disabilities, or provide services associated with or required by people with disabilities.

- **Business Leadership Network (BLN)**, *http://www.usbln.com*, is an employer-led venture of the U.S. Department of Labor, Office of Disability Employment Policy, that promotes best practices to enhance employment opportunities for candidates with disabilities. The BLN provides resources and information to employers committed to the best disability employment practices, accessible products, and exceptional service to customers with disabilities. Local BLN membership chapters offer opportunities to network and local events.

- **Equal Access to Software and Information (EASI)**, *http://www.easi.cc/workshop.htm*, has extensive courseware and training for IT professionals who need to learn more about accessible technology. Of particular note is the online course entitled "Business Benefits of Accessible Information Technology (IT) Design." See *http://easi.cc/workshops/bbaitsyl.htm* for more information. The course instructor is Steven I. Jacobs, president of IDEAL at NCR Corporation.

- **The Job Accommodation Network (JAN),** *http://www.jan.wvu.edu,* represents the most comprehensive resource for job accommodations available, enhancing the job opportunities of people with disabilities by providing information on job accommodations since 1984. In 1991, JAN expanded to provide information on the Americans with Disabilities Act. JAN provides an international toll-free consulting service that provides information about job accommodations and the employability of people with disabilities.

- **The Microsoft Accessibility site,** *http://www.microsoft.com/enable,* provides the most up-to-date accessibility information about Microsoft products. The site contains comprehensive information about accessibility in Microsoft products, information about assistive technology compatible with Microsoft products, training resources, and a free newsletter. Microsoft's Accessible Technology Group manages this site. The group also contributed to this book.

- **Microsoft Developer Network, Accessible Technology,** *http://msdn.microsoft.com/at,* provides resources for developers on how to create accessible technology.

- **Microsoft Windows XP Accessibility,** *http://www.microsoft.com/windowsxp/accessibility,* contains information about the accessibility options in Windows XP Professional and Home Editions.

- **State assistive technology programs** vary widely. The *Assistive Technology Act of 1998* provides funding to states to assist them in developing easily accessible, consumer-responsive systems of access to assistive technology, technology services, and information. Contact your state's program for more information. If you are unable to reach your state's project, contact RESNA's (Rehabilitation Engineering and Assistive Technology Society of North America) Technical Assistance Project at *http://www.resna.org/taproject* or (703) 524-6686 for assistance.

Summary

Although it is possible to develop and implement an accessible technology plan on a case-by-case basis, by using the strategic planning steps outlined in this chapter, you will avoid false starts, decrease costs, and provide higher employee and customer satisfaction. By outlining your vision and objectives first, and then assigning owners to carry out the implementation steps and measure progress, you will gain a far greater level of success that positively impacts many more people in your organization.

The Future
of Accessible
Technology

*Over the next 10 to 15 years, technology has the capacity to
virtually eliminate barriers [faced by people with disabilities]
in the workplace.*

—Steve Ballmer, CEO, Microsoft Corporation

Technology advancements have a mixed track record for access by people with
disabilities. Many advances have made it possible for people with disabilities to
find employment, whereas others have made it harder for some people with
disabilities to use computers. Although assistive technology products have followed these technology advances to provide access where it would otherwise
be impossible and to make it feasible for people with disabilities to be productive in a business setting, they often require reverse engineering to develop
and thus lag behind the technology products that they supplement. Currently,
software and hardware manufacturers must work together to provide the necessary information required for the specialized interfaces needed to meet the
needs of people with disabilities, such as text-to-speech and speech description of the **graphical user interface (GUI)**.

Did You Know?   When the GUI replaced command-line computer
interfaces as the norm, significant development work had to be done to
create screen readers so that computer users who are blind could continue to use their computers. Many people who are blind were very proficient computer users because textual command-line interfaces could
easily work with a text-to-speech interface.

Today, we are on the precipice of revolutionary change in technology.
Computer users are demanding computer user interfaces that are not only
easier to use, but also more flexible and easily customized. They feel that

using a computer is more difficult than it should be. As our population ages, these consumer demands will increase. Computer users also want remote intelligent access from any location. Most importantly, consumers want to choose how they interact with computers. The research and development that is being done to make these changes build on lessons learned when assistive technology first had to meet some of these very same needs. If the technology changes of the next decade maintain these common goals, they will offer significantly improved productivity and increased flexibility for all computer users, especially those with disabilities. They also offer the promise of opening up the power of computer usage to a broader range of people with and without disabilities.

Although it can be difficult to accurately predict the future, we can look at today's research and development projects as indications of where technology is headed. You can anticipate that some of these expectations will be replaced by even greater advancements that are unheard of today.

To look at this exciting future, this chapter will explore

- The trends that provide a glimpse at the technology of the future
- Our view of what the workplace of tomorrow will look like
- How accessible technology will become mainstream in the future

Trends and Expectations

Current research and development projects at Microsoft and other software companies reveal two key themes of future technology: flexibility and customization. Computer interfaces are evolving to adapt to the way that humans interact, think, and organize information. Not only are individuals different in the ways they interact, think, and organize information, but they are also different depending on their environment. For example, an individual using a computer in a quiet office has different preferences than the same individual using a computer in a noisy airport terminal. Seamless customization and flexibility will allow an individual to specify using speech in a quiet office and using a mouse and keyboard when the ambient noise level is above a specified threshold.

Both flexibility and customization are important for everyone, but they are especially important for people with disabilities because they are a critical component of accessible technology.

Although there are many research and development projects going on today, we'll focus on four trends and expectations where we see that flexibility and customization will play pivotal roles in technology. All these trends have the potential to improve productivity for everyone. However, as you'll see, the access potential for people with disabilities is significant.

Did You Know?   Many past technology advancements were originally designed to assist people with disabilities, and their usefulness became ubiquitous. We expect that trend to continue in the future. For example, Herman Hollerith, who experts now recognize as having had a cognitive processing disability, had difficulties remembering school lessons in his youth. In 1886, Hollerith invented the use of punched cards to hold and transport information. His so-called computer became essential because hand tabulation of the U.S. Census was projected to take more than a decade. In 1896, Hollerith founded the Tabulating Machine Company, which later became International Business Machines (IBM).

Intelligent Flexibility and Personalization with Microsoft .NET

By now you have probably heard about the Microsoft .NET platform, the Microsoft strategy to make information available any time, any place, on any device, but you might not know how it will impact your business. Microsoft .NET will provide a collection of Web-based services and technologies that work together to deliver on this strategy. Some of these services and technologies are already available, whereas others are being developed. Although there are many components of Microsoft .NET, we have chosen to discuss those most likely to have an impact on improving the ability of people with disabilities to use computers in a business environment. These include

- Infrastructure and tools that promote flexible computer interactions

- Natural language and speech recognition

- Built-in seamless customization that follows a computer user wherever he or she goes

- The possibilities for an improved user experience for assistive technology

The driving force behind Microsoft .NET is a shift in focus from individual Web sites or devices to new constellations of computers, devices, and services that work together to deliver broader, richer solutions. Using applications built on these services and technologies, people will have control over how, when, and what information is delivered to them. Computers, devices, and services will be able to collaborate directly with each other, and businesses will be able to offer their products and services in a way that lets customers embed them in their own computer environment.

To get a sense of the opportunities that Microsoft .NET will provide business computer users, let's look at today's situation:

- The mechanisms by which people can interact with computers are limited—generally to a keyboard and mouse for input, and a monitor for output—unless the person is using specialized assistive technology.

- User information is principally a local phenomenon. If you log on to your Internet service provider or your company's network from a different computer, your preferences, data, and applications are not accessible.

- Users must directly act on information rather than setting intelligent preferences that automatically act on the user's behalf.

Microsoft .NET promises to address these deficiencies by providing a framework and infrastructure so that the platform and applications built on the platform are easy to use anywhere by anyone. As part of future Microsoft .NET client platforms, Microsoft is building a robust user interface infrastructure and implementation tools that will take technology—including accessible technology—to the next level of intelligent user interactions.

If an application is built using the implementation tools that take advantage of the .NET client infrastructure, it will work seamlessly with assistive technology products without any additional programming. Likewise, assistive technology products using the infrastructure will gain access to countless applications with no additional work. Today, assistive technology manufacturers have to update their products for them to work with new applications and updates of existing applications. This increases the total cost of ownership for a business by requiring more frequent upgrades and additional integration effort. Therefore, Microsoft .NET will eventually lower the total cost of owner-ship for businesses using assistive technology products.

In addition, if your IT developers use the future Microsoft .NET imple-mentation tools to build your business applications, they will automatically take advantage of these capabilities. This means that your business applica-tions will work for all your employees and customers, even when their individ-ual needs are different. This is a substantial benefit for already strapped IT departments and removes the need for customizing each individual's access requirements. Instead, individuals will be able to easily access the applications as they choose, without requiring any additional work by the IT developers.

More Info   Many articles and white papers about Microsoft's .NET strategy are available. To find more information on Microsoft's .NET strategy, access *http://www.microsoft.com/net*.

Flexible Computer Interactions

Microsoft .NET will allow computer users to choose their preferred way to provide, or **input**, information to their computer and to receive, or **output**, information from their computer. These techniques include speech, handwrit-ing, specialized input devices such as a single button switch, and a traditional keyboard or mouse.

For example, using built-in customization capabilities, a computer user could choose keyboard and handwriting as input preferences, allowing her to navigate applications with her keyboard and add text to documents with hand-writing. She might also choose to direct her computer to tell her what it is doing and what choices she can make by actually talking to her and reading the content of her selected documents aloud. Likewise, her colleague could choose a specialized switch device for navigating and entering data and a visual display and text for navigational choices and document content. In both cases, the choices will be easy to make and will work for the operating system and all applications.

Natural Language and Speech Recognition

Today, in order to input information to a computer, a computer user must follow specific steps and make structured choices so that the computer understands what the user intends. This is true even when the computer user is using voice recognition assistive technology. So, for example, if a manager wants to schedule an appointment with an employee, she needs to navigate through a series of menus in a specific order to set the appointment in her calendar application. This might be done with a mouse, keyboard, or voice recognition software. Although voice recognition software is currently very useful as assistive technology, it requires the computer user to speak predetermined phrases in a specific structured order and voice to navigate the menus needed to accomplish tasks.

Current research and development are divided into two approaches that will ultimately converge as part of Microsoft .NET. First, work is being done to allow computer users to type instructions into the computer by using phrases or sentences that are natural to them, in the language of their choice, rather than in predetermined computer instructions. This technique uses **natural language** to direct the computer. You can see the beginnings of this technology in Microsoft Office XP Help's Answer Wizard, which allows you to type a question to obtain help and information. In the future, a computer user would be able to interact with the computer by typing instructions without a predetermined structure or steps. For example, to schedule an appointment, a manager could type, "Make an hour appointment with John at 2 tomorrow to discuss his performance review."

The second area of focus is improved speech recognition. Once these two technology areas are mature, they will be combined to provide speech recognition of natural language. This will allow computer users to talk to their computers using their natural language to accomplish tasks. Although speech recognition of natural languages will become ubiquitous, typed entry of natural language phrases and sentences will also be available. Computer users who cannot speak due to their environment (such as too much noise or the need for privacy) or personal abilities will continue to use typed entry. So, for example, if the manager scheduling the appointment is in an airport, she could type the request. However, in the quiet and privacy of her own office, she might speak the request instead. If she were deaf, she could always choose to type her requests.

Seamless Customization

As Microsoft .NET provides users with more flexibility for how they interact with their computers, computers will automatically adjust to changes in environment and circumstances, providing seamless customization.

For example, say you've chosen speech as your input preference for your mobile device. One day you are in a large conference room waiting for a meeting to begin and the ambient noise gets to a level where speech input is no longer practical. Your mobile device automatically adjusts and switches to your alternate input preference, which is handwriting. The preferences you have chosen will be available to you wherever you go through the use of a **smart card** (which resembles a credit card and contains an integrated circuit and memory that give it a limited amount of "intelligence"), a smart mobile device containing your individual information, or a Web service where you registered your personal preferences. Suppose that you go to the library to do some research using the old stacks and need to use the library kiosk to begin your search. The library kiosk automatically uses your preferences, obtained from the Web service where you registered, and might even download assistive technology from the Web if you require it in order to interact with the system. For someone with a mobility impairment, a wireless switch might be attached to a wheelchair, allowing the person to use the library kiosk without additional assistance. This portable flexibility means that you and your colleagues, based purely on personal preference, can choose to interact differently.

These adaptable systems are especially important for the aging population. As functional limitations occur, more assistance or different modes of interaction might be needed. A person using handwriting for input can continue to use the system even after arthritis prevents him from writing. The system adapts to his needs as they change and allows him to use speech to interact instead.

Improved User Experience for Assistive Technology

Recall that assistive technology products built on Microsoft .NET will use the new interfaces in the .NET infrastructure to gain access to countless applications without additional work. Assistive technology manufacturers will be able to focus more on improving the user experience for their customers by spending their saved development dollars to provide enhanced features.

For example, a manufacturer of a screen enlarger could provide support for **dual monitors** (two monitors working together to show the computer desktop and application windows as though they were one monitor) to greatly improve the usability of its product and increase productivity for its customers. Although support for dual monitors has been available in the Windows operating systems for some time, no assistive technology manufacturer has provided support. Just as someone using a pair of binoculars to view wildlife needs to verify his relative position by looking at the complete viewing area without magnification, a person using a screen enlarger needs to see the orientation of the enlarged area within the overall screen. This means that the enlarged portion can take up only part of the monitor viewing space. With support for dual monitors, the enlarged content could take up one monitor's viewing area, leaving the other monitor's display for orienting the location of the enlarged area.

Did You Know?   John Bardeen, William Shockley, and Walter Brattain, all Bell Labs scientists, invented the transistor in 1948, which is another example of a significant technology advancement originally designed to assist people with disabilities. These scientists were trying to develop more reliable, powerful, flexible, smaller, cheaper, cooler-running, and less power-consuming hearing aids. Sony, convinced this wasn't the best use for the transistor, acquired a license for the technology for $25,000 and later invented the transistor radio.

Communicate and Collaborate Worldwide: Language Conversion

Improved speech recognition capabilities include the ability to perform language conversions. Early products are beginning to appear that convert text in one language to speech in another, and vice versa. A hand-carried language translator can provide opportunities for anyone needing to communicate across language barriers including those barriers produced by hearing loss. In addition to providing language translation to text, current prototype products are also able to provide the translation to a visual representation of American Sign Language (ASL) or other sign language variants.

A person who is deaf or hard-of-hearing can use the device to listen to speech and convert it into text, sign language visuals, amplified speech, or a combination of amplified speech and text. And, even more remarkably, the language used doesn't have to be that of the speaker. Likewise, the person who is deaf or hard-of-hearing can use the translator to "talk" to someone else's translator, converting the text into speech.

These capabilities will extend to video and phone conferencing, truly opening up worldwide communications for everyone.

Managing Data: Intuitive Access to Information

Many of us are inundated with too many files and have difficulty keeping track of them all. When an employee spends precious time looking for a document he knows is stored somewhere on his computer, lost productivity results.

Current research and development is progressing on adaptive interfaces for accessing, storing, and manipulating data. The current computer interfaces for managing data were designed when disk storage was a premium. Now that multi-gigabyte storage devices are cheap and ubiquitous, people have difficulty finding important documents when they need them. Add to this the multitude of information available on the Internet, and the problem is even more serious. With these adaptive interfaces, the actual file and data organization is hidden from the user, and the information is presented in a more meaningful way. For instance, it might be presented by time and purpose of documents. More intelligent search capabilities coupled with sophisticated indexing mechanisms mean that the data can be found quickly and easily. Although this capability helps everyone, it is particularly useful for people with mild memory loss or other cognitive impairments. It also reduces the navigation necessary to find information, which helps people with visual or mobility impairments be more productive.

Did You Know?   Thinking about the needs of individuals with disabilities can broaden the future potential for new technology. Vinton Cerf developed the host-level protocols for the ARPANET in 1972. ARPANET was the first large-scale packet network. Cerf, hard-of-hearing since birth, was married to a woman who was also deaf. He communicated with his wife by using text messaging. Cerf stated, "I have spent, as you can imagine, a fair chunk of my time trying to persuade people with hearing impairments to make use of electronic mail because I found it so powerful myself." (Williams 2000) Had it not been for this experience, Cerf might not have integrated e-mail as part of the functionality of ARPANET, the precursor to the Internet.

Accessing and Managing Appliances with Universal Plug and Play

Appliances that once were usable by most people have become increasingly inaccessible to people with disabilities. Copiers, microwave ovens, and washers and dryers, to name a few, have replaced physical push buttons and dials with touch screens and flat panel buttons for operation. People who are blind or mobility impaired can't use these technology "improvements." They can, however, use the physical push buttons and dials that were replaced. Ironically, manufacturers made these changes to improve the experience for their customers.

A new technology called **Universal Plug and Play (UPnP)** is being used to develop home and office appliances of tomorrow and will address these access issues. UPnP defines a protocol and an **eXtensible Markup Language (XML) schema** that is designed to enable simple and robust connectivity among stand-alone appliances, such as a copier or microwave oven, and personal computers from many different manufacturers. XML helps make the Internet an efficient platform for remote communication by allowing messages to describe their own content. XML is similar to an alphabet, and an XML schema functions as a shared vocabulary for specific business terms and their context.

UPnP is the result of an industry initiative and is a collaboration among more than 400 companies including industry leaders in consumer electronics, computing, home automation, home security, appliances, printing, photography, computer networking, and mobile products. Although UPnP was not initially designed to solve access difficulties, because of its flexible design, it can be used to improve access for people with disabilities.

Using UPnP, home and office appliances—including microwave ovens, copiers, VCRs, thermostats, ATM machines, or kiosks—will be operated by a **controller.** A controller is a computer such as a personal computer, laptop, cell phone, or pager with computer capabilities that include managing e-mail or browsing the Web, or a mobile device that also manages e-mail, calendaring, tasks, and note taking. The controller must be able to communicate remotely using the UPnP protocol and is used by an individual or organization to manage and operate the variety of home and office appliances. Eventually, controllers could be imbedded in a piece of clothing, jewelry, a watch, or even a wheelchair.

One controller can be used to operate any number of different devices in the home or office because UPnP makes it possible to manage an entire range of appliances without special programming. And, the controller can be customized to meet the needs and preferences of the person using it.

The advantage UPnP will offer everyone is the convenience to manage appliances from anywhere. Say you are on the commuter train heading to work and you can't remember if you turned off the oven. Using your mobile device, you can check your oven and turn it off if necessary. A small business could use a computer running controller software to manage the office lights and heating system for cost savings. Everyone will benefit, but specifically people with disabilities who will be able to use an appliance with a specialized controller that works for them.

To provide these advantages, an appliance manufacturer need only define how customers interact and operate their appliances using a predefined XML schema definition. The specific definition is then stored on the Internet to allow access by any UPnP controller.

The mobile device or computer manufacturer creating a controller can then take this development process one step further and provide the software that allows remote access operation of the appliances using UPnP and the XML code describing the possible customer interactions. See Figure 9-1 on the following page. By using a controller tailored to a person's preferences and needs, anyone will be able to access and use any appliance without the appliance manufacturer needing to understand or build to a particular person's access needs. Just as the appliance manufacturer doesn't need to understand the customer's preferences or access needs, neither does the manufacturer of the controller need to understand the specifics of a given appliance or what possible appliances are available.

For example, if the controller is a mobile device, it might have very large buttons for a person who is visually impaired or has dexterity impairments in his or her hands, or it might provide speech controls, which are useful for a wide range of individuals, particularly for those who are blind. Today, if microwave oven manufacturers want to offer models that can be controlled by speech for customers who are blind or visually impaired, they must integrate the speech technology themselves, considerably increasing the microwave oven's manufacturing complexity and costs as well as the retail price. With UPnP, microwave oven manufacturers could offer their customers with visual

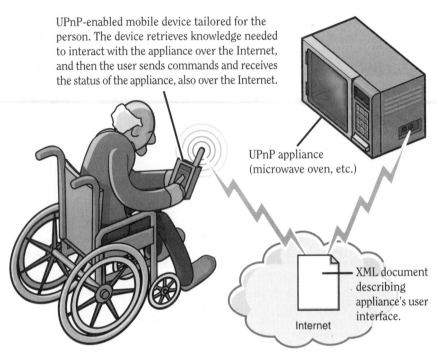

UPnP-enabled mobile device tailored for the person. The device retrieves knowledge needed to interact with the appliance over the Internet, and then the user sends commands and receives the status of the appliance, also over the Internet.

UPnP appliance (microwave oven, etc.)

XML document describing appliance's user interface.

Internet

Figure 9-1.   *Accessing appliances with a UPnP controller*

impairments a microwave that meets their needs through the use of a specialized controller without the additional development complexity and cost.

Also, consider the customer who is deaf. Many people who are deaf use a service dog (a "hearing dog") to inform them when the microwave oven has beeped. The dog requires months of training to be able to notify its owner of various kinds of noises. With UPnP, a microwave oven could inform a deaf consumer's mobile device instead of producing its normal beep. The controller would then flash lights or vibrate as directed by the consumer. In this way, the user would have a specialized type of response regardless of the appliance being used.

By providing flexibility and at the same time reducing the costs of design and manufacturing for that flexibility, UPnP can make access to appliances a problem of the past. Both the appliance manufacturer and the controller manufacturer can focus on their core area of expertise without worrying about the complex matrix of support, making access to a wide range of appliances possible for people with significantly different access needs.

The Workplace of Tomorrow

Now that we have a better understanding of the technology trends of the future, we will look at how this technology will transform and enhance your workplace. In Chapter 2, "Understanding Accessible Technology and Disabilities," we provided examples of how employees now use accessible technology. In this section, we review their current scenarios and look into the future to see how they might be improved.

Doris: the HR Manager

Today

Doris is a human resources manager and is visually impaired. She uses a screen enlargement program.

Tomorrow

Doris continues to use screen enlargement software on her computer but now has a second monitor that allows her to see a broader area of the screen, making her more productive. Doris also had difficulty reading the buttons and small print on the copier and on the office microwave. As a result, she had to memorize the functions she needed to use and had to take extra time when the equipment was upgraded or if she went to another department that used different equipment. Because she now has a mobile device with an enlarged display for controlling all of these appliances, she no longer needs to memorize buttons. Her mobile device tells the copier and the microwave the functions she wants to use. She no longer has any problems when the equipment is upgraded or if she is in another department. Her mobile device works with the new equipment seamlessly.

Robert: the Safety Manager

Today

Robert is a safety manager for a regional department of transportation. He lost a hand in an industrial accident and uses a Half Qwerty keyboard to interact with his computer.

Tomorrow

Although Robert's typing speed is very fast using the Half Qwerty keyboard, he prefers to use the latest speech recognition software. The software has greatly improved since the "old days" when it required exact commands and specific ways of talking in order for the computer to understand. Now he finds that talking to the computer allows him to express his actions in the way that is most comfortable for him. He's even discovered that interacting this way has sharpened his creativity and has simultaneously improved his productivity. He realizes that he feels less encumbered when he isn't typing, which has helped him to focus more on creative solutions to problems he is trying to solve.

Robert recently started using a mobile device designed to allow one-handed operation, which was originally designed for busy executives. It allows him to receive and make phone calls, remotely control his safety equipment, and keep track of his e-mail and schedule. In the past, he occasionally had difficulties with one-hand usage of a new copier or printer at the office. Now he can easily operate them by using his mobile device. He's also discovered that he can use his mobile device to operate the local library's kiosk to find and reserve the new safety management book he read about on the Web.

Steve: the Researcher

Today

Steve is a research assistant who works in the corporate library of a large financial corporation. Steve's specialty is world economics, and he spends most of his day searching and reading statistical information on the Internet. Steve is deaf and takes advantage of visual replacements for sound, such as captioning.

Tomorrow

Steve was recently promoted to research manager, and he now manages a team of five research assistants. Steve still relies on captioning for accessing multimedia, but he's found that more multimedia provides captioning now because it is easier to produce captioning than it used to be. In his team meetings, he uses his tablet computer, which is the size of an average clipboard, to take written notes. He tells his computer what to do by typing English sentences as though he were directing a person. For example, he can type, "open a new Word document called January 7 Meeting Notes." The computer recognizes these sentences and seamlessly allows him to start taking notes. He's also found that he really likes to use handwriting to take notes and to organize his thoughts when producing team status reports. The new software that converts his handwritten English text into German is really beneficial because he can more easily share ideas with a research firm in Germany without having to know German. This language conversion capability allowed his company to expand its business by offering research services in Europe. He and his German colleagues can even communicate live using the software to translate German speech into English text, and vice versa. This technology fully accommodates his deafness in video conference calls as well.

John: the Dental Assistant

Today

John is a dental assistant who had a slight stroke six months ago. He has some muscle weakness and mobility impairments as well as some cognitive loss, which has resulted in mild difficulties with his short-term memory. John's job requires him to work for some part of each day entering and retrieving information from dental patient records using a computer.

Tomorrow

The new natural language interfaces have helped John immensely. He no longer has to remember the computer sequences necessary to accomplish a task. John can now tell the computer in plain English to schedule an appointment or to take his dictation of patient notes. He is amazed at how much more quickly he gets his computer tasks done now. He also finds that he doesn't need additional help from his colleagues like he did in the past.

When John's computer had to be repaired, he was worried that his computer tasks would back up. However, he was easily able to use another assistant's computer because it knew all of his preferences from his smart card and acted just like his own computer. This experience led John to try using the ordering kiosk at his local coffee shop. He was delighted to discover that the coffee shop computer also knew his preferences, also from his smart card, and he was able to place his order without difficulty.

Clair: the Lead Program Manager

Today

Clair is a lead program manager at a large software company. Clair has a learning impairment that targets her reading and writing skills including organization and reference skills. The computer is an essential tool that helps her capture her thoughts "in the moment" and to organize them at a later time.

Tomorrow

Clair has found that now that she can actually "talk" to her computer without having to remember specific commands, she is even more productive than before. As a team manager, she schedules many meetings each week and sends out status reports. She talks to her computer to schedule the meetings and then tells her computer when she wants to start writing status reports. Clair can write her status reports in her own handwriting. Although Clair is a very fast typist, she prefers to first write her thoughts down on paper. She now is more efficient because the thoughts she writes in her own handwriting on her tablet computer are transitioned to text by the computer. Because the computer understands what Clair tells it to do, she finds that she no longer needs to call her company's help desk.

Because Clair's new computer manages her documents for her, she no longer has to keep track of how her reports and research data are actually stored or organized. Her memory and intuition are geared toward time and task, and having all her documents and files presented this way works great for her. She can quickly and easily find the exact report she is looking for.

Accessible Technology Becomes Mainstream

In the next decade, the lines between mainstream expectations for technology and what we now call "accessible technology" will continue to blur significantly. More and more, computers will adjust to a person rather than the person adjusting to the computer. Computer users will want to interact with their computers the way that feels more natural to them rather than learning how to work with a computer and making the appropriate adjustments.

As this transformation occurs, the usability demands of individuals will be much the same as the accessibility requirements people with disabilities have today. Because technologies such as speech recognition and voice output are still relatively new and not as sophisticated as they promise to be, they are often relegated to the realm of assistive technology and early adopters. But as these technologies become more sophisticated, we will witness their transformation. They will be integrated into your average computer.

Conservatively, in the coming decade, all computer users will have sophisticated alternatives to interact with their computers. The average business computer will have built-in flexibility for alternatives such as handwriting and speech recognition. This will change and improve how people—including people with disabilities—interact with an ordinary computer. As a result, assistive technology will also change and might be necessary only for some niche access issues such as providing access for people with a combination of disabilities (for example, people who are deaf and blind or people with extensive mobility impairments).

The most optimistic view of future technology is one where the need for what are now known as "accessible technology" and "assistive technology products" will no longer exist. All technology will be flexible enough to be accessed by anyone in the way that they choose, or for people with disabilities, in the way that they must, given their functional limitations.

As technology progresses, features such as those described earlier in this chapter will be integrated with **Global Positioning System (GPS)**, cell phone, data organizer, and other capabilities into small mobile devices. These mobile devices might be woven into clothing, worn in the ear, attached to a wheelchair, or even become a new form of fashion jewelry. They will not only be able to manipulate our environment by turning lights on or off, or adjusting a thermostat, but they will also inform us of where we are and provide critical information about our environment. This will put everyone in control and allow them to interact and manipulate their environment, regardless of ability, through the method of their choice. Through this technology, we will realize Steve Ballmer's vision, "Over the next 10 to 15 years, technology has the capacity to virtually eliminate barriers [faced by people with disabilities] in the workplace." The next generation of technology will be life changing for everyone, but especially for people with disabilities.

When an employee who is blind can easily navigate through a new office building with no assistance other than the computer he always carries with him as a lapel pin, we'll know the future has arrived.

Glossary

accessibility features   Options within a product that allow a user with disabilities to adjust product settings to his or her personal visual, mobility, hearing, language, and learning needs.

accessible technology   Software and hardware that is flexible and adjustable to a person's visual, mobility, hearing, language, and learning needs and can therefore be accessed by people regardless of their abilities. Accessible technology encompasses three elements: built-in accessibility features, assistive technology products that provide access to computers for people with specific disabilities, and compatibility between the operating system, software, and the assistive technology products.

alternative input device   A tool that allows individuals to control their computers through means other than a standard keyboard or pointing device. Examples include alternative keyboards, electronic pointing device, sip-and-puff systems, wands and sticks, joysticks, and trackballs.

alternative keyboard   A type of alternative input device that is available in different sizes with different keypad arrangements and angles. Larger keyboards are available with enlarged keys, which are easier to access by people with limited motor skills. Smaller keyboards are available with smaller keys (or keys placed closer together) to allow someone with a limited range of motion to reach all keys. Other keyboards available include ones with keypads located at various angles, keyguards, and split keyboards, which divide the keypad into different sections.

assistive technology products   Specially designed products that are chosen specifically to accommodate an individual's disability or multiple disabilities. Also known as *accessibility aids*, these products are developed to work with a computer's operating system and software. Compatibility between the operating system, software, and assistive technology products is a critical component of accessible technology.

augmentative and assistive communications devices   Tools used by individuals with language disabilities who do not have the ability to communicate orally. To communicate, the user either types words and phrases or selects from a series of images that, when arranged in a particular way, generate a phrase. The device then speaks aloud for the individual.

auto-dialer   A product feature that allows a user to dial a number after entering a user-defined, unique code (e.g., "[o" is the code for the "office" number) or selecting a directory listing rather than having to dial individual numbers.

bilateral epicondilitus   Inflammation of the elbows, which can result from on-the-job repetitive motion, such as typing. Also called *tennis elbow*.

Braille embosser   A type of printer that transfers computer-generated text into embossed Braille output.

Braille translation program   Software that converts text scanned in or generated via standard word processing programs into Braille, which can be printed on an embosser.

captioning   The conversion of a soundtrack of a video program into text that can be read on a screen or monitor.

carpal tunnel syndrome   Pain and/or weakness in the hand that is caused by repetitive compression of a nerve that passes through the wrist.

cognitive processing deficit   An inability to attend to and appropriately respond to information presented by sight or sound, and/or the inability to physically respond.

CompTIA (Computing Technology Industry Association)   A not-for-profit trade association that provides computer and communication companies with technology community standards, services, and vendor-neutral technical certification.

controller   A computer such as a personal computer, laptop, cell phone, or pager with capabilities that include managing e-mail or browsing the Web, or a mobile device that also manages e-mail, calendaring, tasks, and note taking. The controller must be able to communicate remotely using the UPnP protocol and is used by an individual or organization to manage and operate a variety of home and office appliances.

device independence   Software that is designed to run on a variety of hardware platforms (e.g., a Web site that can easily be viewed and used on a PC as well as a Macintosh).

Dragon Dictate voice recognition software   A product that enables a user to navigate a computer system and enter text using his or her voice.

dual monitors   Two or more monitors connected to a computer to increase the size of the visible desktop. When this feature is enabled, multiple monitors attached to the same computer act like one large monitor. With certain configurations, the second monitor can also show a zoomed-in view of the first monitor.

electronic pointing device   A type of alternative input tool that allows the user to control the cursor on the screen using ultrasound, an infrared beam, eye movements, nerve signals, or brain waves. When used with an on-screen keyboard, electronic pointing devices also allow the user to enter text or data.

FilterKeys   An accessibility option in Windows XP and earlier versions of Windows that adjusts the keyboard response so that inadvertently repeated keystrokes are ignored. Using FilterKeys, a user can also slow the rate at which a key is repeated when it is held down.

Global Positioning System (GPS)   A radio navigational system in which satellites orbit the earth and transmit time and geographic position. By using a receiver, the user can detect such signals to determine his or her precise geographic location.

graphical user interface (GUI)   A visual computer environment that represents programs, files, and options with graphical images, such as icons, menus, and dialog boxes on the screen.

HotKeys   Keyboard combinations, also known as keyboard shortcuts and shortcut keys, that allow an individual to navigate a computer using keyboard command combinations instead of a mouse. Also, a shareware utility from H2 Software for creating shortcuts to computer tasks that is designed to ease PC navigation. *See also* keyboard shortcuts/shortcut keys.

income protection   An insurance program that provides funds to employees who cannot work and thus cannot earn a living due to an injury or disease.

input   Information a computer user provides to a computer.

IRC (Internet Relay Chat)   A technology that enables users to conduct a live conversation over the Internet by typing messages to each other in real time.

JAWS   A screen reader software program that includes a text-to-speech capability, which enables the computer to speak the contents of a screen to a user with a visual disability.

joystick   A type of alternative input device that can be plugged into a computer's mouse port and used to control the cursor on the screen. Joysticks benefit users who need to operate a computer with or without the use of their hands.

keyboard filter   A software program that include typing aids, such as word prediction utilities and add-on spelling checkers. It can be used to relieve the user from having to make many keystrokes. Keyboard filters enable users to quickly access the letters they need and to avoid inadvertently selecting keys they don't want.

keyboard shortcuts/shortcut keys   Keyboard combinations that allow those who cannot use a mouse or prefer to use a keyboard to select commands and navigate. For example, to move between open documents and programs, you can select Alt+Tab in Windows. These are also sometimes known as HotKeys.

Magnifier   A display utility in Windows XP and Windows 2000 that makes the computer screen more readable by people who have low vision by creating a separate window that displays a magnified portion of the screen. Magnifier provides a minimum level of functionality for people who have slight visual impairments.

Microsoft TechNet   A central information and community resource (available at *http://www.microsoft.com/technet/*) for IT professionals and a source of assistance for Microsoft business products.

MouseKeys   An accessibility feature found in Windows XP and earlier versions of Windows that is designed for people who have difficulty using a mouse. MouseKeys allows the user to employ the numeric keypad to control the movement of the mouse pointer.

Multiple Sclerosis (MS)   A progressive neurological condition that impacts a person's ability to move his or her muscles.

Narrator   A text-to-speech utility in Windows XP and Windows 2000 that provides a minimum level of functionality for people who are blind or have low vision. Narrator reads the text displayed on the screen—the contents of the active window, menu options, or text that has been typed. Narrator is designed to work with Notepad, WordPad, Control Panel programs, Internet Explorer, the Windows desktop, and some parts of Windows Setup.

natural language   A technology approach where computer users type instructions into the computer by using phrases or sentences that are natural to them, in the language of their choice, rather than in predetermined computer instructions.

occupational therapist   A clinician who uses employment activities as part of the treatment of an illness or medical condition.

On-Screen Keyboard   A utility that is part of Windows XP and Windows 2000 that displays a virtual keyboard on the computer screen, which allows people with mobility impairments to type data by using a pointing device or joystick. This utility also includes a scanning option.

on-screen keyboard programs   Software that provides an image of a standard or modified keyboard on the computer screen. The user selects the keys using a mouse, touch screen, trackball, joystick, switch, or electronic pointing device. On-screen keyboards often have a scanning option.

output   Information a computer user receives from a computer.

PaperPort PC   Software that allows users to convert paper to machine-readable documents.

puff-stick   Also called a sip-and-puff system, a straw-like device used by people with mobility impairments to select an item on an on-screen keyboard by puffing into the tool.

reading comprehension programs   Curricula that focus on establishing or improving reading skills through ready-made activities, stories, exercises, or games. These programs can help users practice letter sound recognition and can increase the understanding of words by adding graphics, sound, and possibly animation.

reading tools and learning disability programs   Curricula that include software designed to make text-based materials more accessible for people who struggle with reading. Options can include scanning, reformatting, navigating, or speaking text out loud.

refreshable Braille display   A device that provides tactile output of information represented on the computer screen. A Braille *cell* is composed of a series of dots. The pattern of the dots and the various combinations of the cells are used in place of letters. Unlike conventional Braille, which is permanently embossed onto paper, a refreshable Braille display mechanically lifts small rounded plastic or metal pins as needed to form Braille characters. The user reads the Braille letters with his fingers, and then, after a line is read, refreshes the display to read the next line.

screen enlarger   A mechanism that works like a magnifying glass. Also called a screen magnifier, it enlarges a portion of the screen, increasing the legibility for some users. Some screen enlargers allow a person to zoom in and out on a particular area of the screen.

screen reader   A software program that presents the graphics and text shown on the monitor as speech.

screen review utility A tool that makes on-screen information available as synthesized speech and pairs the speech with a visual representation of a word, for example, highlighting a word as it is spoken. A screen review utility converts the text that appears on screen into a computer voice.

SerialKeys An accessibility feature found in Windows XP and earlier versions of Windows that is designed for people who have difficulty using the computer's standard keyboard or mouse. SerialKeys provides support so that alternative input devices, such as single switch or sip-and-puff system, can be plugged into the computer's serial port.

ShowSounds An accessibility feature found in Windows XP and earlier versions of Windows that instructs programs that usually convey information only by sound to also provide all information visually, such as by displaying text captions or informative icons.

sip-and-puff system A technique that is just one of many different types of switch access that can be used as an alternative input device. In typical configurations, a dental saliva extractor is attached to a switch. An individual uses his or her breath to activate the switch.

smart card A device that resembles a credit card and contains an integrated circuit and memory that gives it a limited amount of intelligence.

SoundSentry An accessibility feature found in Windows XP and earlier versions of Windows that is designed for people who have difficulty hearing system sounds generated by the computer. SoundSentry allows the user to change the settings to generate visual warnings, such as a blinking title bar or a screen flash, whenever the computer generates a sound.

speech recognition system A program that allows people to give commands and enter data using their voices rather than a mouse or keyboard. It is also called a voice recognition program.

speech synthesizer A machine that receives information going to the screen in the form of letters, numbers, and punctuation marks, and then speaks it out loud. Often referred to as text-to-speech (TTS), the voice of the computer is synthesized speech—a distinctive, sometimes monotone voice that is the joining together of preprogrammed letters and words.

StickyKeys An accessibility feature found in Windows XP and earlier versions of Windows that is designed for people who have difficulty holding down two or more keys simultaneously. When a shortcut requires a key combination such as Ctrl+P, StickyKeys enables the user to press one key at a time instead of pressing them concurrently.

Symantec PC Anywhere   PC software that allows users to access office-based computer systems from home.

Systems Management Server (SMS)   A computer that deploys applications, software updates, and operating systems over simple or advanced enterprise networks.

talking and large-print word processor   A software program that uses speech synthesizers to provide auditory feedback of what is typed. A large-print word processor allows the user to view large text on screen without added screen enlargement.

Telecommunications Device for the Deaf (TDD)   A terminal device used widely by deaf people for text communication over telephone lines.

tele-dictation system   A system that takes dictation over a telephone or over Internet-based telephony, returning a text file of the spoken input, generally via the Internet.

telemedicine   The ability to review medical histories, perform examinations, analyze diagnostic tests, and prescribe medication online.

teletypewriter (TTY)   A device for low-speed communications over a telephone line, consisting of a keyboard that sends a character code for each keystroke and a printer that prints characters as their codes are received.

telnet   A functionality that allows a user direct access to data on a remote network.

tendonitis   The inflammation of a tendon that often occurs after excessive use, such as a sports injury, and is generally cured with rest.

terminal emulation mode   A computer, usually PC-based, running software that enables it to imitate a traditional mainframe console and thereby run programs written for and process data originating from a mainframe computer system.

ToggleKeys   An accessibility feature found in Windows XP and earlier versions of Windows that is designed for people who have vision impairment or cognitive disabilities. When ToggleKeys is turned on, the computer provides sound cues when the locking keys (Caps Lock, Num Lock, or Scroll Lock) are pressed. A high sound plays when the keys are switched on, and a low sound plays when they are switched off.

touch screen   A device placed on the computer monitor (or built into it) that allows direct selection or activation of the computer by touching the screen.

trackball   A type of alternative input device that looks like an upside down mouse with a movable ball on top of a stationary base.

Universal Plug & Play (UPnP)   A new technology being used to develop home and office appliances of tomorrow. It defines a protocol and an XML schema that is designed to enable simple and robust connectivity among stand-alone appliances, such as a copier or microwave oven, and personal computers from many different manufacturers.

universal serial bus (USB)   A standard that makes it faster, easier, and cheaper for users to attach and use peripherals, such as scanners, printers, and digital cameras, with their computers.

Utility Manager   A Windows XP and Windows 2000 program that allows users to check an accessibility program's status and start or stop an accessibility program. Users with administrator-level access can configure an accessibility program to start when Utility Manager starts.

wands and sticks   Typing aids used to strike keys on the keyboard. As types of alternative input devices, they are most commonly worn on the head, held in the mouth, strapped to the chin, or held in the hand.

word prediction program   Software that allows the user to select a desired word from an on-screen list located in the prediction window. This list, generated by the computer, predicts words from the first one or two letters typed by the user. The word can then be selected from the list and inserted into the text by typing a number, clicking the mouse, or scanning with a switch.

XML schema   A code scheme that functions as a shared vocabulary for specific business terms and context to be described using XML.

Bibliography

Anthes, Gary H. "Making IT Accessible." *Computer World*, May 2001. Available from *http://www.computerworld.com/cwi/story/ 0,1199,NAV47_STO60856,00.html*.

A.T. Quarterly. "Technology-Related Assistance for Individuals with Disabilities Act of 1988." *A.T. Quarterly*, 5, nos. 2–3 (1994).

Ballmer, Steve. "A Chat with Microsoft's Steve Ballmer." *Business Week Online*, 13 June 2001. Available from *http://www.businessweek.com/ bwdaily/dnflash/jun2001/nf20010613_081.htm*.

Ballmer, Steve. E-mail to Microsoft employees, 18 October 2000.

Blanck, Peter David. "Communicating the Americans with Disabilities Act, Transcending Compliance: A Case Report on Sears, Roebuck, and Co." Washington, D.C.: The Annenberg Washington Program in Communications Policy Studies of Northwestern University, 1994.

Cleghorn, John. Interview by author. 1998.

Cone/Roper. "The Evolution of Cause Branding." Cone/Roper Cause Related Trends Report, 1999.

Conway, Susan, and Char Sligar. *Unlocking Knowledge Assets: Knowledge Management Solutions from Microsoft*. Redmond: Microsoft Press, 2002.

Council on Foundations. "Measuring the Value of Corporate Citizenship." Council on Foundations, 1996.

De La Torre, Gustavo. "Intel Expands Diversity Programs in Four Strategic Areas." *Diversity/Careers in Engineering and Information Technology*, summer/fall 2001. Available from *http://www.diversitycareers.com*.

Digh, Patty. "America's Largest Untapped Market." *Fortune*, March 1998.

Disability Statistics Center. "National Health Interview Survey 1992." Disability Statistics Center (UCSF), 1992. Available from *http://dsc.ucsf.edu*.

Dupont. "Equal to the Task." Dupont, 1996. Available from *http://www.dupont.com/corp/news/daily/2001/dn02_16_01a.html*.

Economist. "Can America's Work Force Grow Old Gainfully?" *Economist*, 25 July 1998.

Employment Management Association. "USWeb Selects NetStart As Internet Recruiting Partner." CareerBuilder. 28 October 1996. Available from *http://corp.careerbuilder.com/cfm/newsview.cfm?type=release&ID=1.*

Falls, Ophelia. "IT Accessibility Hinges on Cooperation." *Government Computer News*, 11 September 2000. Available from *http://www.gcn.com/vol19_no27/interview/2874-1.html.*

Gray, Craig. "Recruiting People with Disabilities as Employees." *Executive Update,* September 2000. Available from *http://www.gwsae.org/executiveupdate/2000/September/electronicissue/Career.htm.*

Henderson, Cathy. "College Freshmen with Disabilities: A Biennial Statistical Profile," *American Council on Education*, 2001. Available from *http://www.heath.gwu.edu/bookstore/pdf/CollegeFresh.pdf.*

Job Accommodation Network. "Accommodation Benefit/Cost Data Report." Job Accommodation Network, 31 October 1998. Available from *http://janweb.icdi.wvu.edu/english/pubs/Statistics/BenCosts1098.html.*

Job Accommodation Network. "Facts About Accommodations." Job Accommodation Network, 2000. Available from *http://www.jan.wvu.edu/media/JANFacts.html.*

Kailes, J.I., and D. Jones. *Guide to Planning Accessible Meetings*. Independent Living Research Utilization (ILRU) Research and Training Center on Independent Living at TIRR, Houston, 1993.

Kay, Alan. "Alan Kay Quotes." December 2000. Available from *http://c2.com/cgi/wiki?AlanKayQuotes.*

LaPlante, Mitchell P., and Dawn Carlson. "Disability in the United States." Prevalence and Causes, 1992. *http://dsc.ucsf.edu/UCSF/pub.taf?_function=search&recid=65&grow=1.*

Lee, Christopher, and Rosemary Jackson. *Faking It: A Look Into the Mind of a Creative Learner.* Westport: Heinemann, 1992.

McAdams, Jerry. "How to Keep Your 50-Somethings." *Harvard Management Update,* September 1999.

Meyer, Ellen. E-mail interview by author. 16 January 2002.

Miyares, Urban. Quoted in Patty Digh, "America's Largest Untapped Market." *Fortune*, March 1998.

National Council on Disability. "Achieving Independence: The Challenge for the 21st Century." National Council on Disability. Available from *http://www.ncd.gov/newsroom/publications/achieving_1.html.*

National Organization on Disability. "Employment Facts about People with Disabilities." National Organization on Disability, 28 June 2001. Available from *http://www.nod.org/cont/dsp_cont_item_view.cfm?viewType= search&contentId=14.*

National Organization on Disability. "Employment Outlook: Reasons for Optimism." National Organization on Disability, 21 September 2001. Available from *http://www.nod.org/cont/dsp_cont_item_view.cfm?viewType= search&contentId=481.*

National Organization on Disability. "The Top 10 Reasons to Hire People with Disabilities." National Organization on Disability, 28 June 2001. Available from *http://www.nod.org.*

Tech Connections. Available from *http://www.techconnections.org.*

The Alliance for Technology Access. *Computer and Web Resources with Disabilities: A Guide to Exploring Today's Assistive Technology.* 3d ed. The Alliance for Technology Access. Alameda: Hunter House, Inc., 2000.

The European Union. "European Year of People with Disabilities." The European Union, May 2001. Available from *http://europa.eu.int/comm/ employment_social/news/2001/jul/eydp2003_en.html.*

Thome, Layne. E-mail interview by author, 19 November 2001.

U.S. Bureau of the Census. *Census Brief,* prepared by the U.S. Department of Commerce Economics and Statistics Administration, Bureau of the Census. Washington, D.C., 1997. Available from *http://www.census.gov/prod/ 3/97pubs/cenbr975.pdf.*

U.S. Department of Labor. "Tax Incentives for Business." Education Kit, U.S. Department of Labor, 1997. Available from *http://www.dol.gov/dol/odep/ public/media/reports/ek97/tax.htm.*

U.S. Food and Drug Administration. "Report on Consumer Focus Groups on Biotechnology." U.S. Food and Drug Administration, Center for Food Safety and Applied Nutrition, Office of Scientific Analysis and Support, 20 October 2000. Available from *http://www.cfsan.fda.gov/~comm/ biorpt.html.*

UnumProvident. "Decision Tree." UnumProvident 1999.

Williams, John M. "How Everyone Benefits from Assistive Tec's Greatest Hits." *Business Week Online,* 20 September 2000. Available from *http:// www.businessweek.com/bwdaily/dnflash/sep2000/nf20000920_400.htm.*

Index

Please note that Appendices A, B, and C are located only on the book's CD. Their page numbers are indicated as "A-," "B-," and "C-," respectively, within the index.

Get a **Free**
*e-mail newsletter, updates,
special offers, links to related books,
and more when you*
register on line!

Register your Microsoft Press® title on our Web site and you'll get
a FREE subscription to our e-mail newsletter, *Microsoft Press Book
Connections.* You'll find out about newly released and upcoming books
and learning tools, online events, software downloads, special offers
and coupons for Microsoft Press customers, and information about
major Microsoft® product releases. You can also read useful additional
information about all the titles we publish, such as detailed book descriptions, tables of contents and indexes, sample chapters, links to
related books and book series, author biographies, and reviews by
other customers.

Registration is easy. Just visit this Web page and fill in your information:
http://www.microsoft.com/mspress/register

Microsoft

Proof of Purchase
Use this page as proof of purchase if participating in a promotion or rebate offer on
this title. Proof of purchase must be used in conjunction with other proof(s) of
payment such as your dated sales receipt—see offer details.

Accessible Technology in Today's Business
0-7356-1501-2

CUSTOMER NAME

Microsoft Press, PO Box 97017, Redmond, WA 98073-9830

MICROSOFT LICENSE AGREEMENT
Book Companion CD

IMPORTANT—READ CAREFULLY: This Microsoft End-User License Agreement ("EULA") is a legal agreement between you (either an individual or an entity) and Microsoft Corporation for the Microsoft product identified above, which includes computer software and may include associated media, printed materials, and "online" or electronic documentation ("SOFTWARE PRODUCT"). Any component included within the SOFTWARE PRODUCT that is accompanied by a separate End-User License Agreement shall be governed by such agreement and not the terms set forth below. By installing, copying, or otherwise using the SOFTWARE PRODUCT, you agree to be bound by the terms of this EULA. If you do not agree to the terms of this EULA, you are not authorized to install, copy, or otherwise use the SOFTWARE PRODUCT; you may, however, return the SOFTWARE PRODUCT, along with all printed materials and other items that form a part of the Microsoft product that includes the SOFTWARE PRODUCT, to the place you obtained them for a full refund.

SOFTWARE PRODUCT LICENSE

The SOFTWARE PRODUCT is protected by United States copyright laws and international copyright treaties, as well as other intellectual property laws and treaties. The SOFTWARE PRODUCT is licensed, not sold.

1. **GRANT OF LICENSE.** This EULA grants you the following rights:

   a. **Software Product.** You may install and use one copy of the SOFTWARE PRODUCT on a single computer. The primary user of the computer on which the SOFTWARE PRODUCT is installed may make a second copy for his or her exclusive use on a portable computer.

   b. **Storage/Network Use.** You may also store or install a copy of the SOFTWARE PRODUCT on a storage device, such as a network server, used only to install or run the SOFTWARE PRODUCT on your other computers over an internal network; however, you must acquire and dedicate a license for each separate computer on which the SOFTWARE PRODUCT is installed or run from the storage device. A license for the SOFTWARE PRODUCT may not be shared or used concurrently on different computers.

   c. **License Pak.** If you have acquired this EULA in a Microsoft License Pak, you may make the number of additional copies of the computer software portion of the SOFTWARE PRODUCT authorized on the printed copy of this EULA, and you may use each copy in the manner specified above. You are also entitled to make a corresponding number of secondary copies for portable computer use as specified above.

   d. **Sample Code.** Solely with respect to portions, if any, of the SOFTWARE PRODUCT that are identified within the SOFTWARE PRODUCT as sample code (the "SAMPLE CODE"):

      i. **Use and Modification.** Microsoft grants you the right to use and modify the source code version of the SAMPLE CODE, *provided* you comply with subsection (d)(iii) below. You may not distribute the SAMPLE CODE, or any modified version of the SAMPLE CODE, in source code form.

      ii. **Redistributable Files.** Provided you comply with subsection (d)(iii) below, Microsoft grants you a nonexclusive, royalty-free right to reproduce and distribute the object code version of the SAMPLE CODE and of any modified SAMPLE CODE, other than SAMPLE CODE, or any modified version thereof, designated as not redistributable in the Readme file that forms a part of the SOFTWARE PRODUCT (the "Non-Redistributable Sample Code"). All SAMPLE CODE other than the Non-Redistributable Sample Code is collectively referred to as the "REDISTRIBUTABLES."

      iii. **Redistribution Requirements.** If you redistribute the REDISTRIBUTABLES, you agree to: (i) distribute the REDISTRIBUTABLES in object code form only in conjunction with and as a part of your software application product; (ii) not use Microsoft's name, logo, or trademarks to market your software application product; (iii) include a valid copyright notice on your software application product; (iv) indemnify, hold harmless, and defend Microsoft from and against any claims or lawsuits, including attorney's fees, that arise or result from the use or distribution of your software application product; and (v) not permit further distribution of the REDISTRIBUTABLES by your end user. Contact Microsoft for the applicable royalties due and other licensing terms for all other uses and/or distribution of the REDISTRIBUTABLES.

2. **DESCRIPTION OF OTHER RIGHTS AND LIMITATIONS.**

   - **Limitations on Reverse Engineering, Decompilation, and Disassembly.** You may not reverse engineer, decompile, or disassemble the SOFTWARE PRODUCT, except and only to the extent that such activity is expressly permitted by applicable law notwithstanding this limitation.

   - **Separation of Components.** The SOFTWARE PRODUCT is licensed as a single product. Its component parts may not be separated for use on more than one computer.

   - **Rental.** You may not rent, lease, or lend the SOFTWARE PRODUCT.

   - **Support Services.** Microsoft may, but is not obligated to, provide you with support services related to the SOFTWARE PRODUCT ("Support Services"). Use of Support Services is governed by the Microsoft policies and programs described in the user manual, in "online" documentation, and/or in other Microsoft-provided materials. Any supplemental software code provided to you as part of the Support Services shall be considered part of the SOFTWARE PRODUCT and subject to the terms and conditions of this EULA. With respect to technical information you provide to Microsoft as part of the Support Services, Microsoft may use such information for its business purposes, including for product support and development. Microsoft will not utilize such technical information in a form that personally identifies you.

- **Software Transfer.** You may permanently transfer all of your rights under this EULA, provided you retain no copies, you transfer all of the SOFTWARE PRODUCT (including all component parts, the media and printed materials, any upgrades, this EULA, and, if applicable, the Certificate of Authenticity), **and** the recipient agrees to the terms of this EULA.

- **Termination.** Without prejudice to any other rights, Microsoft may terminate this EULA if you fail to comply with the terms and conditions of this EULA. In such event, you must destroy all copies of the SOFTWARE PRODUCT and all of its component parts.

3. **COPYRIGHT.** All title and copyrights in and to the SOFTWARE PRODUCT (including but not limited to any images, photographs, animations, video, audio, music, text, SAMPLE CODE, REDISTRIBUTABLES, and "applets" incorporated into the SOFTWARE PRODUCT) and any copies of the SOFTWARE PRODUCT are owned by Microsoft or its suppliers. The SOFTWARE PRODUCT is protected by copyright laws and international treaty provisions. Therefore, you must treat the SOFTWARE PRODUCT like any other copyrighted material **except** that you may install the SOFTWARE PRODUCT on a single computer provided you keep the original solely for backup or archival purposes. You may not copy the printed materials accompanying the SOFTWARE PRODUCT.

4. **U.S. GOVERNMENT RESTRICTED RIGHTS.** The SOFTWARE PRODUCT and documentation are provided with RESTRICTED RIGHTS. Use, duplication, or disclosure by the Government is subject to restrictions as set forth in subparagraph (c)(1)(ii) of the Rights in Technical Data and Computer Software clause at DFARS 252.227-7013 or subparagraphs (c)(1) and (2) of the Commercial Computer Software—Restricted Rights at 48 CFR 52.227-19, as applicable. Manufacturer is Microsoft Corporation/One Microsoft Way/Redmond, WA 98052-6399.

5. **EXPORT RESTRICTIONS.** You agree that you will not export or re-export the SOFTWARE PRODUCT, any part thereof, or any process or service that is the direct product of the SOFTWARE PRODUCT (the foregoing collectively referred to as the "Restricted Components"), to any country, person, entity, or end user subject to U.S. export restrictions. You specifically agree not to export or re-export any of the Restricted Components (i) to any country to which the U.S. has embargoed or restricted the export of goods or services, which currently include, but are not necessarily limited to, Cuba, Iran, Iraq, Libya, North Korea, Sudan, and Syria, or to any national of any such country, wherever located, who intends to transmit or transport the Restricted Components back to such country; (ii) to any end user who you know or have reason to know will utilize the Restricted Components in the design, development, or production of nuclear, chemical, or biological weapons; or (iii) to any end user who has been prohibited from participating in U.S. export transactions by any federal agency of the U.S. government. You warrant and represent that neither the BXA nor any other U.S. federal agency has suspended, revoked, or denied your export privileges.

DISCLAIMER OF WARRANTY

NO WARRANTIES OR CONDITIONS. MICROSOFT EXPRESSLY DISCLAIMS ANY WARRANTY OR CONDITION FOR THE SOFTWARE PRODUCT. THE SOFTWARE PRODUCT AND ANY RELATED DOCUMEN-TATION ARE PROVIDED "AS IS" WITHOUT WARRANTY OR CONDITION OF ANY KIND, EITHER EXPRESS OR IMPLIED, INCLUDING, WITHOUT LIMITATION, THE IMPLIED WARRANTIES OF MERCHANTABILITY, FITNESS FOR A PARTICULAR PURPOSE, OR NONINFRINGEMENT. THE ENTIRE RISK ARISING OUT OF USE OR PERFORMANCE OF THE SOFTWARE PRODUCT REMAINS WITH YOU.

LIMITATION OF LIABILITY. TO THE MAXIMUM EXTENT PERMITTED BY APPLICABLE LAW, IN NO EVENT SHALL MICROSOFT OR ITS SUPPLIERS BE LIABLE FOR ANY SPECIAL, INCIDENTAL, INDIRECT, OR CONSEQUENTIAL DAMAGES WHATSOEVER (INCLUDING, WITHOUT LIMITATION, DAMAGES FOR LOSS OF BUSINESS PROFITS, BUSINESS INTERRUPTION, LOSS OF BUSINESS INFORMATION, OR ANY OTHER PECUNIARY LOSS) ARISING OUT OF THE USE OF OR INABILITY TO USE THE SOFTWARE PRODUCT OR THE PROVISION OF OR FAILURE TO PROVIDE SUPPORT SERVICES, EVEN IF MICROSOFT HAS BEEN ADVISED OF THE POSSIBILITY OF SUCH DAMAGES. IN ANY CASE, MICROSOFT'S ENTIRE LIABILITY UNDER ANY PROVISION OF THIS EULA SHALL BE LIMITED TO THE GREATER OF THE AMOUNT ACTU-ALLY PAID BY YOU FOR THE SOFTWARE PRODUCT OR US$5.00; PROVIDED, HOWEVER, IF YOU HAVE ENTERED INTO A MICROSOFT SUPPORT SERVICES AGREEMENT, MICROSOFT'S ENTIRE LIABILITY REGARDING SUPPORT SERVICES SHALL BE GOVERNED BY THE TERMS OF THAT AGREEMENT. BE-CAUSE SOME STATES AND JURISDICTIONS DO NOT ALLOW THE EXCLUSION OR LIMITATION OF LIABILITY, THE ABOVE LIMITATION MAY NOT APPLY TO YOU.

MISCELLANEOUS

This EULA is governed by the laws of the State of Washington USA, except and only to the extent that applicable law mandates governing law of a different jurisdiction.

Should you have any questions concerning this EULA, or if you desire to contact Microsoft for any reason, please contact the Microsoft subsidiary serving your country, or write: Microsoft Sales Information Center/One Microsoft Way/Redmond, WA 98052-6399.